Economic Diplomacy

Also of Interest

The Politics of East-West Trade, edited by Gordon B. Smith

Strategic and Critical Materials, L. Harold Bullis and James E. Mielke

The Political Environment of Economic Planning in Iran, 1971–1983: From Monarchy to Islamic Republic, Hossein Razavi and Firouz Vakil

The Gulf and the Search for Strategic Stability: Saudi Arabia, The Military Balance in the Gulf, and Trends in the Arab-Israeli Military Balance, Anthony H. Cordesman

†*The Foreign Policies of Arab States,* Bahgat Korany, Ali E. Hillal Dessouki, et al.

Political Risk in the International Oil and Gas Industry, Howard L. Lax

OPEC, the Gulf, and the World Petroleum Market: A Study in Government Policy and Downstream Operations, Fereidun Fesharaki and David T. Isaak

Oil Strategy and Politics, 1941–1981, Walter J. Levy, edited by Melvin A. Conant

The Geopolitics of Energy, Melvin A. Conant and Fern Racine Gold

Economic Coercion and U.S. Foreign Policy: Implications of Case Studies from the Johnson Administration, edited by Sidney Weintraub

†Available in hardcover and paperback.

Westview Special Studies in International Relations

Economic Diplomacy: Embargo Leverage and World Politics
M. S. Daoudi and M. S. Dajani

The 1983 collapse of world oil prices revived memories of a time only a decade earlier when the price of a barrel of oil did not exceed three dollars. By the late 1970s, spot market prices had reached peaks of forty dollars a barrel. A major role in creating these new realities was played by the 1973/1974 Arab oil embargo, which formed the psychological, political, and market conditions for the dramatic price surge. This important study probes the embargo in detail, thoroughly examining its history, the motivations that caused it, and its ripple effect on world politics and the international economic order. The authors carefully examine the interruption of oil supplies to Western Europe during the 1956 Suez Canal crisis, the growing momentum of Arab oil leverage beginning with the First Arab Petroleum Congress in 1959, the decline of the oil companies' domination of the petroleum industry, and the Arab political environment between the 1967 Arab defeat and the 1973 Arab oil embargo. The book concludes with a chapter addressing the lessons to be learned from these recent embargoes.

Dr. M. S. Daoudi is director of International Industrial Investments, a company specializing in industrial projects in the Middle East. He is a political economist who holds doctoral degrees from the University of South Carolina at Columbia and the University of Texas at Austin and has taught at both universities. He recently completed a study dealing with the longevity of OPEC. **Dr. M. S. Dajani** holds degrees in business, economics, government, and international relations. At present, he is working on a book on international politics, the United Nations, and the Palestine question. Drs. Daoudi and Dajani are the authors of *Economic Sanctions: Ideals and Experience* (1983).

Economic Diplomacy: Embargo Leverage and World Politics

M. S. Daoudi and M. S. Dajani

Westview Press / Boulder and London

Westview Special Studies in International Relations

Copyright © 1985 by Westview Press, Inc.

Published in 1985 in the United States of America by Westview Press, Inc., 5500 Central Avenue, Boulder, Colorado 80301; Frederick A. Praeger, Publisher

Library of Congress Cataloging in Publication Data
Daoudi, M. S.
  Economic diplomacy.
  (Westview special studies in international relations)
  Bibliography: p.
  Includes index.
  1. Petroleum industry and trade—Political aspects—
Arab countries. 2. Arab countries—Foreign economic
relations. 3. Arab countries—Foreign relations.
I. Dajani, M. S. II. Title. III. Series.
HD9578.A55D36 1985   327.1′11   84-15217
ISBN 0-8133-0101-7

Printed and bound in the United States of America

10   9   8   7   6   5   4   3   2   1

To
King Hussein Ibn Talal
and to the memory of
King Faisal Ibn Saud and
President Gamal Abdel Nasser

Three towering leaders of our time,
each of whom inspired a nation in his own way

Contents

Acknowledgments

This book has taken us nearly eight years, during which time it benefited from our association with a number of people who deserve particular mention. First and foremost, we record with pleasure our personal gratitude to James A. Bill, Carl Leiden, and Raymond A. Moore, whose direction and guidance helped to clarify and develop our ideas, and whose continued faith and encouragement brought this work to its final fruition. We are also indebted to Richard Portes, Donald Weatherbee, Hafez Farmayan, Robert Stookey, Janice J. Terry, Kenneth Perkins, Norman Schofield, Thomas D. Kelly, Robert Wirsing, Natalie K. Hevener, and James N. Roherty, who read either parts or the entire manuscript and offered valuable comments and suggestions.

This is hardly the place to acknowledge accumulated professional debts. Nevertheless, during these eight years several other people have introduced us to new ideas and helped us find our way through the often dark pathways of research, both in formal class discussions and intellectual exchanges and in informal conversations: Richard Kraemer, Henry Dietz, Morris Blachman, Margit Resch, Faust Pauluzzi, Robert L. Hardgrave, Jr., Daniel R. Sabia, Jr., Robert F. Gorman, Donald L. Fowler, Peter C. Sederberg, John S. Stolarek, and Elizabeth Fidlon. All provided their time and learning kindly and unreservedly.

For friendship and support we would also like to express our deep gratitude to Joe Sessi, Farouk Abu Innab, Maher Masri, Raja Shehadeh, Michel Tobbeh, Antoine Sansour, Mahmoud Shurayh, Ragheb Kiblawi, Fathi Kurd, and Michel Stephan. Two individuals deserve special note: Rajai K. Dajani and Anmar Hmoud.

Finally, we owe special thanks to the staff of Westview, whose high professional standards have improved the quality of this book. Needless to say, the responsibility for the contents of the book and the opinions expressed in it are our own.

M. S. Daoudi
M. S. Dajani

Introduction

The collapse of world oil prices in 1983 has revived old memories of a time when the price of a barrel of oil did not exceed three dollars. What seems incredible is that those old memories go back only about a decade—to 1973. Since then, oil prices have jumped from less than three dollars a barrel to an official twenty-four dollars a barrel, reaching by the late 1970s spot-market peaks of forty dollars a barrel. A major role in creating this new reality was played by the 1973/1974 Arab oil embargo, which created the psychological, political, and market conditions for the price surge. Surprisingly enough, no major study has probed this episode in detail or thoroughly examined its background, motivation, objectives, and impact on world politics and the international economic order. To do so is precisely the purpose of this study.

It was in October 1973 that for the first time in recent history the use of a single commodity as an international political instrument had global repercussions. Though it was implemented only partially, the 1973/1974 Arab oil embargo sent shock waves through the entire world's economy, particularly in those industrial states that depended heavily on imported oil to maintain their high energy consumption. At the same time, the embargo undermined the existing political and economic global orders, introducing new centers of power that the major powers could not ignore, while a general public alarm focused the world's attention on the scarcity of the global energy supply and the growing need to locate new energy sources.

The embargo illustrated the dynamic use of the three tools—military, economic, and diplomatic—on which foreign policies depend. In October 1973 Arab oil producers denied oil to the West, hoping that the United States and Western Europe would pressure Israel to withdraw from the occupied Arab territories. The embargo was lifted in March 1974 as a result of intense diplomatic efforts; however, no sooner was it lifted than some of the Arab oil producers began to hint that it might be reimposed. This led the United States in January 1975 to threaten to use force should the continuous flow of oil to the West be seriously interrupted.

It is the purpose of this book to examine such uses of economic resources and raw materials as political leverage in international affairs by investigating the power of one specific resource—oil. We analyze the Arab oil-producing nations' use of the oil weapon to influence the foreign policy of a number of major Western nations. We explore multivariate dimensions of the "oil weapon," tracing its use in historical, political, and cultural contexts, and then focusing on three specific episodes in which use of the weapon was contemplated, seriously considered, and then actually accomplished: the 1956 Suez crisis, the 1967 Arab oil embargo, and the 1973/1974 embargo. In addition, we explain how the Saudi perception that the United States held the key to resolving the Arab-Israeli conflict precipitated the policy that led eventually to the 1973 embargo. Saudi Arabia's relations with the West, particularly its economic and political dependence on the United States, played a major role in both determining how oil was deployed as a political weapon and imposing limits on its use.

Massive political, economic, and social developments within the Arab world and on the international scene between 1956 and 1973 caused a profound shift of attitudes toward viewing oil politically, rather than strictly economically. In studying the significance of the use of oil as a political weapon, one question continually arises: How free were (and are) the Arabs, particularly Saudi Arabia, to use oil as a political weapon? Or, narrowly stated: Did Saudi economic, political, military, and technical dependence on the West in general and the United States in particular dictate caution, tact, and prudence in its use of the "oil weapon," and, if so, to what extent? This study tests and identifies the limits of using economic instruments as substitutes for force in achieving political goals.

In the Middle East, the first and major use of the oil weapon took place in 1951 when Prime Minister Mohammed Mossadeq of Iran nationalized the British Petroleum's (BP) fifty-year-old concession.[1] In retaliation, all major international oil companies imposed an oil boycott on Iran, which eventually brought the country to the brink of economic collapse and paved the way in 1953 for the coup that restored Shah Mohammed Reza Pahlavi to the Iranian throne.[2]

Chapter 1 studies the first aftershock of the Mossadeq experience: the interruption of oil supplies to Western Europe during the 1956 Suez crisis. This interruption resulted from the blocking of the Suez Canal and the sabotage of oil pipelines in Syria that carried Iraqi and Saudi oil to the Mediterranean for shipment to Europe. The United States was then able to use the tactic of delaying oil deliveries to exert pressure on the British government, first to stop fighting, and second to withdraw all armed forces from Egypt. France, similarly vulnerable to oil shortages, was left with no option but to follow suit. Israel, too, was vulnerable to the economic and political leverage of the United States and was forced eventually to withdraw. Militarily, the combined powers of Britain, France, and Israel could have defeated the small army of Egypt and occupied Egyptian strongholds on the banks of the Suez Canal; indeed, these forces could have accomplished any military task assigned to them. But in the final analysis economic and political considerations, not military power, decided the issue and obliged the tripartite alliance to withdraw.

In the postwar period, Europe was shifting its source of primary energy from coal to oil, but it produced only about 10 percent of its own oil. A continuous flow of oil was necessary for the maintenance and growth of the European economy. An energy crisis was averted in 1956 because the United States made its oil readily available; however, the economic impact of this short interruption served as a signal and a discomfiting reminder of the intimate connection between the Western economies and Mideast oil. Throughout the Suez crisis, Saudi Arabia ignored Egyptian calls to nationalize its oil industry in retaliation for the Anglo-French invasion of Egypt. Political antagonisms in the Arab world and the traditional rivalry for Arab leadership between Saudi Arabia and Egypt contributed to the Saudis' reluctance to use oil as a political weapon. However, the Saudis' lack of administrative authority over the policymaking processes of the multinational oil companies' Arabian operations rendered it virtually impossible that there could be any agreement with the Egyptian demands.

Many books and articles have analyzed the Suez affair.[3] Some give a general treatment of the crisis. Others reflect the policies, positions, and views of the various actors that were involved either directly (Egypt, Israel, Britain, France, the United States, the Soviet Union, the United Nations) or indirectly (Australia, the British Commonwealth, Canada, India, South Africa, Hungary, China, and West Germany). Divergent legal analyses have been offered, as well as discussions from military and strategic perspectives. Some writers have claimed to know the "secrets" or "inside story" of the crisis. One even saw a "sequel" to the crisis. However, most published works, including those that purport to deal with the economic impact and consequences of the conflict, have dealt only incidentally with the role played by economic leverage in resolving the crisis. Chapter 1 attempts to address this aspect of the Suez crisis in detail.

Chapter 2 considers the 1967 Arab oil embargo of Britain, the United States, and West Germany.[4] Powerful pan-Arab and domestic pressures on the conservative elites of the oil producers obliged the governments of Saudi Arabia, Kuwait, Libya, and the Gulf sheikhdoms to join Iraq and Algeria in cutting back production and imposing an embargo on oil. However, because of their strong economic, military, and political ties to the West, the oil-producing conservative regimes made no serious attempt to enforce the embargo. But even if they had intended to do so, in practical terms they were in no position to act because the multinational oil corporations were in full control of all phases of the Arab oil industry: exploration, production, transportation, refining, and marketing.

Chapter 3 traces the growing momentum of Arab oil leverage from the First Arab Petroleum Congress in 1959 to the 1973 Arab oil embargo. It defines the conflicting relationship between the oil companies and the host governments, focusing on the growth of an oil culture among the elites of the Arab oil-producing nations and on attempts by these elites to increase the producing governments' control of oil-production policies.

Chapter 4 analyzes how the conflict of interest between the host countries and the operating companies increased tension and created a tug of war in which relinquishment of old concessions, participation agreements, and nationalization acts diminished the multinationals' domination of the petroleum industry and dramatically shifted the oil power structure.

Chapter 5 scrutinizes the Arab political environment between the 1967 military defeat and the 1973 oil embargo. This environment played a major role in determining both the employment of the oil weapon and the constraints imposed upon it. The discussion puts the 1973 embargo decision into focus by analyzing the domestic and international political developments that preceded and conditioned it. Whereas up to mid-1972 only radical Arab governing elites had sought to employ oil as a political weapon, subsequent political tension in the Arab world caused even the conservative elites to begin to view oil politically rather than commercially. These complex developments forced countries like Saudi Arabia, the world's number one oil-exporting country and the leading force that had sought to dissociate oil from politics, to unsheathe the oil weapon and wave it in the faces of its Western allies. Although in 1956 Saudi Arabia had ignored Egyptian calls to nationalize oil in retaliation for the Anglo-French invasion of Egypt, and although in 1967 the Saudis gave only lip service to the use of oil as a political weapon against the United States, Britain, and West Germany, by 1973 the king of Saudi Arabia, Faisal, had taken the lead in threatening to use, and later in actually using, oil as a political weapon against the United States and Western Europe in order to force an Israeli withdrawal from the Arab territories occupied in 1967, particularly East Jerusalem. An analysis of these political developments within the producing nations and of their growing power to control crude-oil production (though not distribution and marketing) helps to shed light on the strengths and weaknesses of the Arabs' use of oil as a political weapon in 1973/1974.

Against this background, Chapter 6 probes in detail the specific application of the oil weapon. Shipments of oil to Western Europe and the United States were interrupted, causing shortages and creating the conditions that allowed the Organization of Petroleum Exporting Countries (OPEC) to assume unilateral control over oil prices, causing tremendous dislocations in the world's economic order.[5] This chapter traces the developments that occurred between October 1973, when the embargo was imposed, and March 1974, when it was lifted. It analyzes the embargo's objectives and assesses its achievements, the factors that mitigated its impact, and the world's reaction to it. The chapter concludes with a discussion of why, despite oil's indubitable economic and political leverage, and despite all the drums and trumpets accompanying its deployment, the oil weapon was not fully mobilized in support of Arab political goals in October 1973.

Chapter 7 puts forth a number of conclusions. Just as oil power should not be overestimated, it should not be underestimated. Even in times of oil oversupply, the Western nations' economies remain heavily dependent on oil as their primary source of energy, and because other sources are failing to compete successfully with oil in terms of safety, practicality, and low cost, the use of oil as a political weapon still poses a serious threat to the consumer nations. The consumers' counterleverages lie in their ability to conserve and cooperate, acting together as one body in their bargaining with the producing nations. There can be little doubt that the current dependent, asymmetrical relationship between the United States and Saudi Arabia is changing. Saudi reaction to the Camp David agreement and U.S. reaction to the peace initiative of Crown Prince Fahd (now king) show that Saudi and U.S. interests in the Middle East can diverge and that in such instances neither party is averse to pursuing an independent policy. Nevertheless, the U.S./Saudi relationship is becoming increasingly symmetrical and interdependent. If this trend continues, it may have profound implications for any future Arab hopes of using oil as a political weapon.

Falling oil prices and a world energy glut in the early 1980s, generated by conservation, fuel-switching, and new non-OPEC finds, have given rise to a certain euphoria that the oil leverage is no longer viable and that the consumer, not the producer, holds the trump card in the oil-political game. But it may not be long before this optimism fades away, for the supply curve is quite fragile and could easily break. Low oil prices could put an end to the costly new fields that recently increased world oil production; turmoil in the Middle East generally or the Gulf in particular, or political instability in a major oil-producing country such as Saudi Arabia could halt oil shipments; or consumers could relax their vigilance, spur energy consumption, and renew pressure on supplies. Ten years after the 1973/1974 Arab oil embargo the United States, its main target, still imports nearly a quarter of its oil, and oil still represents nearly 40 percent of the country's energy consumption. Consequently, renewed U.S. dependence on OAPEC (Organization of Arab Petroleum-Exporting Countries) oil remains a distinct possibility. Both the United States and Western Europe remain vulnerable to oil-supply interruptions and future price increases.

The Leverage of Oil, 1956

Nationalization of the Suez Canal

From the day Gamal Abdel Nasser assumed the leadership of Egypt in 1954, following the dismissal of Mohammed Naguib, Egypt's first president, Nasser realized that the real challenge to his power lay in the success of his economic measures at home.[1] He had inherited serious economic problems: a rapidly growing population in a country that had a limited strip of fertile land. The curbing of the landlords, the education of a backward people, and the introduction of social welfare and health measures had scarcely been touched in the period of British administration.[2] The idea of building a high dam at Aswan was conceived to irrigate a much larger area of the country and to provide a livelihood and housing for more people in Upper Egypt. Because the Aswan project was much beyond Egypt's financial and technical capabilities, Nasser sought help from Western governments;[3] initially he obtained promises of $55 million from the United States and $15 million from Britain, and then $200 million from the World Bank after the other offers were forthcoming.[4] But as relations between Egypt and Britain and the United States worsened, the whole enterprise began to take a different course.

Before 1952 British-Egyptian relations were generally tense, marked by moments of bitter political conflict. Following the Egyptian revolt of 1952, relations acutely deteriorated.[5] The new Egyptian leader made serious and continuous attempts to reduce British hegemony in Egypt and the rest of the Arab world; on its part, the British government responded by launching a campaign to check his growing prestige. Nasser perceived that, once Britain was weakened in the Middle East, Egyptian influence over the oil-rich, strategically located Arab states would increase and France would become more vulnerable in Algeria. Peter Mansfield in *The British in Egypt* (1971) offered a British perspective on the two countries' worsening relations:

Relations between Britain and Egypt had already deteriorated sharply since the false dawn of the 1954 agreement. The Eden government had numerous grievances against Nasser's Egypt: first the challenge in the Sudan, then its wider support for anticolonial movements throughout Africa, and finally the outspoken opposition to Britain's plans for an anti-Soviet Middle East Defense Organization—the Baghdad Pact.[6]

Nasser's recognition of Communist China,[7] a possible alternative source of arms, proved fatal to the U.S. decision to lend Egypt the money needed to build the Aswan Dam. As Townsend Hoopes wrote in *The Devil and John Foster Dulles* (1973): "In Dulles' pantheon of devils, the Red Chinese represented perhaps the highest and purest evil, and this view was shared by a large majority of the Congress, the press, and the American people."[8] Furthermore, Egypt's arms agreement with Czechoslovakia[9] and its dealings with the Soviet bloc caused some hesitation in Washington, both in Congress and in the Eisenhower administration, particularly because the Jewish lobby was exerting great pressure on the administration to cancel the deal.

Rumors emanating from Cairo that the Soviet Union might take over the financing might have been designed to push the United States into a final favorable decision. They had the opposite effect. On July 19, 1956, Secretary of State John Foster Dulles announced that, conditions having changed, the American offers of aid were no longer in effect.[10]

Dulles maintained that the United States had withdrawn its offer of assistance mainly because "the ability of Egypt to devote adequate resources to assure the project's success has become more uncertain than at the time the offer was made."[11] The London *Economist* reported on 28 July 1956 that Selwyn Lloyd, who had replaced Harold Macmillan as foreign secretary, had serious doubts with regard to the feasibility of the dam project: "We came to the conclusion that the Egyptian government would no longer be in a position to devote to the dam project the degree of priority necessary to secure its success."

In reaction to the offer's recision, Nasser issued a decree nationalizing the Suez Canal Company and taking over "all its property and rights pertaining thereto" to finance the costs of the dam program and related works from Suez Canal revenues. In the nationalization speech, delivered to a mass rally in Alexandria on 23 July 1956, Nasser explained that the initial U.S.-British grant for the dam had been for $70 million over five years, while the canal earned the equivalent of $100 million yearly, and that Egypt had been getting only £1 million out of the company's £35 million in earnings (nearly $2 out of every $70).[12]

Military Intervention

The Egyptian nationalization of the Suez Canal constituted a major challenge to Britain's authority in the Middle East as well as to its prestige on the international scene. In the words of Robert R. Bowie:

> As [Prime Minister Anthony] Eden and his Cabinet perceived the situation, the seizure imperilled much more than the Canal. At stake was the whole British position in the Middle East. If unchecked, Nasser would exploit Arab nationalism to dominate the region, including the sources of Middle Eastern oil which had become the lifeblood of the British and European economies. Nasser's action and speech were only the final proof that the West could not compromise with him.[13]

Eden, whose health and domestic political base were deteriorating, found in the canal seizure adequate justification for the use of force.[14] The act itself was taken in such a defiant mood that Eden felt he could not easily brush it aside. Only four days later, he tersely told the House of Commons that Britain could accept no arrangement for the future of the Suez Canal that left the waterway "in the unfettered control of a single power."[15] Eden made clear that he regarded this policy not merely as an *obiter dictum* but as a doctrine applicable, presumably, *after* as well as *before* 1968, when the canal's concession expired: "It is upon this that we insist . . . nothing less than this can be acceptable to us."[16] Britain's anxious mood was more explicitly expressed in a cable that Eden sent to President Dwight D. Eisenhower shortly after the nationalization: "My colleagues and I are convinced that we must be ready in the last resort to use force to bring Nasser to his senses."[17]

The British government was in such a militant mood that it chose not to heed the warning of the Soviet foreign minister, Dmitri Shepilov, that the military preparations already undertaken by the British and the French could lead to war in the Middle East. In an address to the conference of the twenty-four signatories to the 1888 Istanbul Convention that began on 16 August 1956, Shepilov warned: "One cannot fail to see that such a violation would not be confined to a local conflict in the area of the Suez Canal. It could flare up into a large conflict which could cover the area of the Near and Middle East and possibly go outside these limits."[18] Even U.S. uneasiness about British military intentions did not deter Eden from proceeding with his plans to go to war over Suez should Nasser fail to back down, which he showed no intention of doing. Actually, Eden had reached his decision more than four months before the Suez invasion. When advised of his options by his foreign minister, Anthony Nutting, Eden exploded: "But what's all this nonsense about isolating Nasser or 'neutralizing' him, as you call it? I want him destroyed, can't you understand? I want him removed."[19]

In Egypt, Nasser made it quite clear that he would not even discuss any terms that would take the Suez Canal "out of the hands of Egypt and put it into some other hands." This attitude enforced Britain's resolve to impose a solution on Egypt by force. The United States urged caution, but both Britain and France were convinced, though for different reasons, that Nasser must be taught a lesson that could prove useful to other nationalist leaders in the Third World who might in the future entertain similar ideas.[20] As Israeli Minister of Defense Moshe Dayan wrote in *Diary of the Sinai Campaign* (1966), already the British were "preparing to topple Nasser, who is a common enemy of theirs and Israel's," to safeguard "Britain's position in the Middle East as a power that stands firmly on her rights in the Suez Canal."[21] In his book *Full Circle* (1966), however, Eden made an effort to downplay imperialistic intentions while stressing the commercial and strategic actions involved:

We estimated that the United Kingdom had reserves of oil which would last for six weeks, and that the other countries of Western Europe owned comparatively smaller stocks. The continuing supply of fuel, which was a vital source of power to the economy of Britain, was not subject to Colonel Nasser's whim. More than half of Britain's annual imports of oil came through the Canal. At any time the Egyptians might decide to interfere with its passage. They might also prompt their allies to cut the pipelines. We had to gauge the implications of bringing oil from the Persian Gulf by the long haul around the Cape of Good Hope.[22]

The key to French hostility "was the Algerian rebellion which had erupted in late 1954. Despite heavily expanded forces, France had failed to suppress the rebels. In their frustration, French leaders, including [Premier Guy] Mollet, attributed their failure largely to Nasser's support for the Algerian rebels."[23]

As for Israel, three main bases for foreign policy had emerged since 1948: first, to secure the ratification of the territorial status quo; second, to obtain foreign assistance, not only to attain economic self-sufficiency but also to counteract the effects of the Arab economic boycott and the restrictions on Israeli navigation in Arab-controlled waterways; and third, to prevent a possible large-scale return of Arab refugees.[24] The Egyptian affront to Britain gave Israel an opportunity to join an alliance to overthrow the Nasserite regime, which posed a serious challenge to Israel's existence, and also to secure free navigation through the Suez Canal and the Strait of Tiran.

Thus Britain, France, and Israel each had its own objectives, and their common enemy was Nasser.[25] Accordingly, an alliance was established primarily to overthrow Nasser and force Egypt to drop its claim to sole control of the Suez Canal. As the most influential power among the three, both regionally and globally, Britain was mainly responsible for inviting France and Israel to coordinate their international behavior in pursuit of this goal. With all their resources pooled, the three allied nations launched their planned attack on Egypt. On 29 October 1956, Israeli troops moved into the Sinai under the pretext that hostile activities by Palestinian commandos had been renewed. Israeli Prime Minister David Ben-Gurion kept his intentions secret even from his cabinet until the last moment, informing it only one day before the attack was launched.[26] This step was worked out in advance to give the British and French governments a pretext to intervene on the grounds that such intervention was necessary to protect the Suez Canal.[27] Thus the Israeli move was immediately followed by both governments' giving the Egyptian and Israeli ambassadors an ultimatum, stating that France and Britain would occupy key positions in the canal zone unless Egypt and Israel stopped hostilities forthwith.[28] Eden told the Commons that both governments had been told that if they did not comply within twelve hours, "United Kingdom and French forces will intervene in whatever strength may be necessary to secure compliance."[29] The Egyptians rejected the ultimatum as tantamount to surrender of sovereignty. On 31 October 1956, after announcing that British and French troops would be landing in the Suez zone to "secure" navigation through the canal, the British and French began their military operations against Egypt. From 1 November to 6 November, Egyptian targets were hit by the three powers and Egypt's small army was easily overcome.

The invaders' tactical objectives were the occupation of the canal's main towns, which could give them a strong bargaining chip in later negotiations and an easy psychological victory that they hoped would activate opposition forces in Cairo to bring about the downfall of Nasser. To facilitate this, the invaders' media concentrated on the man rather than the issue to give the Egyptian people the impression that the belligerency of the invaders was due to Nasser's personal character, rather than the cause he was fighting for.[30] They attempted to make it seem as if his removal alone could restore peace to the area. To the rest of the world, the triple alliance put up a front that showed them unwilling to give in to pressure without an Egyptian announcement of a denationalization act and the restoration of the old state of affairs in the region.

In the field, the triple alliance had no cause to complain. Their armies were able to score easy victories against the ill-equipped, disorganized, and vastly inferior Egyptian army. Israeli advances into the Sinai were hardly delayed, while the Anglo-French forces, in full command of the air and with considerable troops at their disposal, easily overcame what small, though heroic, resistance they encountered. However, even this weak Egyptian resistance helped to buy Nasser the time he needed to outrun the Anglo-French attempt to delay a United Nations resolution calling for a ceasefire and to influence a U.S.-Soviet diplomatic intervention against the invaders.

Throughout the military intervention, the United States assumed a leading role in opposing the tripartite attack on Egypt. President Eisenhower pieced together the Anglo-French-Israeli collusion, which had been planned without consulting the United States. "The President was very angry," wrote Peter Lyon in *Eisenhower: Portrait of the Hero* (1974), "but it was a carefully frigerated wrath. From that moment Eden's ambitions were destined to go smash."[31] In their book *United States Foreign Policy and World Order* (1976), James Nathan and James Oliver added that "the last thing Eisenhower needed going into a presidential campaign was a war in the Middle East in which two NATO allies were acting in clear violation of international law."[32] M. S. Venkataramani analyzed and interpreted the U.S. response by strongly emphasizing U.S. economic and strategic interests in Middle Eastern oil. He wrote: "One of the most important factors that influenced the course of U.S. diplomacy before and during the Suez crisis was oil. American actions can be seen in proper perspective only in the light of a careful examination of her strategic and economic interests in oil production, refining and marketing in both Western Europe and West Asia."[33] Strategic interests were involved because Europe's military forces, as well as NATO forces in Europe, were highly dependent on Middle Eastern oil.[34]

The Soviet Union joined the United States in its efforts to pressure Britain, France, and Israel to withdraw. On 1 November the UN General Assembly carried a resolution urging the three invading nations to desist by sixty-two votes to two (Britain and France), with seven abstentions.[35] However, despite U.S.-Soviet pressure, Britain and France did not seem willing to give in without at least an Egyptian announcement of a denationalization and the restoration of the prenationalization state of affairs. But the deteriorating economic position of Britain, "largely as a result of the decline of oil supplies and the unwillingness of the United States to help,"[36] made the British government reconsider. The run on sterling reached such dangerous proportions that the devaluation of the pound was becoming imminent.[37]

Heavy U.S. pressure was applied on the three allied invading powers to accept a ceasefire and withdraw their forces. President Eisenhower "employed diplomatic and economic instruments against both the Israelis and the Anglo-French effort."[38] In addition to political endeavors, the U.S. president

> hit the British at their most vulnerable point—their economy. As October turned to November it became apparent that the pound sterling was under immense pressure and the United States was not only doing nothing to help but may, in fact, have encouraged the drain of reserves. Specifically, in the week of November 5 the Bank of England was forced to draw down its gold and dollar reserves by some 15 percent to meet the demands for gold and dollars from holders of sterling—more than $250 million. Much of the large-block selling was taking place in New York, and there was speculation that it was being initiated by the Treasury Department at Eisenhower's direction. Foreign Secretary MacMillan now warned Prime Minister Eden of British economic collapse. MacMillan knew that there was no help in Washington. The British knew that they would receive a financial transfusion only if there was an immediate cease fire.[39]

In *American Foreign Policy Since World War II* (1977), John Spanier asserted the importance of the U.S. actions:

> America's opposition to the Suez invasion was the decisive factor in stopping the fighting. Egypt had already blocked the canal, and the Syrians had cut the pipelines running across their country from Iraq. Britain was therefore dependent upon American oil to replace its losses from the Middle East; and the Administration threatened to use this economic sanction if Britain did not cease the attack. Faced with this dire prospect— plus opposition to the invasion within Britain, the Commonwealth (Canada, India, and Pakistan), and the United Nations—the British government accepted a cease-fire and later withdrew its forces; France and Israel had little choice but to follow suit.[40]

The desperate state of the pound sterling as a result of the crisis and urgent need for oil forced the British government to agree to a ceasefire on November 7. The French followed suit as they were also vulnerable on the monetary issue and were equally jeopardized by the prospect of a severe oil shortage. "France," reported the *Economist* on 10 November 1956, "like Britain, will pay a stiff economic price for its action in Egypt." The interruption of oil supplies was expected to strike "a severe blow at the French balance of payments."[41] Rationing had already begun in both countries, and winter was fast approaching.

Before Suez, 73 percent of Europe's oil had come from the Middle East (one-half of that through the canal), but with the canal closed and the Syrian pipelines destroyed, Europe was drawing only 9 percent of its total requirements from the area; because only 27 percent came from non–Middle Eastern sources, this meant that total supply was down to 30 percent of normal.[42] A supplement from the United States was urgently needed, but continuous European calls failed to activate the Middle East Oil Emergency Committee—a committee created by the U.S. government after the first phase of the Suez crisis to draw up plans for increases in oil production in the United States and Venezuela, the creation of a tanker pool, and possibly also special arrangements to finance the purchase of dollar oil.[43] The work of this committee was suspended early in November, and the U.S. government indicated that it would take no official action until the British and French troops had been totally withdrawn. The U.S. presidential elections were close and supporters of the Eisenhower administration wanted to be able to take credit that it had produced not only prosperity at home but peace abroad. "Most Americans," reported the *Economist* on 10 November 1956, "sick at heart, believe that this attack [the Soviet invasion of Hungary] was encouraged by, if not the direct result of, the immoral and out-moded 'gunboat diplomacy' which the British and French were pursuing on the Suez Canal."[44]

Moreover, in addition to its "distaste for the British and French action,"[45] the Eisenhower administration feared the implication of the Anglo-French action in terms of increasing Soviet influence in the Middle East. Thus, the United States decided to let the Middle East Oil Emergency Committee lie dormant, as U.S. interests were directly involved:

> American companies controlled nearly 60 percent of the oil produced in the Middle East in the first half of this year [1956]. The charmed life of Tapline, the continuation of Saudi Arabian production, and the Arab tolerance of American oil companies in the other Middle Eastern countries owes much to the refusal of the United States to endorse the British and French intervention. Official American offers, even now, to ease the burden for Britain and France might end this tenuous immunity.[46]

The United States, whose Middle Eastern policy was largely responsible for the Suez crisis,[47] had earlier "pledged to finance the dollar costs of European purchases of Western Hemisphere oil if the Suez Canal was closed."[48] But now, even though the administration would have liked to rush oil to Western Europe to replace the lost supplies, the major U.S. oil companies, which had shown no reluctance to provide the extra supplies needed in Europe within the limits of the antitrust and oil conservation laws, advised caution to the U.S. State Department. They warned that such a course would risk all the reserves of the region and perhaps provoke action against U.S. holdings.[49] Meanwhile, the U.S. secretary of the interior made it quite clear that the government had no intention of rationing U.S. supplies in order to release more oil for export, though to abandon Britain, France, and the rest of Western Europe completely would be to lose historic allies and customers. As a result, the diplomatic strategy was "to promise oil but to go slow in delivery, first to ensure the end of hostilities and second to secure withdrawal from Egypt of the invading armies."[50] This approach resulted in an outcry in Britain that the United States was using oil as a lever to "exert the maximum pressure to get the Anglo-French forces out of Egypt."[51] Other European newspaper editorials accused the United States of having imposed "oil sanctions" and engaging in "oil blackmail."[52]

Withdrawal of Invading Forces

On 22 November, the British and French governments notified the United Nations that a phased withdrawal of forces would begin as the United Nations Emergency Force (UNEF) achieved strength in the area. In the words of Charles Robertson, "the decision was a painful one, based largely on continued pressure from the United States. Secretary of the Treasury Humphrey had told the British that no American financial aid would be forthcoming until such a statement was made."[53] The *New York Times* reported on 22 November 1956 that the "growing oil shortage," coupled with U.S. unwillingness to organize any program to supply oil until the UN resolution was accepted, were responsible for the Anglo-French decision. By mid-November UN troops arrived in the canal zone, but only on 30 November 1956 did the U.S. president "permit the United States petroleum industry to coordinate the efforts they [had] been making individually to assist in handling the oil supply problem resulting from the closing of the Suez Canal and some pipelines in the Middle East."[54] On 22 December the last British and French troops departed from Egypt.

Israel refused to withdraw, fearing that Egypt would deny use of the canal to Israeli ships and other ships bearing Israeli goods. This Israeli failure to comply with UN resolutions ordering a withdrawal from the Gaza Strip and Sharm el-Sheik invited a stern warning from the man who had proposed the UNEF to maintain the truce, Lester B. Pearson, that "such intransigence invited economic sanctions."[55] In response, the Israeli foreign minister, Golda Meir,

> expressed surprise at the strength of the pressure being exerted on Israel. Acknowledging that the military operations had produced a psychological reaction, she mentioned there had been other "aggressions," notably in Kashmir and Hungary, which had not stimulated the same reaction in the General Assembly.

"We have considered this question of sanctions carefully," she said. "And we have decided we cannot give in to such a threat. Sanctions will cause terrible hardship among us, but we cannot forgo our right to self-defence. Whatever happens we shall not give in.[56]

In analyzing the impact of the threat of sanctions on Israel, the *Economist* wrote on 23 February 1957:

The public has taken the threat of economic sanctions with astonishing calm. It is difficult to say whether this calmness flows from a secret belief that at the last moment sanctions will not materialise or from confidence that Israel will be able to weather the storm. The first explanation can be deduced from paragraphs in the papers which explain that the General Assembly is only empowered to recommend sanctions and that a resolution of the Security Council is needed to impose them—in which case Israel believes that France would use its veto.

Nevertheless, it was the effect of other U.S. "private" sanctions that had already been imposed that was beginning to be painfully felt in Israel.

Nobody, however, can clearly envisage what economic sanctions would mean for the economy and for daily life in Israel. The man in the street is only now beginning to realise that the United States imposed its "private" sanctions immediately after the outbreak of the Sinai campaign. Since then Israel has received no money from the grant in aid for 1956-57; this should have amounted to $25 million. Nor has any surplus food been received; $17.5 million worth should have been shipped to Israel. Finally, technical aid worth $4 million has also been stopped. These three items make a hole of $46 million in Israel's dollar income. In addition the country has now to pay much more for its oil—the only fuel in the country—as the price of oil and of transport has gone up steeply. Thus the drop in Israel's dollar income is already estimated at roughly $80 million out of about $470 million.[57]

Inducing Israel to relinquish the territory gained in the invasion was no easy task. Though Prime Minister Ben-Gurion announced that his forces would leave the Sinai, he continued stalling and on 23 January 1957 declared that Israel would retain the Gaza Strip and all of the west coast of the Gulf of Aqaba. But in spite of the tremendous pressure built up in the U.S. Congress and in the media in support of Israel's stance, President Eisenhower, in late February 1957, sent Ben-Gurion a stiff note warning that unless his forces left the Sinai the United States might vote for UN sanctions against Israel and cut off U.S. aid. Moreover,

Secretary of State Dulles threatened to withdraw the privilege of income tax deductibility for contributions to the United Jewish Appeal.[58]

Continued pressure from the United States, the Soviet Union, and the world community gave Israel no choice but to comply.[59] On 1 March 1957 Foreign Minister Meir announced that all Israeli forces would withdraw, and on 16 March they did so.[60]

The Interruption of Oil Supplies

Though the currently accepted interpretation of the yielding of the French and British to withdrawal demands puts more weight on the political and diplomatic factors, economics were even more crucial to the outcome of the issue, and oil was among the most decisive components.

Since the early fifties, there had been a growing increase in traffic through the Suez Canal. The sea route from the Gulf to Britain via Suez is about 6,500 miles, as against 11,300 miles around the Cape of Good Hope. The Suez Canal acquired "particularly great importance as an oil transportation artery, offering Middle East oil the shortest outlet to the European and U.S. markets."[61] Oil tankers accounted for nearly 76 million tons of the total 116 million tons shipped through the canal in 1955.[62]

By the time of the Suez crisis, European demand for oil (about 2.5 million barrels per day) was supplied mainly by the Middle East. About 0.8 million barrels a day were moved from the Middle East fields to Mediterranean ports and thence transshipped to Europe by tankers;[63] another 1.2 million barrels a day came directly from the fields along the Gulf via the Suez Canal; the remaining 0.5 million barrels were supplied by non-Arab oil producers. The pipelines bringing the oil from the fields to the Mediterranean passed through one or more countries with whom arrangements were made and transportation taxes paid. However, no matter what agreements were signed, it was extremely difficult to maintain adequate security along the pipelines due to the large area they covered, particularly when the Arab governments concerned chose to overlook nationalists' efforts to block the flow of oil. The Trans-Arabian Pipe Line Company (Tapline), for example, operated in four countries, any of which could block the flow of oil. Of its 1,068 miles, 25.8 miles were in Lebanon, the Mediterranean terminus; 79.1 miles were in Syria; 110 miles were in Jordan; and the balance were in Saudi Arabia, where it originated.[64] That line was moving about 325,000 barrels of oil a day for transshipment, mostly to Europe. The other pipelines to the Mediterranean were from Iraqi fields. One line extended from the Kirkuk fields passing through Syria to Tripoli on the Lebanese coast. Another line bypassed Lebanon, terminating at Banias on the Syrian coast. These lines had a combined capacity of about 500,000 barrels a day.[65]

Only two days after the meeting of the executive council of the International Confederation of Arab Trade Unions, Radio Cairo reported that the council had told Arab workers that "the time has now come to cut off oil supplies from Britain and France—if necessary by blowing up the pipelines."[66] In his book *Nasser* (1972), British Foreign Minister Nutting wrote:

> When, in response to Arab Trade Unions demands for the sabotage of Western-owned oil pipelines, the Syrians decided to blow up the three most important pumping stations on the Iraq Petroleum Company's pipeline to Tripoli, Nasser opposed even this limited demonstration of Arab solidarity. The Joint Command telegraphed to Damascus saying that sabotage of the pipelines would be "injurious to the interests of other countries not implicated . . ." and should therefore be called off. The message arrived too late to prevent the demolition teams fulfilling their allotted task. Nevertheless, Nasser's advice made some impact on the excitable Syrians, sufficient at any rate to obviate any similar action against the American-owned Trans-Arabia pipeline (Tapline), which escaped unscathed from the Suez War.[67]

Three of the pumping stations of the Iraq Petroleum Company (IPC) were blown up, cutting off the flow of oil. One day later, on 3 November 1956, an Iraqi government spokesman confirmed that the flow of Iraqi oil had stopped from the Kirkuk fields "for the time being."[68] This action was taken in spite of the fact that the Iraqi and Saudi Arabian governments had requested the Syrian government four months before to take all necessary steps to protect the pipelines "in order to prevent the West having an excuse for aggression."[69] According to the London *Evening Standard* of 7 November 1956, the Iraqi premier, Nuri Sa'id, warned Syria in August that "if there is any serious interruption of the flow of Iraqi oil to the coast, Iraqi troops will be used to safeguard the pipelines." Sa'id did in fact station Iraqi troops conspicuously on the Syrian borders. However, this show of force failed to prevent Arab nationalists from blowing up the pumping stations on the Kirkuk-Homs pipeline. The pro-British Sa'id government was even embarrassed on a second count. The oil pipeline from Kirkuk in Iraq to Haifa, Israel, supposedly unused since 1948, was blown up at two places in northern Jordan, setting fire to the oil, which, in the words of the London *Times* on 14 November 1956, "flooded out." The *Manchester Guardian* on the same day reported that "flames were seen over a wide area and eyewitnesses said oil was gushing out over the land." How oil came to be in the pipeline remains an enigma because pumping to Haifa had been banned by Jordan since the Arab-Israeli war of 1948. An IPC spokesman responded that "the oil seen was what was remaining in the pipeline when the Iraqi government banned the supply of oil to Haifa in 1948."[70] However, that explanation was not convincing to many in the Arab world.

The sabotage of the IPC pipelines cut Iraq's main export channel from its large northern oilfield to the Mediterranean. At an early stage in the Suez dispute, the Iraqis had suggested to London that "if the quarrel with Egypt over the canal were at some moment to run high, it might be prudent to stop pumping for a spell in order to safeguard the installations," but they were discouraged by the British, whose overconfidence was very much regretted later.[71] The Saudis, "as a precaution against a similar assault on revenue, insured against sabotage by cutting off relations with Britain and France; but the Iraqis were ill placed to make a corresponding move on account of their membership in the Baghdad Pact."[72] King Saud closed the pipeline from Dhahran, Saudi Arabia, to the Bahrain refinery—a fact too often overlooked. He also imposed stringent conditions on the distribution of oil shipped from Saudi Arabia by tanker, giving the *Economist* on 9 November 1956 reason to conclude: "If other governments respect Arab sovereignty, oil will flow whether it is owned by Arabs or westerners; if they do not, it will not." The point is further illustrated by the Syrian reaction to the British request for immediate repair of the damaged pipelines. In mid-November, the Syrian minister of public works issued a statement saying that no repair would be permitted until "the forces of aggression have left Egyptian soil."[73] In addition to the sabotage of the IPC pipelines there were explosions of sixteen bombs in parts of the Kuwaiti oilfields in early December 1956, causing fires and pipeline damage but no appreciable drop in total oil production.[74] Similarly, in Qatar the local pipeline was cut, but it was repaired within twenty-four hours.[75]

The sabotage of the IPC's pipelines to the Mediterranean and the blocking of the Suez Canal forced most Western European countries to ration petroleum.[76] By these two routes, slightly over 2 million barrels of oil had flowed to the Mediterranean every day.[77] According to Charles L. Robertson,

In the months before the Suez Canal was blocked and the Iraqi pipeline sabotaged, Europe had imported close to 3,000,000 barrels of crude petroleum and petroleum products every day. Of these, approximately 1,410,000 came from the Persian Gulf through the Suez. Another 50,000 from the Far East also came through the canal. Through pipelines to Eastern Mediterranean ports came 680,000 barrels, 100,000 were imported from the Soviet Union and its satellites (chiefly Rumania), 570,000 came from the Caribbean area, and only about 40,000 to 50,000 barrels per day were shipped from the United States Gulf Coast.

Now only one pipeline was left open from the rich Middle East oil fields to the Mediterranean: Trans-Arabian Pipeline, through which 330,000 barrels flowed each day. The charmed life of the Tapline, in contrast with the sabotaged Iraqi pipeline, was the result primarily of its American ownership and American opposition to the Anglo-French-Israeli invasion.[78]

In an effort to downplay the importance of the Suez Canal as a lifeline to Europe, executives of the oil companies were hinting in July 1956 that "tankers hauling Middle Eastern oil to the nations of the Western world could avoid the Suez Canal without affecting significantly the flow of oil to these nations."[79] Nevertheless, other authoritative sources warned against such views, asserting that "any interruption of shipping in the Suez Canal would have an immediate effect on oil supplies in Western Europe."[80] Western political circles seemed not to appreciate this impact fully. In an editorial article that discussed Suez and the oil supplies for Western Europe, the London *Financial Times* reported on 11 August 1956:

At present 67 million tons of oil a year pass through the Canal, most of which goes to Western Europe. Rerouting of all supplies around the Cape of Good Hope would be beyond the capacities of the world's tanker fleets, although a certain amount of tanker capacity could be made available in an emergency. A gap in Europe's oil requirements would remain which could only be filled by oil from the Western Hemisphere. If the Canal were closed Europe might have to import up to 35 million tons per annum of oil from the Western Hemisphere. This is based on the assumption that oil shipments from the Middle East to the United States would not come to a halt.

In Kuwait the rate of oil production was cut to only a quarter of normal output due either to lack of enough tankers to transport the oil or to the boycott of British tankers, while in Indonesia, wharf laborers protesting against the Anglo-French action in Egypt obliged the oil companies to cut production in Indonesia by 60 percent to prevent storage tanks from overflowing.

Economic Impact of the Oil Crisis

By the early 1950s demand for oil was growing fast.[81] On 19 November 1956 the *Financial Times* wrote:

Exclusive of the Soviet sphere, the quantity of energy effectively consumed by the world was about two and one-half times higher in 1955 than in 1920. While more coal is being used than was the case 35 years ago, coal's relative contribution has come down from five-sixths to less than half the world's energy requirements. The effective consumption of petroleum fuels, including natural gas, has risen on the other hand from 15 percent to just over half of the total.

In terms of world crude oil production, this has involved an increase from about 100 million tons in 1920 to about 700 million tons in 1955, the latter quantity being nearly three times the corresponding figure just before the last war.

In an article published in the British *National Bank Review* and extensively quoted in the Edinburgh *Scotsman* of 19 November 1956, Lord William Fraser Strathalmond, chairman of British Petroleum (1941–1956), emphasized the importance of oil in the modern world. He focused his analysis on the close correlation between a prosperous standard of living and the consumption of energy. He pointed out that the traditional source of energy—the coal industry—was having difficulty maintaining output and that for the next decade or so developments in the nuclear field could be expected to make only a marginal contribution to the world's energy needs. In consequence, Strathalmond argued, dependence on oil in the near future would become greater rather than less. The next stage in his analysis was to consider where the world's supplies of oil were to be found, throwing into bold relief the strategic significance of the Middle East. While at the time "that area accounted for only about one-quarter of the world's output of oil, it met about four-fifths of the needs of all Western European countries. Thus, about 50 percent of Britain's oil supplies in 1955 came through the Suez Canal and another 25 percent through the Syrian pipeline."[82] The United States and other producers, including Venezuela and Iran, were in a position to supply most of Europe's requirements, but there were financial as well as political difficulties involved. Europe was already having difficulties in getting enough dollar exchange to pay for imports other than oil; now payments for the non-Arab oil as well had to be in dollars rather than sterling, which meant more economic hardships.

Oil-supply interruptions caused the Western European countries concerned to focus on two main problems: (1) Where could they procure sufficient oil to keep their industries going? and (2) How could they finance the much greater cost of this extra Western Hemisphere oil in dollars? As time dragged on without a resolution to the crisis, economic conditions in Europe worsened, with predictions that the oil shortage might become even more acute in January and February of 1957.

The British economy suffered more than the European continent because British industry was much more dependent on seaborne trade. Further, by the midfifties British industry had an unprecedented dependency on oil rather than coal as an energy source. About two-fifths of British crude steel was produced in oil-fired furnaces, and in 1955 the British glass industry used oil as fuel for manufacturing over half of its production.[83] With the canal closed, the pipeline blocked, and prospects of obtaining adequate U.S. supplies dim, Britain imposed severe restrictions on the use of oil at home. Nevertheless, by late November, "normal supplies dropped by 40 percent,"[84] and it was uncertain when, if ever, they would be restored or their loss made good from the Western Hemisphere. Stocks were falling and the country then had some idea of the difficulties with which it would be faced.

In France the government established a provisional oil conservation scheme in the hope that gasoline rationing would not prove necessary. Already there had been a big reduction in motoring, in part because of the difficulty in finding gasoline (distribution to the retailers had been severely cut). By mid-November the French authorities were still doing their best to persuade a skeptical public that no other form of rationing threatened them. Commodities such as sugar became scarce, owing to the rush of would-be hoarders, although in fact France's own sugar production that year presented a different problem—a surplus of about 30 percent.[85]

Many "bystander" countries in Europe also suffered serious economic consequences as a result of the Suez crisis. In a report on the general European situation, the *Financial Times* of 20 November 1956 wrote:

> The German stock position became known to be much less encouraging than was suggested earlier, and in France there were serious fears of a sharp setback to production. Even the Scandinavian countries depended on oil to a much greater extent than was generally realized. What was more, European oil supplies were interdependent. Italy, for example, which got 96 percent of its crude oil from the Middle East, exported considerable quantities of refined products to Switzerland, Greece, and Turkey.

In several continental countries, drastic measures had already been taken, such as bans on weekend motoring and limitations on the range of movement of private cars. Many countries were applying short-term measures of economy. These varied from cuts of 33 percent and of 20 percent in bulk oil supplies made by France and Switzerland, respectively, to cuts of 10 percent made by Belgium and Norway and a mere 5 percent by Italy. West Germany relied for the time being on an increase in gasoline prices of up to 20 percent.[86] Sweden introduced measures to reduce consumption by about 20 percent. As a result of the gasoline crisis, Volvo, Sweden's leading car manufacturer, cut its production by 30 percent.[87] Sunday and holiday journeys were banned in Belgium, while a Sunday ban on private motoring in Holland was coupled with a call for a voluntary 10 percent reduction in oil consumption.[88] France, Germany, and Britain went so far as to open negotiations with the Soviet Union and Rumania on possible purchases of oil to tide them over their present shortages.[89] Even Israel, which had accumulated considerable stocks prior to the commencement of hostilities in October 1956, began to feel the pinch in view of the uncertainty of future supplies following the cessation of shipments from the Soviet Union and general pressure on Western Hemisphere supplies.[90]

Gasoline rationing was only a hint of the total impact resulting from the closing of the Suez Canal and the sabotage of the IPC pipelines. The additional cost to Europe of transporting oil around the Cape of Good Hope was estimated by François-Georges Picot, director-general of the Universal Suez Canal Company, to be £54 million per month.[91] British Minister of Fuel and Power Aubrey Jones made the statement that the "additional freight costs of shipping oil around the Cape of Good Hope may be of the order of 2 pounds a ton."[92] Most of this additional cost was passed on to the consumer, the governments taking only part of the burden. Furthermore, a shortage of ships caused by the longer voyages around the cape interrupted the movement of imports and exports and led to a reduction in output in some industries. A necessary further cut in fuel oil consumption caused shorter working hours and unemployment. A prolonged stoppage of oil would have had consequences throughout the Western economy, particularly because Europe was living off its stockpiles of oil, the quantities of which were not disclosed.

The damage to the world's economy inflicted by the closure of the Suez Canal was reflected in: (1) the upsetting of established sea routes, leading to (2) increased total freight costs and shifts in the direction of foreign trade, (3) slowing down of the economic development of individual countries and regions, (4) increasing lengths of transportation routes, (5) sharply increased charges for shipping, insurance, and other costs.[93]

Analyzing the effects of the Suez developments on the European economy, George Parkhurst, vice-president of the Standard Oil Company of California (Socal) and a director of the Arabian-American Oil Company (Aramco), stated that

First, there is the cost of the military operation in Egypt.
Second, there is the high cost of shipping dry cargoes as well as oil by circuitous routes.

Third, there is a loss of trade resulting from limited transportation facilities. *Fourth,* there is the inflation of tanker rates, which have gone sky high. *Fifth,* there is the purchase of oil in the Western Hemisphere—the United States and Venezuela—for dollars.

I venture to predict that the term "dollar shortage" will again become a familiar one in reference to the European economy.[94]

However, these economic consequences could have been more severe had a serious oil shortage developed. John M. Blair observed:

2,165,000 barrels per day of the Eastern Hemisphere supply (west of Suez) had been moved via the canal and the Middle East pipelines. Nonetheless, no shortage developed, as the affected areas received slightly more than 90 percent of the supplies prior to the stoppage. These additional supplies were made possible by increased production, by heavy stock withdrawals during November and December, and by numerous unusual operations ... particularly in the United States.[95]

Another oil expert, P. H. Frankel, shared similar views:

The petroleum supply problem during the Suez Crisis was never one of a shortage of oil itself; with the exception of Saudi Arabia's ban on supplies to Britain and France all the oil was available as before, but owing to the closure of the Suez Canal and to the sabotage of more than half of the pipeline capacity, the available tanker fleet—fully used already before the Crisis—did not suffice to carry to its normal destinations the whole of the quantities hitherto shipped from the Persian Gulf, the latter having by the closure of the Canal suddenly become so much more distant from Europe.[96]

Frankel concluded:

In the end the repercussions of the Suez Oil Crisis were less drastic than they were at the time expected to be. This was due to the warm winter, the fact that demand was also for some other reasons below estimate and, to a great extent, to the skill with which all parties concerned handled their problems, handicapped as they were by being allowed to take all steps they could think of short of the effective ones. However, most people who are aware of the facts involved know how narrowly we escaped being faced with a very ugly situation.[97]

The economic effects of the closure of the Suez Canal and blocking of the IPC pipelines as well as the reduction of oil production in the Middle East due to the absence of tankers to carry oil westward proved to be only discomfiting reminders of the close connection between the

Western European economy and Middle Eastern oil. A 1957 report of the oil committee of the Organization of European Economic Co-Operation (OEEC) concluded with the following farsighted note:

> The safe-guarding of European oil supplies will require the concentrated efforts of both Governments and industry. As we have emphasized, by no means all the favourable factors which applied in the winter of 1956-57 could be counted upon to recur in the event of any future disruption of supplies. The successful surmounting of a major threat to the economy of Europe should not be allowed to lull Member countries into a sense of false security.

2
The Leverage of Oil, 1967

The Saudi-Egyptian Axis: The Politics
of Divergence, 1956–1967

In the aftermath of the Suez crisis, the Arab world was exposed to an unending stream of nationalistic and revolutionary propaganda emanating from a number of Arab capitals, particularly from Cairo. The failure of the tripartite invasion increased Egypt's stature in the Arab world, which Egypt exploited to promote its own ideas of social change and economic development. The dramatic military invasion and subsequent withdrawal of all military forces from Egypt produced a highly charged emotional atmosphere in the Arab world, arousing a fervent sense of nationalism among the Arab masses. This in turn created for Egypt a receptive political environment in which to pursue its revolutionary aspirations to lead an anticolonial drive in the Middle East to terminate all foreign influence.

Immediately after the Suez crisis, Arab nationalism reached such an emotional pitch that even the highly influential (but pro-Western) government of Nuri Sa'id in Iraq, at the time Egypt's only serious rival for Arab leadership, could maintain its hold on power for only eighteen months. In their book *Politics in the Middle East* (1979), James A. Bill and Carl Leiden elaborated:

> Nuri had consistently clung to his British friendships in good times and bad, and had incurred considerable distrust from many of his own officers as a result. After all, the Western defense alliance, in which Iraq alone of all the Arab states participated, was called the *Baghdad* Pact: Radio Cairo spoke for many Arabs in denouncing the Iraqi government's attachment to what it called Western "imperialism."[1]

Dissatisfaction with Nuri and his pro-British government climaxed when, in July 1958, the Hashemite monarchy in Iraq was overthrown in the bloodiest coup d'etat in modern Arab history, a blow that jolted the

Arab world and struck fear into the hearts of Arab monarchies and pro-Western regimes.

In its propaganda campaign, Cairo (later joined by Damascus and Baghdad) aimed at undermining the Arab pro-Western autocracies and monarchies, particularly those in the oil-rich Gulf states. This effort was intended to aggravate these countries' internal tensions and to drive a wedge between the ruling elites and the masses in hopes that one day the chasm would be so wide that it would lead to revolution. Throughout the late 1950s and early 1960s numerous civil disturbances, military coups, and political upheavals occurred within the Arab world. Several key issues, including anticolonialism, Arab unity, socialism, and economic reform, were the underlying factors creating this unrest, but undoubtedly the Palestine question was one of the most complex and explosive among them. Few Arab leaders thought in terms of compromise with Israel; those who dared to, like Tunisia's President Habib Bourguiba, were exposed to intense public campaigns aimed at discrediting them and undermining their regimes.[2] Others questioned more discreetly the extent to which Arab militancy should manifest itself in military adventures against the militarily more powerful and technologically advanced Israeli state.

Earlier efforts by the various Arab governments to determine a unified course of action against their common enemy had often faltered. This led many observers, both foreign and Arab, to a habitual skepticism about whether these regimes could act in concert given their different images of the world, different attitudes toward foreign powers, different political systems and ideological orientations, and, most significantly, their conflicting national interests. This pessimism was based not on conjecture, but rather on actual experience in Arab politics and on well-founded projections into the future of the way the Arab political system had functioned in the past.

The widening rifts among the Arab regimes led to their eventual polarization into two opposing camps. One camp, labeled "revolutionary," consisted of Egypt, Syria, Iraq, Sudan, Yemen, and Algeria. The other, labeled "conservative," consisted of Saudi Arabia, Jordan, Libya (before the 1969 coup), Kuwait, the Gulf emirates, Tunisia, and Morocco. Lebanon, a fragile, laissez-faire democracy, aspired to play a "neutral" role in the conflict, although at times the intense quarreling would spill across its borders, causing temporary disruptions of Lebanese political equilibrium. George Lenczowski in *U.S. Interests in the Middle East* (1968) explored this aspect of the Arab political structure:

> The basic conflict between the revolutionary and conservative camps was over the future of Arab political and economic development. The revo-

lutionary camp espoused, at least in theory, a radical transformation along socialist lines. The conservative camp wanted to pursue evolutionary developments, taking into account local characteristics and the traditional element of society. President Nasser of Egypt has been the major, though not unchallenged, leader of the revolutionaries. For most of this period King Faisal of Saudi Arabia has been the most prominent conservative leader. The foreign policy alignments of the camps tended to follow their domestic orientation: the revolutionaries being pro-Soviet and the conservatives pro-American. Their views on the question of Israel also tended to follow their internal divisions. The conservatives, although verbally supporting the general Arab position on Israel, were reluctant to see open conflict renewed.[3]

Cairo's claim to leadership of the "revolutionary" camp was based on two major recent political events that had captured the imagination of the Arab masses: the 1952 Egyptian revolution and the 1956 nationalization of the Suez Canal. In contrast, following the Iraqi coup, Riyadh's claim to leadership of the "conservative" camp was based mainly on religious and economic factors. Saudi Arabia is the country in which Islam originated and from which it spread. It has the two most holy cities of Islam, Mecca and Medina. Thus, Saudi monarchs have traditionally been the guardians of the Muslim holy places, particularly the Kaabah, to which all Muslims are called upon to make a pilgrimage at least once in their lifetime. Saudi Arabia was also the most influential among the Arab oil producers because of its enormous proven reserves.[4]

The traditional Saudi-Egyptian rivalry transcends the personalities of Nasser and Faisal. In 1818 Egypt invaded and occupied areas of the inner Arabian peninsula in an effort to check the kingdom's rapid expansion. Not until 1840 did internal problems draw the Egyptian forces back home. From the time of the consolidation of their rule in 1932,[5] Ibn Saud and his family had perceived that the greatest threat to their new kingdom was from the Hashemites to the north, with whom Saudi Arabia shared a long land border. But the 1952 Egyptian revolution changed those calculations drastically. In the few years following the takeover of Egypt by young, ambitious, and zealous military officers, the Saudi rulers attempted to coexist with the new Egyptian regime. The deposed Egyptian king, Farouk I, had not been popular with the Saudis, and the new Egyptian leaders promptly made what appeared to be a dutiful pilgrimage to Mecca and Riyadh. In return, Saudi Arabia cut diplomatic relations with Britain and France in support of Egypt during the 1956 Suez crisis. Between 1958 and 1967 Saudi-Egyptian relations became more aggravated than they had ever been before. Unresolved problems accumulated, spreading mutual distrust, which in turn deterred any genuine effort at coordinating policies or unifying a position on any major Arab or international issue. The uncompromising, ideological, and vocal conviction of the Egyptian leadership that there could be no compromise with "reaction," either domestically or in inter-Arab politics, led both King Saud and his successor, King Faisal, to view the danger to their regime's national security and political stability as coming not only from communism or Israeli militarism but also from "radical Nasserism."

With the development of radio communications, the Saudis' perception of Egyptian threats intensified. Previously, when communications in the Middle East were slow, the Saudi monarchs had felt that the desert could insulate them from the political unrest that seethed elsewhere. Accordingly, they made few efforts to promote development or invest in public works, education, or health services; oil revenues were treated as the personal income of the sovereign and were used largely to finance his political aims and to promote royal comfort.[6] Saudi monarchs felt that their prestige as the keepers of the Muslim holy places was to some extent sufficient to protect them against Arab radicalism. King Saud attempted to compete with Nasser by trying to extend Saudi influence to other Arab countries, but isolated himself in 1958 by financing an abortive plot to assassinate Nasser. As his poor administration and enormous expenditures began to exceed all limits, Saud was replaced in 1964 by his younger brother, Prince Faisal.[7]

The new Saudi monarch used his oil revenues, the domestic peace his accession to power had brought about, and staunch U.S. political support to attempt to counterbalance Nasser's revolutionism. But Faisal was an introverted conservative who possessed none of Nasser's personal charisma. His basic problem was the absence of a highly educated elite who would carry the burdens of a rapidly expanding government and help him in his efforts to build a modern state. Moreover, Faisal's attempts to assume the role of an international Islamic leader were not notably successful. He did convene a number of Islamic conferences that he hoped would transcend the limits of the Arab world, but Nasser's persistent attacks on these efforts, linking them with imperialism and foreign powers and portraying them as fronts for Western dominance in the area, robbed them of the massive support they had been expected to gather. Furthermore, the lack of concrete programs weakened Faisal's aspirations of building a religious alliance and left many Islamic countries disenchanted. As his challenges to the Egyptian leadership faltered, Faisal confined himself more and more to his own kingdom, pursuing an isolationist policy, fostering those Arab regimes and monarchies feeling the heat of Nasser's revolution, and leaning more and more on U.S. political support and military aid.

Egypt Asserts Its Leadership of the Arab World, 1956–1967

In his *Philosophy of the Revolution* (1954),[8] Nasser wrote of "heroic and glorious roles which never found heroes to perform them." For centuries since the death of Saladin, the Arabs had searched for a leader to give them the dignity denied them by centuries of foreign domination. From the depths of this unresolved crisis, Nasser was "the one leader who both stood for the things—the self-respect, the unity, the independence—the Arabs craved for, and had the ability to convey these aspirations to the rest of the world."[9]

With unremitting energy, Nasser rekindled the imagination of those Arabs who were young, frustrated, and resentful of the lid that had been clamped onto their political aspirations by the traditional oligarchy, and he struck fear into the hearts of the feudal and aristocratic classes who had long controlled the people's daily lives. To the poverty-stricken, underfed, medically neglected, uneducated masses spread over Egypt[10] and the rest of the Arab world, he was a hope for a better tomorrow— the aspirations of a nation molded in the texture of a single man.[11] Arabs who felt oppressed by foreign powers, absolute monarchs, and rigged parliaments saw in Nasser a long-awaited answer to their prayers. In the Muslim majority, he stirred a yearning for the glories of the early days of Islam. To Arab nationalists, he embodied defiance and challenge to Western domination of Arab affairs. Political mistakes made by the British, French, or Americans in the Middle East added to his stature. Though Egypt's need for funds was pressing, Nasser refused to compromise with any source that offered conditional aid. More significantly, he resisted becoming corrupt. To this very day, the "Cairo Tower," which graces the landscape across the Nile, stands as a reminder of how the Egyptian leader in 1955 responded to a "personal gift" of three million dollars from President Eisenhower's executive budget.[12] Such attitudes enhanced Nasser's stature in the eyes of his fellow Arabs, who came to view him as a sovereign who could be trusted.

Under Nasser's charismatic leadership, Cairo exercised an unprecedented and perhaps unwarranted influence on Arab politics.[13] Crucial decisions needed Nasser's approval to be implemented: The Baghdad Pact, which the Western powers hoped to use as a bulwark against communism and Arab nationalism, failed to materialize solely as a result of Cairo's opposition. A Radio Cairo criticism of any political plan in the Arab world crucially affected its fate, no matter what other Arab country supported it. Cairo's influence was felt even in the internal politics of other states as Nasser strove to upset the political stability of conservative or traditional Arab autocracies. It was felt particularly in Saudi Arabia, where "most Saudi nationalists . . . continued to look to President Nasser instead of King Saud for personal inspiration."[14] This obviously earned Nasser the enmity of several other Arab regimes, particularly as his efficient propaganda machine could now reach even those Arabs living in the farthest corners of the Arab world.[15]

In 1956 the first major crisis that Nasser faced was the tripartite attack on Egypt. The failure of this invasion left him an Arab hero; while Eden fell, Nasser survived, gaining the reputation of a national savior. Two years later Nasser's prestige was enhanced by Egypt's union with Syria, but Syria's withdrawal from the United Arab Republic in 1961 dealt a blow to both Nasser's prestige and Egypt's pivotal position in the Arab world. The conservatives were encouraged and Nasser accused "reactionism, imperialism and its agents" of having joined forces and "succeeded in separating Syria from Egypt."[16] The year 1962 was characterized, in the words of political scientist A. I. Dawisha, "by an environment of rigid political polarization between Egypt and the conservative camp led by Saudi Arabia, which was perceived by the Egyptian leadership as the bastion of reaction and the major agent for imperialist ambitions in, and conspiracies against, the Arab world."[17]

The Saudi-Egyptian politics of divergence widened dramatically when a military coup in Yemen in September 1962 succeeded in declaring that country a republic, precipitating a civil war between the Egypt-backed Republicans and the Saudi-backed Royalists.[18] Nasser, who had overcome his aides' urgings to intervene militarily against the secessionists in Syria one year before in a bid to "preserve Arab blood," took a diametrically opposite stand on the Yemeni issue; Egyptian troops were posted to support the Republican army in the civil war.[19] Among other factors, this decision may be attributed to Nasser's desire to regain the initiative in the Arab world that Egypt had lost after the Syrian secession. Consequently, the Yemeni civil war became a war by proxy between "progressive" and "conservative" Arab regimes. It widened the rift between the two regional powers. Saudi Arabia backed the Yemeni Royalists, seeing an imminent peril in Egyptian thrusts toward the Saudi Arabian southern borders, which could expose it to military attack and nourish domestic dissent, while Egypt, ambitious to make Yemen a symbol of the "inevitable" primacy of the "Arab revolutionary tide" over the "forces of reaction," supported the Republican army at the cost of many lives on both sides and an alarming drain on the Egyptian treasury. The Yemeni war became Nasser's "Vietnam."[20] He later admitted that Egyptian involvement had been a "miscalculation," and that he "never thought that it would lead to what it did."[21]

By early 1964 Nasser succeeded in terminating, temporarily at least, the political polarization in the Arab world when he convened an Arab summit conference in Cairo to discuss the Israelis' projected diversion of the River Jordan. Saudi-Egyptian tensions eased, and Nasser's conciliatory attitude toward Faisal resulted in the resumption of diplomatic relations between the two countries in March of the same year. In the wake of this summit conference,

> the ideological confrontation between the "progressive" and "conservative" camps subsided considerably. The perception of the "battle of life or death" between socialism and reaction . . . was gradually replaced by an attitude of tolerance and a tacit acceptance of the differing political and social systems. Haykel's theory of the primacy of the revolution over Arab solidarity was, at least for the time being, put on ice, as the Arab world entered a period of peaceful coexistence. Consequently the propaganda war was discontinued by all parties and an atmosphere of almost complete tranquillity reigned over the Middle East for the first time in nearly ten years.[22]

In this atmosphere of reconciliation, the protracted political and military conflict over the control of Yemen ebbed when a ceasefire agreement between Nasser and Faisal was reached in August 1965. This truce, known as the Jedda Accords, required Nasser to withdraw his overextended Egyptian troops from the perilous Yemeni mountains; a caretaker coalition government was to be formed to rule Yemen until a plebiscite could be held to determine what kind of permanent regime the country was to have. Although this truce helped decrease the intensity of the war, the terms of the agreement were never put into effect, and Nasser's ambitions to impose a progressive regime on Yemen's feudal people and to extend his influence into the Gulf emirates and the southern peninsula were dashed by successive military setbacks. However, though neither military setbacks nor political conciliation failed to put an end to Egypt's presence in the Arabian peninsula, both undermined Nasser's influence there.

It was not long before tensions between Cairo and Riyadh began to mount once more. In his bid to build himself up as an international Islamic figure, Faisal toured some Islamic countries in late 1965 and early 1966, calling for an Islamic summit in Mecca later in 1966. Nasser perceived Faisal's initiative "as a new drive to isolate Egypt and the rest of the progressive forces in the Arab world."[23] In an interview with Moscow's *Izvestia*, Nasser declared that "the forces of colonialism and reaction inside and outside the Arab world are launching a new offensive, and therefore, all progressive forces inside and outside the Arab world should close their ranks, solidify their unity and redouble their vigilance, and thus become effective."[24]

Nasser's suspicions that there was an "antiprogressive leadership conspiracy" were compounded when Britain and the United States announced a major arms sale to Saudi Arabia in December 1965. In his editorial in the Cairo daily *al-Ahram* of 29 April 1966, Editor-in-Chief Mohamed Haykal contended that this conspiracy was "a part of the colonialists' reactionary onslaught against the national revolutions in Asia, Africa, and Latin America." The phase of Arab solidarity was clearly ending, and Egypt felt once more that it needed to go on the offensive against reactionary regimes.[25] Nasser himself had become increasingly convinced that there was an international "imperialist" plot against Egypt. Thus in a major speech on 22 July 1966 he returned to the theme of "imperialism" in alliance with "reaction" plotting against progressive and "socialist" systems and publicly announced the end of the period of "peaceful coexistence" by declaring Egypt's refusal to attend the forthcoming Arab summit conference.

Fearing Israeli-Western collusion against Syria, Egypt signed a defense alliance with the Syrian government on 4 November 1966, which asserted that aggression against either state would be regarded as an attack on the other. This perception of an Israeli threat started the downward spiral that led in June 1967 to the most disastrous confrontation of Nasser's entire career.[26]

The 1967 Oil Embargo: Adversaries as Allies

The situation in early June 1967 was much more critical than the 1956 Suez affair. "An Arab-Israeli war, regarded by both sides as a life and death struggle, would be a much nastier affair than Suez, and the passions it generated would be more intense and more widespread," wrote David Hirst in the London *Guardian* on 29 May 1967.[27]

The atmosphere of crisis that prevailed in late May 1967 prompted Iraq to invite other Arab oil producers to come to Baghdad on 4 June to discuss the situation. On 1 June oil ministers from a number of Arab oil-producing countries accepted the Iraqi invitation. Three main items were on the conference's agenda:

1. to stop the shipments of Arab oil to any country that supported or participated in any attack on an Arab country or violated Arab territorial sovereignty;
2. to warn foreign oil companies operating in Arab countries either to cooperate with the decisions of the conference or risk losing their concessions; and
3. to ask all Islamic and friendly oil-producing countries to stand united with the Arabs over the sale of oil to their enemies.

Two difficulties faced the conference. The first was whether the countries whose economies did not depend on oil, such as Egypt, would be able to persuade oil-dependent countries to imperil their national economies and risk the loss of their best markets. While two-thirds of Iraq's production traveled through vulnerable pipelines in Syria, most Saudi oil was transported by tankers that loaded cargoes in the Gulf. The second problem was whether any embargo that might be agreed upon could be enforced. The oil companies that operated in the Middle East under profit-sharing agreements with the different countries were mainly U.S. and British, making it most unlikely that those companies would carry out the dictates of the conference.

With the outbreak of the Arab-Israeli war on 5 June, the Baghdad conference felt an urgency to express solidarity with the Arab com-batants—Egypt, Syria, and Jordan.[28] Toward this end, the oil ministers of Iraq, Saudi Arabia, Libya, Kuwait, Algeria, the Gulf sheikhdoms of Bahrain, Qatar, and Abu Dhabi,[29] and the representatives of Egypt, Lebanon, and Syria agreed to "stop all shipments of oil to any nation assisting Israel in its aggression against Arab countries."[30] Though some of the ministers present had reservations and wanted to confer with their governments first, the conference decided to establish an embargo against oil shipments destined for the United States and Britain, as it was widely believed that U.S. and British planes had given air cover to Israel and that British aircraft had bombed Arab targets. In his book *America and the Arab States* (1975), Robert W. Stookey explained:

> The remarkable skill of the Israeli air force in the first hours of the battle, notably the rapid turnaround achieved between sorties, made possible an attack greatly exceeding in intensity what [Jordan's King] Hussein and Nasser believed possible with the number of aircraft known to be in Israel's inventory. They leaped to the conclusion that American planes from Sixth Fleet carriers and British aircraft from Cyprus were participating in the onslaught. Without regard for the publicly known disposition of the Sixth Fleet, whose fighting units the United States had carefully kept well west of the troubled area, and without consulting the Russians, who as usual were keeping the American fleet under tight surveillance, Nasser declared to the world on June 6 that the United States and Britain were assisting in the Israeli operations.[31]

The 1956 experience had taught the conferees that, unless contained or absorbed, the spontaneous anger of the Arab masses could prove destructive. The situation in 1967 seemed ripe for a repetition as for quite some time before the outbreak of hostilities Cairo and Damascus had been overtly urging the destruction of Western-owned installations in the event of any Western intervention in support of Israel.[32] Similar urgings at the time of Suez had led directly to the sabotage of the IPC pipeline. Israeli victories on the battlefield inflamed the feelings of outrage among the Arab masses. The International Confederation of Arab Trade Unions called on all Arab oil states to join in the embargo. It also urged workers to blow up pipelines and oil installations in any Arab nation that refused to comply with the embargo.

Anti-American riots broke out in Saudi Arabia on 7 June, obliging Aramco to suspend all its operations and to evacuate some of its personnel. In Libya, workers seized the terminals and offices of Oasis Oil Company and stopped operations for five hours until the Libyan authorities removed them. In Kuwait, where the bulk of oil production is controlled by the Kuwait Oil Company, oil installations were placed under army guard. In Bahrain, two refineries were shut down because of a labor stoppage. Anti-Western feelings were running high, mainly because Israel's devastating victory had been achieved by using Western-supplied weapons, making words such as Phantom and napalm into household words overnight.[33]

This explosive situation posed a serious political problem for the oil-producing governments, mainly Kuwait, Libya, and Saudi Arabia, none of which had a secure grip on power. Under the circumstances, it seemed expedient for those countries to demonstrate true Arab sentiments by joining the embargo against Britain and the United States.

Arab Rivalries Return

Once the peak of emotional intensity caused by the war had subsided, internal conflicts among the various Arab states began to reassert their primacy over the common cause against Israel. Disagreements about the oil-embargo strategy began to revive the old prewar "revolutionary/reactionary" antagonism, which had been muted by the necessity of Arab solidarity against Israel.[34] While Egypt, Syria, Algeria, and Iraq were demanding that the embargo be continued, Saudi Arabia, Kuwait, and Libya wanted it lifted. Other sources of inter-Arab differences were: (1) strategic, i.e., Egypt's growing alignment with the Soviet Union, a move opposed by the Saudis, who desired that the Arabs depend instead on Islamic countries; and (2) geopolitical, i.e., Faisal's insistence that Egyptian forces be withdrawn from Yemen as a prerequisite for any Yemeni settlement.

The rivalry was crystallized when the foreign ministers of the thirteen Arab League states met in an emergency session in Kuwait on 18 June 1967 to discuss the embargo. A proposal made by Egypt, Iraq, Syria, and Algeria for a complete stoppage of production failed in the face of strong opposition from Saudi Arabia, Kuwait, and Libya. The moderate oil producers were apprehensive that their national economies might be endangered as a result of the loss of oil revenues. Another inhibiting factor was the 1951 experience of Iran, whose oil exports had been stopped during the nationalization dispute. When the Iranian fields began production again in 1953, key markets were found tied to long-term contracts elsewhere. In addition, many Western nations had been imposing a strict embargo on Soviet oil imports for fear that the Soviet Union might cut off oil supplies in an emergency or for political reasons. The moderate Arab producers feared that a total ban would classify them as unreliable suppliers and cause them to lose long-term markets. In the end a compromise was reached. While the proposal for a complete stoppage was rejected, it was agreed to continue the embargo against the United States and Britain. The embargo was also extended to West Germany because of German military and financial aid to Israel, and in particular because of Germany's sale of gas masks to Israel shortly before the fighting broke out. An embargo on oil shipments to Rhodesia and South Africa, imposed before the war, remained in effect. To those targets, Iraq, acting alone, added Italy for its pro-Israeli attitude in the United Nations.

By early July a number of steps were being taken to ease the tense European oil-supply situation. Iraq, which since the war had imposed a total embargo on shipments, began to resume oil exports to "friendly countries." In Libya, a general strike by the oil workers in protest against "Anglo-American support for Israeli aggression" had been preventing oil shipments from the main port of Tripoli since the beginning of the war. Strenuous efforts on the part of the Libyan government to end the total ban in favor of a limited embargo against Britain, the United States, and West Germany remained unsuccessful. The Libyan government's hands were tied because it was being accused of having allowed the United States to use the Wheelus base in Libya against the Arab nation during the June war. Not until early July, when a new Libyan government was appointed, were oil shipments resumed to "friendly countries" such as France, Italy, Spain, Greece, and Turkey. The official Libyan news agency described the embargo against "other Western European countries" as "becoming worthless," because other producers were not enforcing it. The newly appointed prime minister, Abdel Qadir al-Badri, issued a tough policy statement reaffirming that Libya, "which was losing around $1.5 million daily in oil revenues," was "fully committed" to the embargo resolutions passed at the Arab oil ministers' conference in Kuwait and that it would "sacrifice development projects for its principles."

At the same time, Saudi Arabia's media stepped up the number of commentaries and statements pointing out that the embargo was impairing the economies of Arab oil-producing countries more than those of the target countries. By publicizing such a viewpoint, Saudi Arabia was implying that it had decided to take the lead at home and abroad in pressing for an end to the embargo. In an interview with the Saudi daily *al-Madina al-Munawarah* published on 29 June 1967, Saudi Oil Minister Sheikh Ahmed Zaki el-Yamani questioned the value of the embargo and argued that if it continued the Arabs stood to lose as much economically as they had already lost territorially. Yamani urged other Arab oil-producing countries to study what he called "the serious impact on their economies" that would result from the continued halt of oil production and asserted that the embargo was turning out to be a double-edged weapon as the Arabs began to realize that they were not the West's only source of oil.[35] To presage its possible lifting of the embargo, Saudi Arabia began to stress that its justification for the embargo had disappeared after Jordan's King Hussein stated during a visit to the United States in late June that he was unsure whether U.S. or British aircraft carriers had actually participated in the Israeli attacks against the Arab countries in the June war.[36] In an official statement made on 7 July 1967, the Saudi Arabian government called for an end to the Arab oil embargo against Britain and the United States. The Saudi statement said: "Now that it has been established that there was no evidence of British and American aircraft helping Israel in last month's war, there is no reason to continue the ban on exporting oil to the two countries."[37]

This Saudi antiembargo trial balloon was attacked fiercely by other Arab governments, which accused the Saudis of "deserting" the Arab cause.[38] On 8 July the Egyptian radio and press responded that the Saudi statement had been a "shock to Arab public opinion" and that if the Saudis lifted the embargo they would be "undermining Arab solidarity" in the present crisis.[39] The Egyptian media gave great prominence to an attack on the Saudi monarch by the Cairo-based Arab Lawyers' Federation, which declared that King Faisal's deicision to resume pumping was "a stab in the back coming not from imperialism or aggression this time but from an Arab state which should have been in the vanguard in defending Arab honor."[40] The federation urged all Arabs to work against the Saudi decision and "not allow anyone to plot against Arab national interests." The semiofficial *Egyptian Gazette* wrote on 10 July 1967:

Saudi Arabia lost nothing in the battle. It did not participate militarily against Israel despite its declarations of support for the other Arabs, declarations which were empty words. Now it is seeking to profit by sending its oil to the U.S. and Britain, caring nothing for the difficulties in which the Arabs find themselves and caring nothing for their rights. The mere withholding of oil by all the Arabs until the U.S. and Britain agree to cease their support of Israel and to acknowledge the Arabs' rights would probably in itself force those two countries to toe the line. By imposing other sanctions, including the closure of the Suez Canal, there could be little doubt of a favorable outcome. It cannot be denied that the sacrifice is not small. But the Arabs are prepared for this. It is part of their battle, in which all the people are ready to take part.

In *al-Ahram's* weekly editorial published 14 July 1967, Editor-in-Chief Haykal criticized the Saudis' justification of their projected resumption of oil shipments to the United States and Britain, stating that "America's stand at the United Nations proved beyond the least shadow of a doubt America's support of Israel." Haykal wrote:

When the destiny of the Arab nation is at stake, the Arabs should not let Faisal's stand determine the future of the whole nation.

However, it is easy to refute King Faisal's arguments used to justify all his attitudes.

King Faisal began to set the stage for the resumption of pumping oil to the USA and Britain on the grounds that he has no proof that the USA and Britain directly participated with Israel in the war launched against a number of Arab countries which is in fact a war against the whole Arab nation.

It is easy to ask King Faisal the following question: What is Israel, originally and basically, your Majesty?

Isn't she the base established by imperialism to serve as a bridgehead to threaten the whole Arab nation, and as a barrier dividing the continuous expanse of Arab land?

And who supplies Israel with money and arms which she used in her aggression launched recently and previously?

Where did Israel get this number of planes which range between 1,200 and 1,500? And where did she get the pilots?

The Unified Arab Command had estimated—and this happened in your presence—Israel's first line planes at 300. Yet Israeli planes which raided the Jordanian front alone on June 6, according to the assessments made by King Hussein and his Command, reached 400.

The Jordanian radar networks testified that the American and perhaps the British aircraft carriers had participated in giving Israel an air cover. King Hussein has sent the records of the radar networks to the UN. This means that he found something which had definitely aroused his suspicions.

It is a real shame that your Majesty insisted afterwards on the statements which King Hussein made during his visit to the USA, in which he said that he was not sure that the American aircraft carriers participated in the battle.

Those statements have their own circumstances and grasping at them would be a heavy burden on Jordan which is suffering from her wounds.

Furthermore, the USA did not deny, nor can she deny, that thousands of American volunteers arrived in Israel two weeks before the aggression. There were pilots and this has now become indisputable. And before their arrival, their American planes were flown to Israel after the insignia of the American Air Force were removed and painted over with the Israeli Star of David.

If the U.S. did not participate in the battle with the aircraft and pilots of the American aircraft carriers, America participated with her aircraft and pilots from her bases in America and Europe.

By this America participated directly in the battle by giving air cover to Israel.

In Iraq, both government officials and civic organizations denounced the Saudis' anticipated lifting of the embargo. The government described the Saudi decision as "a stab in the back of Arab unanimity" at a critical stage in modern Arab history and "a flagrant challenge to the Arab will which considers oil the mightiest weapon in the battle."[41] Dr. Mahmud al-Homsy, chairman of the Iraqi Society of Economists, described the Saudi stand as "treason"[42] and asserted that the elimination of the Saudi regime should be the major objective of the Arab liberation movement: "Such regimes constitute a break in the Arab front which must be repaired." The chairman of the Iraqi Association of Teachers, Khalil Marzuk, called the Saudi decision "a treacherous act which served the interests of America and imperialism."[43] Yemen also denounced the Saudi decision as a violation of the resolutions of the Baghdad oil conference, describing it as "a failure by Saudi Arabia to fulfil her obligations towards the entire Arab nation, and new evidence that this country's rulers are not prepared to shoulder their responsibility in facing the aggression."[44] A statement by the Front for the Liberation of Occupied South Yemen denounced the Saudi position: "Britain is still practicing terrorist actions against Arab people in Aden. To give them oil is a stab in the back of Arabs and disrupts Arab unity needed in the battle for our destiny."[45] Algerian radio attacked Saudi Arabia for renouncing the general Arab agreement to ban deliveries of oil, charging the Saudis with "treason against the Arab struggle."[46] In Lebanon, a wave of criticism swept through political circles, and Damascus Radio exhorted all Arab workers "to frustrate the reactionary plans to supply the imperialists with Arab oil."

The former Saudi oil minister, Abdullah al-Tariqi, in exile in Beirut, argued that Saudi Arabia would suffer no great losses of income if oil shipments to the United States and Britain were not resumed. Using figures to support his argument, Tariqi asserted that in 1967 Saudi Arabia would continue to earn from oil exports the same revenue as it had earned in 1966 even if the embargo continued, because the imports of the United States and Britain were matched by the 1967 increase in Saudi oil production. Tariqi maintained that Western losses because of the embargo exceeded Arab losses and added that the embargo would eventually compel those countries to change their political attitudes.[47] Similar views were echoed by other Arab states and organizations.

This vehement Arab opposition obliged the Saudi government on 12 July officially to deny all reports that it intended to lift the embargo against Britain and the United States and to maintain that "King Faisal had made no decision on resuming the oil supplies."[48] At the same time, the Saudi government allowed Tapline, the U.S. company that handled the 1,068-mile oil pipeline from Saudi Arabia to the Mediterranean, to resume oil exports.[49] Also on 12 July, Saudi Oil Minister Yamani flew to Kuwait to try to persuade that country to join the Saudi attempt to lift the oil embargo. Yet in spite of Saudi disenchantment with the embargo, Sheikh Yamani at the end of two days of unsuccessful talks with Kuwaiti officials "reiterated that Saudi Arabia was observing the boycott of countries which supported Zionist aggression."[50]

Egypt Reverses Its Position

In the aftermath of the June war, the Arab masses looked to Nasser to restore their lost honor and self-respect. The Egyptian leader directed Egyptian policies toward "liquidating the traces of aggression" and securing a just settlement for the Arab-Israeli conflict. His immediate goal was to strengthen his weakened grip on the levers of power in Egypt and undermine extremist opposition by taking over both the premiership and the secretary generalship of Egypt's only official party, the Arab Socialist Union.

Internationally, though the Egyptian regime was becoming increasingly dependent on the Soviet Union for arms, Nasser's strategy centered around returning to Egypt's traditional policy of nonalignment and exhausting all diplomatic means of rallying international opinion to press for Israel's withdrawal from the occupied Arab lands. Toward that end, Nasser allowed his confidant Haykal to advocate the restoration of diplomatic relations between Egypt and the United States. The justification for Haykal's *volte-face* in early August 1967 was that "a head-on clash with the U.S. was, and still is in my opinion, an error which we cannot afford and for which we are not equipped." Even the Soviet Union, Haykal wrote, sought to avoid such a clash. Consequently, Haykal argued that the reestablishment of relations with the U.S. was vital to enable Egypt to maintain a balanced international policy.

On the Arab level, Nasser assigned high priority to peaceful coexistence and sought to end the bipolar structure of Arab politics. Egypt therefore moved to mend its relations with Saudi Arabia and the other conservative Arab regimes, taking a major diplomatic step toward ending hostilities between the two camps at the Arab Foreign Ministers' Meeting in Khartoum, Sudan, in early August.

Arab Foreign Ministers' Meeting

An Egyptian offer submitted to the August 1 Arab Foreign Ministers' Meeting of terms for the settlement of the conflict with Saudi Arabia over Yemen represented a breakthrough that changed the general situation of Arab politics. The proposal called for the immediate revival of the Jedda Accords, which had been concluded between President Nasser and King Faisal in August 1965 to end the Yemeni civil war.[51] At least five reasons lay behind the Egyptian decision:

1. Cairo needed to form a solid common Arab front to deal with the urgency of Israel's occupation of Arab territories and to map a joint Arab strategy to carry on the political, economic, and military struggle in the wake of Israel's June victory.

2. Cairo needed to muster all the military strength it could inside Egyptian borders to defend itself against further perceived Israeli threats; Nasser was anxious to bring the estimated 20,000 Egyptian soldiers back from Yemen, both to strengthen Egypt's own defense lines that faced the Israelis across the Suez Canal and to pare military expenses.

3. Cairo hoped that Saudi goodwill and close connections with the United States might help bring about a peaceful settlement of the Arab-Israeli conflict. Moreover, Egypt needed Saudi financial support to meet its exceedingly grave economic problems.

4. Cairo no longer felt the need for an Egyptian military presence in Yemen. The British decision fixing the definite date of January 1968 for the independence of Aden and the withdrawal of British troops led Nasser to judge that Saudi Arabia would no longer represent a danger to the Yemeni republic.

5. Cairo hoped that resolving the Yemeni conflict would smooth over the deep and bitter rift between Egypt and Saudi Arabia and end the Arab cold war, which had become Nasser's main preoccupation.

To put the plan into effect, Egypt proposed the formation of a committee of three Arab states—one to be chosen by itself, a second by Saudi Arabia, and a third by the Arab foreign ministers themselves. The Saudi government reacted favorably to the Egyptian initiative.

Once the thorny issue of Yemen was resolved, the major issue facing the conference became the oil embargo. On this the ministers remained split. Iraq, demanding that the embargo be continued indefinitely, placed before the conference a proposal that called for a complete stoppage of all Arab oil exports to the West, the nationalization of foreign monopolies, and the withdrawal of Arab funds from Western countries. Tunisia, Libya, Kuwait, and Saudi Arabia urged moderation, arguing that such measures could harm the Arab nations themselves and pointing out that the embargo had already damaged the Arab economies. Kuwait called for "more far-sighted and practical attitudes" in dealing with the embargo issue.

Despite dissent over the embargo, the Arab Foreign Ministers' Meeting achieved a climate of sufficient agreement to warrant the convening of an Arab summit meeting. Egypt's ceasefire offer had proven instrumental in persuading the foreign ministers that the atmosphere for a summit was favorable. The resolutions adopted by the foreign ministers were not published for "security reasons." However, a communiqué issued on 8 August 1967 reflected the new, more cooperative mood, stating that the ministers of economy, finance, and oil would meet in Baghdad on 15 August to discuss the oil embargo and other economic reprisals against Western states accused of "aiding the Israeli aggression." Furthermore, the communiqué declared the reactivation of the Arab "solidarity pact," signed at the third and last Arab summit held in Casablanca, Morocco, in September 1965, which involved a pledge to halt inter-Arab propaganda attacks.

Meeting of Arab Ministers of Economy, Finance, and Oil

In a crucial meeting that could have affected the international oil outlook for years to come, the Arab Ministerial Conference convened in Baghdad on 15 August 1967 to prepare recommendations on how economic measures could best be used to strengthen the Arab position in the aftermath of the June war. On the meeting's agenda were four specific plans: (1) Algeria's proposal that the large Arab financial deposits in Britain and the United States be withdrawn; (2) Iraq's proposal that all Arab oil supplies be cut for a period of three months so as to exhaust Western European stocks; (3) Kuwait's proposal that a joint Arab fund for "war and reconstruction" be created, with headquarters in Kuwait and with an initial capitalization of £100 million; and (4) Egypt's proposal for the creation of an Arab petroleum organization along the lines of OPEC. Egypt, a non-OPEC member, had been a major campaigner for the establishment of such an organization.

The most controversial of these proposals was the Iraqi call for a shutdown in oil exports by all Arab producers for three months, starting 1 September in order to hit Europe's peak winter demand for fuel. This was to be followed by a selective embargo in which supplies would flow again to "friendly nations" in sufficient quantity to meet their domestic demand. These countries would have to guarantee that no oil would be reexported. The plan further called for partial and "phased" nationalization of foreign interests in the Arab oil industry, designed to produce a "catastrophic oil shortage" in the developed countries, which would then be forced to exert pressure on Israel to withdraw. The plan was endorsed by Egypt, Syria, and Algeria, but met with rigid opposition from Saudi Arabia, Kuwait, Libya, Tunisia, Morocco, and the Gulf sheikhdoms.

Timed to coincide with the opening of the conference, Saudi Arabia's official radio attacked the continued embargo of oil exports to the West. Commenting on the Baghdad meeting, the broadcast maintained that both the embargo and the call for nationalization "run counter to Arab interests."[52] Arguments in favor of lifting the embargo were based on the following considerations: (1) lack of evidence that the U.S. and Britain had supported Israel with air cover as had been assumed initially; (2) Arab need for oil revenues to rebuild their economies; (3) perceptions that continuing the embargo was causing the Arab world to become overdependent on the Soviet Union, while its removal would bring in the West as a counterweight to communist influence; and (4) fears of a possible British intervention in Kuwait and other Arab oil-producing countries. By the end of their meetings, the Arab ministers failed to agree on a collective strategy for cutting off Arab oil, though they did agree to continue the embargo. However, Saudi Arabia added the proviso that the Arab oil-producing countries should have the freedom to meet at any time in the future to reconsider the embargo in the light of new developments. In addition, the conferees recommended that the following resolutions be submitted for final approval to the Arab summit conference to be held in Khartoum on 29 August 1967:

1. Petroleum is an effective weapon in the battle and pumping must be stopped totally, not merely partially, but permanently until the consequences of Israeli aggression have been eliminated.
2. The Arab summit in discussing this matter should take into consideration the consequences of such a step on Arab states in general and on oil-producing states in particular.
3. Arab oil-producing countries should meet to work out joint plans with regards to the oil embargo.

4. Withdrawal of Arab funds from the U.S. and Britain, with the conversion of these funds into currency other than sterling or dollars.

5. A contraction in the volume of Arab investment abroad and the withdrawal of all investment from the U.S. and Britain.[53]

It was decided that these recommendations not be made public. Instead, the conference issued a brief, noncommittal communiqué that made no reference to nationalizing foreign oil companies or to an embargo on oil exports. The communiqué merely stated that the talks had been characterized by a "spirit of Arab solidarity" and that the conferees "unanimously agreed on positive resolutions."[54] Publicly, "the conference managed to preserve an outward show of unanimity," and observers judged that "one more hazard has been overcome in the arduous ascent towards the summit."[55] It was at this summit that a final decision was taken by Arab heads of state on the oil embargo.

The Fourth Arab Summit Conference

The task of rebuilding Egypt after a defeat of such magnitude required superhuman capabilities. Egyptian losses amounted to nearly $2.2 billion in arms and military equipment in addition to the loss of the annual income from the Suez Canal and the Israeli occupation of the Sinai oilfields and the strategic Strait of Tiran.

Nasser, who had withdrawn the resignation he had tendered immediately after the swift collapse of his army, embarked on the task of rebuilding. He possessed administrative skill and was still popular among his Egyptian countrymen and the Arab masses. To create a new Egypt, Nasser was in urgent need of Arab moral, political, financial, and diplomatic support. And it was the rich oil-producing countries, notably Saudi Arabia and Kuwait, which had the most potential to offer. For this reason Nasser, who had earlier declined to attend Arab summit conferences, eagerly smoothed the way toward the long-awaited Fourth Arab Summit Conference, which convened in Khartoum on 29 August 1967 to map out strategy to restore Arab strength in the wake of the June war.[56] Throughout the conference Nasser gave priority to a policy of conciliation and appeasement. Resuming the leading role he had played before the war, the Egyptian leader stressed Arab unity, while at the same time "rejecting all solutions offered because they constituted surrender, which we refuse . . . we have no other way but resistance."

The Khartoum conference saw the completion of a mediated agreement between Nasser and Faisal over Yemen. The accord, a difficult act of statesmanship for the Egyptian president, improved Nasser's image at home and abroad and eased his relations with moderate and conservative

Arab leaders. It enhanced King Faisal's prestige and stature, and it created a climate in which Arab regimes were more willing and able to discuss their differences. The conference overrode Syrian and Iraqi entreaties to approve a three-month total cutoff of Arab oil "to induce the West to put pressure on Israel."[57] Throughout the summit King Faisal pleaded forcefully for the rebuilding of Arab strength with all available resources, the most important of which was income from oil.

The resolution finally adopted by the twelve-nation summit made no specific mention of a resumption of oil shipments. It said, however, that because oil production was an effective measure to consolidate Arab economies and help those countries whose economies had been affected by the war to face any possible economic pressure from outside, "it had been decided that oil-producing countries should resume full production."[58] In exchange, the oil states—Saudi Arabia, Kuwait, and Libya—agreed to pay £135 million ($378 million) a year in aid to Egypt and Jordan to help those countries restore their economies and military strength. Syria, which had absented itself from the conference, lost the conferees' favor. In return for the aid, the oil states got a tacit approval to resume oil shipments to Britain, the United States, and West Germany without being subjected to embarrassing cries of "treason" and "sellout." The subsidy, representing approximately 20 percent of the annual revenues from oil of these three states, was to continue until the "consequences of the Israeli aggression have been eliminated."

The summit also decided not to withdraw the Arab dollar and sterling deposits from U.S. and British banks. Nasser agreed to both decisions and also agreed to make no further efforts to export the Egyptian revolution to the monarchies. Other resolutions adopted by the summit were:

- to establish an Arab Development Fund;
- to take all necessary steps to consolidate Arab military strength to face any possible aggression;
- to work on eliminating all foreign military bases on Arab territory;
- to coordinate political and diplomatic policies to ensure an Israeli withdrawal from Arab territory; and
- to assert that the responsibility for eliminating all traces of Israeli aggression rests upon all Arab states.

At the end of the summit the Arab heads of state agreed in the conference communiqué

to unite their political efforts on the international and diplomatic level to eliminate the effects of the aggression and to insure the withdrawal of the aggressive Israeli forces from the Arab lands which have been occupied since the 5 June aggression. This will be done within the framework of the main principle to which the Arab states adhere, namely: no conciliation with Israel, no recognition of Israel, no negotiations with it, and adherence to the rights of the Palestinian people in their country.

The carefully worded communiqué made no reference to the resumption of diplomatic ties with Britain or the United States. Though the summit agreed that there would be no recognition of Israel, the Arab leaders present were disposed to end the state of belligerency with Israel as part of an overall Middle East settlement. They accepted joint responsibility for Soviet-U.S. mediation to achieve Israeli withdrawal from the occupied Arab territories.

The summit, which had begun in a somber mood amid serious doubts as to whether it would achieve anything, ended as a victory of reason over sentiment; realism over idealism; moderation over extremism; diplomacy over war; unity over fragmentation. In general, the conference marked a victory for King Faisal, owing to Egypt's dire financial straits. Saudi Arabia contributed from its oil revenues a major share of the Arab subsidy to Egypt. This cash subsidy worked well for Saudi Arabia and the other Arab oil-producing countries, which desired a return to the normal channels for selling their oil. But even though Egypt became financially dependent on Saudi Arabia, King Faisal was hardly a competitor for Nasser's pan-Arab leadership. Arab leaders like Algerian President Houari Boumediene (1965–1978) stood a better chance than the pro-Western Saudi monarch. Boumediene had come through the June defeat with increased prestige, and his country had, with its own war of national liberation, provided the only modern Arab epic. But Algeria's ability to take up the leadership of the Arabs for the recovery of Palestine was limited because of its location two thousand miles away.

In Khartoum, Nasser embraced Faisal and an uneasy truce began. With the loss for an indefinite time of its canal revenues, most of its tourism, and a large part of its oil, it was clear that Egypt could not afford the luxury of an exclusive "revolutionary" policy. While an Arab revolutionary commented, "The tragedy of Khartoum is that Nasser, symbol of Arab revolution, has become a moderate," Arab moderates and conservatives judged the summit a "triumph of realism."[59] British Foreign Minister Nutting observed:

For Nasser this was undoubtedly the most difficult, if not crucial, of all Arab summit meetings. Not only did Syria boycott the conference, but his Iraqi allies also joined with the Algerians and Shukairy, who represented the PLO, in trying to put Egypt in the dock for having abandoned the struggle and accepting a cease-fire when the Israelis had reached the Canal. The Iraqis also pressed for a boycott on sales of Arab oil to the West and for the withdrawal of Arab deposits, estimated at 4,000 million pounds, from British banks. Nor were those who favoured a more realistic approach of much help in contesting this hard-line approach. While they refused to cripple themselves by imposing oil sanctions on the West, they nevertheless declined to take the lead in advocating a settlement with Israel for fear of being branded as traitors to the Arab cause.[60]

In his influential weekly column entitled "In Frankness" for the Cairo *al-Ahram*, Haykal, President Nasser's unofficial spokesman, commented on the decision of the summit to lift the oil embargo:

The proposal to establish an embargo on Arab oil was not adopted because it was not feasible. The arguments of the oil-producing countries indicated that the embargo was possible theoretically, but impossible practically. It is to be noted that the export of oil from Arab countries did not stop for more than a few hours directly following the aggression, and that Arab oil continued to reach the countries from which it was supposed to be withheld—the United States, Britain, and West Germany. The rise in oil prices was not because of an embargo, but because of the closure of the Suez Canal.

Then let the exports of oil proceed, but let oil bear its share of the cost of the military and political battle which falls well within the realm of the possible. To be fair one must say that the oil-producing countries deserve our appreciation. Saudi Arabia, Kuwait and Libya will contribute 135 million pounds annually to the military and political battle, until the consequences of aggression are removed.[61]

On 2 September 1967 Saudi Arabia became the first country officially to announce its resumption of oil shipments "to all countries without exception." It was soon followed by other Arab oil producers.

In summary, as far as oil supplies were concerned, the 1967 Middle East crisis produced the following concrete effects:

1. Closure of the Suez Canal, cutting off shipping routes through the canal to Western Europe;
2. Imposition of an oil embargo on shipments to the United States, Britain, and West Germany;
3. Brief interruptions of oil operations in a number of producing nations as a result of strikes, disruptions, or threats of sabotage.

As for the embargo itself, there was an initial five-day total prohibition of oil pumping and export by all Arab producers beginning 5 June 1967; then there was a subsequent nineteen-day embargo of shipments to the United States and Britain; this was followed by a selective embargo that lasted until 2 September 1967 against the United States, Britain, and West Germany imposed by a number of the Arab oil producers.

A Comparative Analysis of the 1956 and 1967 Suez Closures

No close parallel can be drawn between the 1967 and 1956 Suez Canal closures. The closure in 1956 caused chaos, resulting in the rocketing upward of freight rates and ship values to four times their precrisis levels. In contrast, while the canal in 1967 was still an important waterway for oil trade, it was less vital than it was before the 1956 closing in the wake of the British-French-Israeli invasion. Whereas in 1956 about 60 percent of Britain's oil came through the canal, only 25 percent came through it in 1967. The importance of the Suez Canal had been diminished by four main factors:

1. The coming into service of new supertankers of over 100,000 tons capacity to transport the oil around the Cape of Good Hope without great economic loss. Between 1957 and 1967 the average size of a tanker in the world fleet increased by 76 percent and the total tonnage by 123 percent.[62] Due to the oil glut and low demand in June 1967 as compared to October 1956, the time factor lost its significance.
2. The availability of tankers to transport the oil was crucial. It was the shortage of tanker transportation rather than the shortage of available oil that caused much of the 1956 oil crunch. Whereas in 1956 tankers were in short supply even in normal times, by 1967 there was a tanker surplus. Remembering the 1956 experience, oil companies were employing more ships than they needed to safeguard against closure of the canal.
3. Subsequent discovery and development of vast new oilfields west of Suez—in Libya, Algeria, and Nigeria.
4. Increasing amounts of Gulf oil reaching the Mediterranean ports through pipelines. In 1956 "more than 80 percent of Western Europe's oil came from the Persian Gulf area, and had to pass through the Suez Canal. In 1967 the proportion was less than 60 percent."[63]

However, the closure of the Suez Canal did cause Britain and West Germany, as well as the rest of the European nations, some discomfort and distress, because it cut off most of the oil from Gulf countries. The 1967 closing of the Suez Canal had the following impact:

1. It resulted in longer transportation routes because Gulf oil had to be rerouted around the Cape of Good Hope; this led to an increase in the prices of crude generally as the oil companies began to pass on their extra transportation costs. This raised freight costs for other commodities such as grain as well. According to the London *Times* of 6 June 1967: "A trip from Basra on the Persian Gulf to London via the Cape of Good Hope involves an extra 4,800 miles steaming. At the average speed of 13 knots, it would require 38 days against the normal 22. The difference of 16 days, therefore, pushes up the voyage costs by £7,200 and, even after deducting about £2,000 for Canal dues and disbursements there would be a higher wage bill to foot."
2. It generated cooperation between the Soviet Union and the British and French oil companies as the Soviets began to export oil to Western Europe from the Black Sea;
3. It increased the valorization of non-Gulf crude oil due to the geographic advantage, raising the prices of Iraqi and Libyan crude;
4. It benefited South Africa, which transformed some of its harbors into major bunkering stations;
5. It accelerated the construction of supertankers.

The 1967 Arab Oil Embargo: An Assessment

According to the communiqué issued by the oil ministers following the Baghdad oil conference of 5 June 1967, the embargo was aimed at countries that "commit or take part in aggression against the sovereignty or territory or territorial waters of any Arab state" (see Appendix A). By "aggression the conference meant: (1) direct armed aggression on the part of any state in support of Israel; (2) provision of military assistance to the enemy in any form whatsoever; (3) attempts to secure the passage of commercial vessels through the Gulf of Aqaba under military protection of whatever form.

Soviet Response to the Embargo

Throughout the embargo the Soviet Union pursued the policy that the interdiction of oil was "a concrete and effective expression of Arab solidarity and a form of opposing the Israeli aggression and those who inspired it."[64] Writing in the Moscow journal *International Affairs*, L.

Sedin asserted: "A powerful weapon in the hands of the Arab countries is the oil boycott. This is the first time in the history of the Middle East that the western world has been made to feel who is the real owner of the Arab oil. Let us add that the Western Powers depend heavily on Arab oil."[65]

Following the Khartoum summit, the Soviet press supported the new Arab position of resuming oil shipments to the West, observing that "it was . . . a matter of sober calculation. Refusal to pump oil for the United States, Britain, and Federal Germany caused no actual shortage of oil and oil products in Western Europe."[66]

Objectives of the Embargo

The 1967 Arab decision to enact an oil embargo against selected, presumably hostile, countries was intended to serve two declared objectives: (1) to deter Western nations from lending their military support to Israel in its war with the Arab confrontation states; and (2) to punish those nations that would not heed Arab warnings and actively intervened on Israel's side by supplying it with arms and ammunition.

However, a careful analysis of the situation, particularly in the aftermath of the war, brings to the fore other important, though implicit, purposes that the embargo hoped to achieve, such as:

1. Retaliatory action taken against countries perceived to have intervened on Israel's side or supplied Israel with the weaponry that made it possible to inflict heavy losses on the Arab side;
2. A gesture of solidarity taken by the oil producers to express their devotion to the Arab cause;
3. A precautionary initiative designed to reduce the possibility of sabotage by Arab nationalists, by depriving extremists of an excuse to damage oil installations belonging to Western oil companies;
4. An insurance policy taken out by the oil producers against future civil disorders and political opposition;
5. A safety valve to relieve pressures to nationalize the foreign oil companies operating in Arab countries.

Factors Softening the Embargo's Impact

The news of the 1967 oil embargo was taken calmly in the nations placed under the embargo. The reasons for the equanimity were:

Availability of Stock. At the time of the embargo, reserves in the consumer countries were high—about four months' consumption.[67] Those reserves were adequate enough to allow normal consumption until emergency measures could be put into effect.

Availability of Tanker Transport. There was abundant tanker tonnage to transport oil around the southern tip of Africa without great economic loss.

Availability of Alternative Sources. The limited shortages in supplies resulting from the Arab oil embargo were offset by other non-Arab sources such as Iran, Venezuela, and the United States. In contrast with 1956, the United States from the beginning took the lead in efforts to avert an oil crisis by making its supplies available to Western Europe. According to the authoritative trade journal the *Petroleum Economist,* "the U.S.A. was able to help the Free World with a dramatic increase in domestic production; this made over 1 million barrels a day available to Western Europe, by exports and the diversion of supplies previously intended for the U.S.A."[68] In his book *Power Play: Oil in the Middle East* (1973), Leonard Mosley elaborated on this point:

> OPEC as a body had not been asked to institute an oil stoppage, but its two principal non-Arab members, Iran and Venezuela, might have been expected to aid their fellow members' boycott by limiting their own operations to the rate of shipments prevailing before the Six-Day War. Instead, they stepped up production to take advantage of all the shortages their Arab confreres and the closing of the Suez Canal had caused. For some time the shah of Iran had been agitating for a considerable increase in the output of oil from the consortium's fields; but the consortium, all of whose member companies had interests in other parts of the Middle East, had so far resisted, on the grounds that taking more from Iran would mean taking less from Saudi Arabia, Abu Dhabi, Iraq and Kuwait, thus arousing Arab hostility. Now they did not need to exercise such restraint, since the Arabs had halted oil shipments from these countries. The result was a tremendous rise in Iranian sales to Britain and Germany, the two main targets of the Arab boycott. Venezuela, whose usual principal market was the United States, also increased its shipments to Europe.[69]

This policy of non-Arab oil producers increasing their output to meet any probable oil shortage in Europe led to optimism in official circles. "Oil is not scarce; and even allowing for the foreign exchange element, it is cheap in real terms," stated the British minister of power, Richard March, who apparently did not allow the crisis in the Middle East to divert him from the lines of his long-term energy policy.[70] On their part, the Arab countries made no serious efforts to enlist the support of non-Arab producers to reduce or at least maintain their oil output at preembargo levels.

Geographical Spread of Production Areas. By 1967 more oil was being produced in the non-Arab world than in 1956, causing Arab oil to lose some of its strategic significance.

Western Control of the Oil Industry. The Arab producers had virtually no control over the operations of the multinational oil companies who were in charge of Arab as well as international oil resources. The Arab political analyst Fawwaz Trabulsi observed: "At first, many hopes were placed on a prolonged Arab embargo on oil destined to the U.S. and Britain, which would bring about Western pressure for a quick Israeli withdrawal. This plan was soon dropped: the regimes of the oil-producing countries of the Middle East do not control their oil."[71] Moreover, the oil companies were generally British, French, Dutch, and U.S.; they shared the oil on a contractual basis and controlled the existing marketing systems.

Causes Underlying the Embargo's Failure

The 1967 Arab oil embargo failed to have a "dramatic effect" on the economies of Western nations. Ten reasons underlay this failure:

Absence of a Unified Arab Embargo Policy. The tidal wave of emotion that swept the Arab world following the outbreak of hostilities with Israel in June 1967 imposed severe pressures on the various Arab oil-producing countries to express solidarity with the combatant Arab states. However, in their handling of the matter, the oil producers acted more like a *posse comitatus*—summoned suddenly to Baghdad to discuss the crisis and placed under heavy pressure to "do their duty." This meant employing oil as a political weapon against any Western country that supported Israel. Having performed this duty and returned home, many troubling questions began to arise in the states imposing the embargo with respect to the embargo's purpose, its targets, duration, effectiveness, and justification.

Lack of a Uniform Interpretation of the Embargo. The Arab producers' failure to agree on a uniform interpretation resulted in technical and procedural difficulties in implementing the embargo. For example, Algeria and Libya did not in fact place an embargo on West Germany; Iraq for a few weeks imposed a total ban on oil exports; and Saudi Arabia and the Gulf sheikhdoms stopped all their oil operations only for about a week.

Lack of Will and Determination. The oil producers lacked will and determination to make the oil weapon highly effective. The Saudis, at odds with Nasser and threatened by his regime for more than a decade, were not eager to enforce an embargo aimed at their Western allies in order to bail Nasser out of his problems. As the area's largest producer of oil, the Saudi attitude was crucial, the more so because of Saudi influence on other conservative Arab oil-producing states. It was obvious that the Saudis became involved with the embargo solely to avoid alienating themselves from the Arab world, with all the implications that such a move would have had for the stability of the Saudi regime. By giving lip service to the embargo, the Saudis managed to keep themselves inside the Arab policymaking process and to step into part of the power vacuum that had been created by Nasser's humiliating military defeat. However, it was not long before an opportunity presented itself for King Faisal to lift the embargo without damaging his image in the Arab world—by pledging to pay a sum of money to those Arab countries affected by the war.

The Short Duration of the Embargo. Failure to prolong the embargo beyond the target countries' tolerable time limits prevented it from having a disruptive effect on their economies. A six-month stoppage of oil exports was "estimated as necessary to put a squeeze on Europe,"[72] beyond which oil stocks and emergency supplies would be seriously low. Daniel Crecelius wrote: "Faisal had made a symbolic attempt to help the Arab cause during the war by declaring an embargo of Sa'udi oil against the West, but his lifting of the embargo after only one week not only angered Arab radicals but deprived this ultimate Arab weapon of a true test of its potency. With enough oil in storage, Europe did not even feel the pinch of the embargo before it was lifted."[73] As for the United States, J. Cordell Moore, assistant secretary of the interior, stated on 10 June 1967: "If the present shutdown continues for more than a few weeks a critical transportation and supply problem will develop which cannot be solved by individual efforts of oil companies."[74]

Prolonged disruption of Middle East supplies would have seriously affected countries in the western Pacific and Southeast Asia, which got the bulk of their requirements from the Middle East. In addition, it could have had a "creeping effect" on world supplies, resulting in serious shortages over the long term, because the longer it takes for normal trading conditions to be restored, the greater the tendency to cause economic dislocations in the consuming countries.

Switching of Supplies. Rerouting of oil shipments, particularly supplies already on the high seas, was hard to detect and made it possible for nations under the embargo to obtain supplies. Though written guarantees that oil cargoes would not reach the target nations were demanded before loading any tanker, it was virtually impossible to detect the final destinations of these cargoes, especially of refined oil, due to transshipment. This was made more difficult because there was no move by the oil producers to impose quotas on the amounts of oil shipped to individual countries. Leakage to target countries was inevitable. European countries such as France, Belgium, the Netherlands, Luxemburg, and Spain continued to receive oil from Arab sources; oil supplies were thus being rerouted through third parties. An emergency plan to circumvent the embargo was approved by the Organization for Economic Cooperation and Development (OECD) at a meeting in Paris on 13 June 1967. The plan involved sharing terminal, pipeline, tanker, and storage facilities. On their part, the major U.S. oil companies made concerted plans that involved mobilizing a special tanker fleet to move alternative North and South American oil supplies to Western Europe.

Selective Nature of the Embargo. Because the embargo was selective, it did not result in a decrease in production. As oil was available, the oil companies possessed sufficient supplies to allow them to divert oil intended for countries under the embargo to other destinations. This freed oil that ordinarily would have gone to those destinations from the non-Arab producers, such as Iran, Nigeria, and Venezuela, to be exported to the target nations. Robert A. Wright, writing in the *New York Times* on 17 June 1967, maintained that "should there be a complete embargo, however, there would indeed be a world oil crisis. The Arab nations account for 21 percent of world oil production. It is believed that production increases in Iran, the United States, Canada and Latin America could replace only about one-third of that loss. Permanent replacement supplies would take years to develop."

Flexibility in the Pattern of International Oil Traffic. The interlocking distribution system of the Western oil companies allowed oil to reach target nations even though direct shipments were prohibited. Most of the oil multinationals were owned by U.S. and British companies. Because the companies had wells in several parts of the world, they could stop shipments from Kuwait to Britain, for example, send the oil due for Britain to a third country, and then reroute it from thence to Britain.

The Seasonal Factor. Although the 1956 oil crisis took place in October when winter was approaching and demand for oil was high, the 1967 embargo took place in June at the beginning of summer when demand for oil in the Northern Hemisphere is seasonally low. Pipelines, too, vary seasonally in importance—only when winter approaches does their closure become an acute problem. In summer the pipelines were used relatively less, and the oil companies used their option to ship oil from the Gulf ports rather than risk pipeline sabotage.

Lack of a Unifying Arab Oil Forum. No organization existed in which the Arab oil-producing states could sit down together, discuss their problems, and plan a unified oil policy. As will be shown later, the formation of OAPEC in 1968 was a major element that made the 1973 embargo more effective, as OAPEC played a leading role in formulating Arab oil policies, acting as a lens to bring divergent Arab views into focus.

Lack of U.S. Vulnerability. The United States, the main target of the embargo, was not affected seriously because its imports of Middle Eastern oil were insignificant. It was able to make up the loss by removing the ceiling from domestic production. As Thomas Barger pointed out in *Arab States of the Persian Gulf* (1975):

> Even more important to the failure of the 1967 embargo was the fact that the United States imported very little Arab oil, and the shut-in capacity of the United States oil fields was considerable. U.S. "conservation" operated largely through the import quota system, and the Texas Railroad Commission had left available an unused domestic producing capacity. So during the embargo the United States was able to increase its production rapidly, not only to supply its own needs, but also to help the European countries affected.[75]

Restraints on Oil Producers

In their efforts to use oil as a political weapon the Arab oil-producing countries were restrained by two factors:

1. The producing nations were dependent on oil revenues to meet government expenditures, including the salaries of the army and civil service, particularly as most of them had no other substantial source of foreign exchange. In Kuwait, oil income accounted for 97 percent of the government's revenues; in Saudi Arabia the figure was 87 percent; and in Iraq 62 percent.[76] In the absence of alternative markets, the loss of royalty payments for an indefinite period meant serious economic problems. Some producers, like Kuwait, had huge monetary reserves, while others, such as Iraq, required steady oil revenues to remain solvent.

2. Most of the oil producers were engaged in ambitious development projects that they were reluctant to discontinue because such a move would create unemployment and feed political unrest.

Backlash Against the Embargo

In the long term, the decision to bring oil into the political arena led the consumer nations to intensify their efforts to diversify sources of supply. Consequently, the United States, Western Europe, and Japan began thinking in terms of long-term contracts with non-Arab suppliers, where political risks would be lower. In addition, consumer nations sought to reduce their dependency on Middle East oil by earmarking large amounts of capital for oil exploration in Asia, Australia, and North America.

Economic Impact of the Embargo

In spite of all the above factors, the economic impact of the oil embargo and the blocking of Suez Canal traffic was pervasive and profound for three main reasons.

1. A cessation of the oil flow from the Arab countries compelled Britain to dip into its reserves of foreign currencies in order to purchase oil. This placed the pound sterling under heavy pressure. Tanker chartering, shipping detours, and replacements from other oil-producing regions allowed Britain to receive needed oil, but only at a higher cost. This inevitably affected the balance of payments as Britain had to buy large quantities of oil from expensive U.S. and Venezuelan fields.

2. Not all alternative sources could be relied upon to fill the gap in the world oil supply. Iran was wary of offending the Soviet Union, while Nigeria was threatened by the disruption of a civil war.[77] The London *Guardian* warned on 7 June 1967:

> Since both Britain and the rest of Western Europe take about two-thirds of their oil from the Arab countries, the effects of a prolonged embargo could be very serious. The gap, in fact, is one that could not possibly be filled in the short run. Of the alternative suppliers, Nigeria is now scarcely more secure than the Middle East. Iran has oil to spare, but will be wary of offending her Russian neighbour. As for Venezuela and the United States—the other big oil producers—the problem is one of pipelines, ports, and ships. These simply do not exist at the present on a scale sufficient to meet Europe's needs, even if the heavy cost in foreign exchange could be met.

3. Though the United States got most of its oil from North and South America, a large proportion of the oil used in the Vietnam War came from the Middle East. "About 40 million barrels of oil are needed each year for the war in Vietnam, of which nearly half is from the Arab countries." Consequently, the disruption of oil shipments to the United States had serious strategic implications as it "threaten[ed] the broad security interests of the United States."[78] The U.S. Department of Defense immediately moved to assure sufficient supplies for Vietnam and other installations abroad. According to the *New York Times* of 11 June 1967, the Gulf area accounted for 65 percent of the 120 million barrels the Department of Defense moved annually for Southeast Asia and the western Pacific. The cost of this supply was nearly $240 million, and the added cost to carry supplies from other sources was estimated at $21 million a month. As Thomas F. Brady of the *New York Times* noted: "The only pressure the Arab countries can put on the United States through oil is to halt the oil that goes from the Arab states to Vietnam for the war. The United States Navy has a contract to buy Saudi oil from the Arabian American Oil Company at a rate reported to be 100,000 barrels a day. If the Saudi boycott is maintained this oil will have to go to the Far East by longer routes."[79]

Utility of the Embargo

In spite of its proclaimed failure to achieve a dramatic political and economic impact, one cannot but acknowledge that the 1967 Arab oil embargo did have some utility in the following ways:

1. It marked the first time that the Arab oil producers used their oil collectively as a political weapon.
2. It exposed the deficiencies and obstacles that needed to be overcome in subsequent embargoes.
3. It focused attention on the role played by the oil companies in controlling this vital natural resource.
4. It helped maintain the perception that the Arab governments were doing something in retaliation for their military defeat. This helped relieve domestic pressure on those governments and released some of the tension that had built up among the Arab masses.
5. It helped restore some of the Arabs' self-confidence and self-esteem that had been shattered by their defeat on the battlefield.
6. It allowed the Arab oil producers to surmount the psychological barrier of imposing an oil embargo.
7. It marked the first attempt by weak nations "to impose their will on the foreign policy of Great Powers."[80] It somewhat restrained U.S. foreign policy behavior. As long as the embargo had not been lifted officially, the United States refrained from taking actions that could have been interpreted as hostile to the Arab countries in order not to give the producers proper cause for strict enforcement.[81] Not long before the lifting of the embargo, however, under "pressure from American Jews, the United States sold fifty F-4 Phantom jets to Israel."[82]
8. Being the first episode of its kind in history, the perceived failure of the embargo[83] created a widespread misconception in diplomatic and academic circles that a future Arab oil embargo could not be sustained and that the Arabs could never muster the strength needed to mount a long-term oil embargo. This led Western policymakers to undervalue the significance of Arab oil, causing them to be caught in 1973–1974 unprepared for a serious oil shortage.

Perhaps most significantly, the 1967 Arab oil embargo laid the groundwork for the 1973/1974 oil embargo, which had greater international political and economic implications than its unfortunate predecessor. Chapter 3 will discuss and analyze the major developments between 1967 and 1973 that lent Arab oil leverage vastly greater power, authority, and influence.

3
The Growing Momentum of Arab Oil Leverage, 1959–1973

As the Arab oil ministers were preparing their papers for the June 1967 oil summit meeting (presumably to take action on a proposal to impose a partial boycott of Arab oil exports to nations supporting Israel), one common thought must have crossed their minds: To what extent could they exercise their influence on the oil companies operating within their domains without clashing with these companies or antagonizing their home governments? Technically, the Arab oil producers had no legal right to dictate an embargo to the oil companies unless they chose to exercise the authority inherent in their political power as sovereign, independent nations.

The Concession Agreements

Following World War II, the major U.S. and European oil companies rushed to consolidate their control over Middle Eastern oil resources "to satisfy their increasing needs for foreign reserves." That area "not only gave promise of a treasure of oil, but it was also one where political and private barriers did not appear to be insuperable."[1] Those were the days of oil scarcity, high freight rates, and a keen strategic concern over access to oil resources. Commercially, the Middle East offered huge reserves of oil, high profits, and virtually no risks. Politically, the area absorbed the keen attention of U.S. policymakers, who sought to secure access to those oil resources.[2] Consequently, the international oil companies (the only parties with the necessary funds, industrial skills, and assured access to the consuming markets) sought and obtained the sole rights to exploit and develop the oil resources of the Middle East countries. These rights were conceded to the companies in the form of concessions, usually defined as licenses "granted by the state to a private individual or corporation to undertake works of public character over a considerable period of time, and involving investment of more or less large sums of capital."[3] In return, the host government received a stipulated royalty per ton of oil once production began. This made the host countries and emirates only lessors and royalty collectors, without administrative authority over the policymaking or decisionmaking processes of the companies that were developing their oil resources.

The concession agreements, obtained at a time when the Gulf emirates and Arab states had no other national income source, were tipped in favor of the companies, who were given a free hand to look for, exploit, refine, export, price, market, and distribute the oil produced.[4] Usually negotiated with single rulers and procured through large bonus payments involving a certain amount of political intrigue,[5] these agreements covered "the granting of rights for research, extraction, export, and sale of petroleum, the exclusive rights to build pipelines, immunity from taxes and customs dues and the payment of royalties."[6]

The scope of these agreements included most or all lands held by the ruler or government involved and included no provisions for the relinquishment by the companies of parts of any unexploited area.[7] This gave the companies the right to retain all the areas covered by the agreement, even if they neither fully exploited the production potential of the areas at their disposal nor allowed others, including the leasing governments, to exploit them. Countries where little or no oil had been found, Libya, for example, enticed the oil companies into accepting the costly risks of exploration by offering them highly favorable terms. The duration of the concessions extended over very long periods. The Saudi Arabian principal concession agreement was supposed to run until 1999, the Iraqi agreement until 2000, and the Kuwaiti agreement until 2026.[8]

Profit-sharing agreements usually provided for a royalty, generally one-eighth of the value of the oil produced, to be paid to the government whether the company made a profit or not. This assured the government a minimum revenue tied to the volume of oil produced. The profit-sharing agreement usually came into play when the income remaining with the oil company (before it paid income tax to its own government) began to exceed the total of royalties, local taxes, import duties, and other payments to the government of the producing country; income tax was then levied to adjust the total payments by the oil company to one-half its net income. Having handed over half of its net income, the oil company was usually—though not always completely—exempted from all other forms of taxation. Income tax was levied by the British, U.S., or other foreign governments only on the share of the profits retained by the oil company, and the company could offset against this tax liability the income taxes that it paid to the government of the producing country.[9]

By the close of the 1950s, substantial differences of opinion between the producing countries and the oil operators began to accumulate.[10] The concession agreements came under strong attack from Arab officials and oil experts on both ends of the political spectrum. Fuad Rouhani in *A History of OPEC* (1971) pointed out that "during the 1940s the feelings of discontent generated by the regimes of concessions, bringing about the conviction that the status and obligations of foreign operators had to be subjected to a new order, rose high among many producing countries."[11]

One of the main critics of the oil concessions was former Saudi Oil Minister Tariqi, described by *Time* magazine (27 April 1959) as "the unquestioned spokesman of the new generation of Arab experts in oil." While in charge of Saudi oil affairs, Tariqi's primary policy was to insist that Aramco grant Saudi Arabia new concessions on more favorable terms: "Under the present concessions, we're like merchants. We lose control of the oil once we get paid our fifty percent production tax. The oil industry is not controlled by Saudi Arabia, but by foreigners. They don't take Arab oil to the ultimate markets as Arabian companies; they transfer it to a foreign marketing company that we have no control over."[12] In another interview (with the Saudi daily *al-Yamamah* on 18 December 1959) Tariqi maintained:

> These early concession agreements were grossly unfair to the host countries and enabled the concessionaire to control the economy of the host country, drain its resources, and impede its development. The role of the early Arab negotiators could only be condoned if it were remembered that they were unsophisticated, that special circumstances obtained at the time and there was a pressing need to conclude these early agreements.[13]

Other oil producers shared similar views. In an official memorandum issued in 1961, the Iraqi government gave the following account of the historical background of the concession of the Iraq Petroleum Company:

> After World War I, Iraqi oil was coveted by the imperialists and became the object of fierce competition among the governments of the allied countries and the major oil companies. Subsequently, the companies came to an agreement among themselves for monopolizing Iraqi oil and exploiting it under the worst possible terms for the host country and at the least possible cost to themselves, without regard to the interests of the people of occupied Iraq. This injustice to Iraq was done at a time when the country was not an independent sovereign state, but under the direct control of the British mandatory power. The IPC concession agreement was based on a vague promise made to the Turkish Petroleum Company by the Ottoman Government before World War I. Had it not been for the

direct British rule in Iraq at the time, no sovereign state should have recognized the validity of such a vague promise or granted the company an important concession without first inviting bids from other interested parties.[14]

By 1967, however, more important than this sort of rhetoric was the changed climate of opinion in which the oil multinationals were operating. These were times utterly different from those that prevailed before. First, the oil multinationals no longer had the field to themselves. The impact of the independent oil companies—the newcomers—in the Middle East was already significant.[15] Independents usually had neither the resources nor the inclination to hold back production from their newly won reserves. Second, the Organization of Petroleum Exporting Countries was beginning to make its presence felt, and the oil companies were starting to take its resolutions more seriously.[16] Third, no matter how safe the multinational companies' contractual rights looked on paper, these agreements had an anachronistic flavor in an era of awakened nationalism, particularly as a new breed of Arab oil technocrats was pressing hard for a review of the concession agreements and their impact was beginning to be felt.

A New Breed: The Oil Technocrats

Phenomenal political, social, and economic developments in the Middle East presented the Arab governments with further cause for dissatisfaction with the concession agreements. New agreements between some oil-producing governments and nonmajor newcomer oil concerns, who offered better terms than those already established and a higher revenue per barrel (for example, the Saudi agreement with a Japanese concern), gave the Arab governments no alternative but to make an effort to press for a review of the concession agreements and a more active role in the area's only major industry. But such an attitude would not have been possible or practicable if it were not for a newly emerging elite class of oil professionals who took it upon themselves to generate, at the popular level, more involvement and interest in the oil business.

In the vanguard of Arab thought and action in oil affairs were young "new men" whose views and aims were greatly at variance with those of the oil companies and their executives.[17] Rejecting what the industry considered made economic sense or what it believed was fair, equitable, and possible, these Arab oil experts (among whom Mahmoud Zayd and Mohamed Salman of Egypt, Abdullah Tariqi of Saudi Arabia, and Dr. Nadim Pachachi of Iraq stand out) were putting forth many suggestions and demands. In time, these demands made up a consistent pattern of claims for fuller participation in the development of Arab oil, for new financial arrangements, and for more Arab involvement in all phases of the business under Arab management.[18] Further, these technocrats asked many questions. Some of these were whether the Arab oil-producing countries were receiving a fair share of the profits from the oil discovered by others in their lands, whether the existing concessions were unfair or outmoded and should therefore be revised, whether the Arabs should be consulted and share in decisions as to price changes, and what should be done about the worldwide pricing systems and other major operating practices of the industry.

Five distinct features marked the philosophy of these "oil technocrats." First, they insisted on the need to enlighten the masses on the oil issues by providing the public with all it needed to know about oil. That step, they hoped, would lead to the emergence of an enlightened, responsible, and well-informed public opinion that would constitute an invaluable basis of support for their ideas and policies. Tariqi, for example, as soon as he assumed the office of minister of petroleum and mineral resources of Saudi Arabia in 1958 introduced an entirely new style into official Arab dealings in oil.[19] He made great efforts to explain to the general public the specific aims and achievements of his oil policy. He was always ready to express his views both in interviews with the press and in specially written articles. He also encouraged others to do likewise. Articles on oil affairs and the complicated issues of the industry began to appear in the Saudi press. Surprisingly enough, the public received these with warmth and interest. Meanwhile, another prominent figure among the oil technocrats, Dr. Pachachi, minister of national economy under the old Iraqi regime, made other attempts to interest the public in oil affairs on a serious level. In his book *Iraqi Oil Policy, August 1954 to December 1957*, Pachachi expressed the opinion that the Iraqi public had the right to know how the government administered that vital sector of the national economy. He stressed that it was the duty of every Iraqi oil official to keep the public informed on all developments in the oil industry. He emphasized that officials should use every available opportunity to obtain new concessions and benefits from the oil companies operating in Iraq and to make every effort to create a suitable atmosphere for negotiations.

Second, the oil technocrats stressed the importance of a pragmatic approach to oil affairs. It was in the interest of the producing governments, they insisted, to dissociate matters related to the oil industry from politics and from the views of individuals. They themselves were not affiliated with any political party or interest group, and their appeal to public opinion was from the beginning essentially apolitical. They owed their positions to their technical education rather than to any political bargaining or pressure, and many harbored no political ambitions of their own.

These youngish men differ rather significantly, to the casual observer at least, from the similarly aspiring intelligentsia of other developing societies. Their education is sometimes technological rather than legal. Their ladder of advancement has not been primarily political, but within the semi-technical administrative departments that each of the host governments had necessarily created to handle its contacts with its tenant company. Their political influence is likely to depend upon their successes in dealing, on behalf of the host government, with the oil companies. This in itself might tend to canalize their radicalism into seeking always to improve the bargain that the governments get. The better that bargain, the better their chance of achieving, say, the economic development that they believe their country needs.[20]

Third, the technocrats insisted that "Arabization" or full Arab participation be realized by "new deals" in oil, achieved through the regular channels of normal negotiations and friendly dialogue, rather than through nationalization or unilateral action. Moderates by temperament and pro-Western by education, they demanded objectives that were capable of fulfillment, with give-and-take on both sides of the negotiating tables. Such an attitude, they hoped, would avoid conflicts with the Western governments, for whose ideals and beliefs they held the deepest respect. All avenues that would alienate them from the Western governments or deprive them of Western aid and technology, thus placing them at the mercy of the Eastern bloc, were abandoned. They firmly believed that only through such a policy of "modernization and objectivity" could the Arabs maximize their gains from the oil industry.

Fourth, these oil technocrats recognized that Arabization of the oil industry was in the long run the most effective way of ensuring that Arab oil resources would benefit the Arab countries themselves. However, Arabization, they felt, could not be realized until a well-trained, competent class of Arab experts and technicians had been created in the several phases of the industry—a class of experts who could challenge the companies on particular issues and who would ensure a gradual and peaceful transfer of control to the producing governments. With such an objective in mind, they encouraged young, intelligent, educated Arabs to seek employment in the oil industry and to develop technical expertise on as large a scale as possible.

Fifth, these oil technocrats put great emphasis on the need to unify Arab oil policies.

Since the technocrats had no political commitment they inevitably found themselves moving closer and closer to their counterparts in other Arab countries, whose problems and aims were essentially the same. Thus the unification of Arab oil policies developed into an integral part of the technocrats' ambitions. The unification of Arab oil policies had three main attractions. It would enable the technocrats (1) to exchange information on oil matters, (2) to widen the basis of their public support, and (3) to strengthen their hands vis-à-vis the oil companies through the possibility of taking collective action.[21]

The oil technocrats felt that a unified Arab oil policy would present a solid front to the companies that could increase their countries' revenues and provide them with other benefits from the industry. Further, it could facilitate long-term common oil-policy planning with the rest of the Arab oil-producing countries.

Political Polarization of Arab Oil Policies

With petroleum's role becoming more vital in international politics, the Arab oil-producing governments began to feel the need to coordinate their oil policies in order to get a bigger share of the oil income. The Arab League charter contains provisions requiring cooperation among member countries in all their various affairs, with particular emphasis on the key industry, petroleum. At its fourth meeting, held in late May 1957, the Arab League Council approved the recommendation of the Arab Petroleum Experts Committee and the suggestion of the secretary general to hold an Arab petroleum conference, first, "to encourage an awareness of and an interest in petroleum affairs in the Arab countries and the assessment of the extent of its importance in their economy,"[22] and second, "to exchange technical, economic, and legal information on the oil policies followed by individual countries, the desire being to achieve such a measure of coordination as would lead to fruitful cooperation."[23]

The First Arab Petroleum Congress was held in Cairo, 16–23 April 1959. Its "purely scientific and cultural" nature was overcome by a strong political undercurrent. However, the technical and educational aims of the congress provided the main motif throughout the sessions, "only to provide a primary common ground with the companies."[24]

From the beginning it was apparent that there was a very wide knowledge gap between the Arabs and the companies. As one paper at the congress pointed out, there was still no standardized equivalent in Arabic for many of the technical terms used in the oil industry. Arabic technical terminology in this field had not developed, as it had, for example, in the field of medicine.[25] Interest in spreading knowledge about oil among their own people was clearly apparent on the Arab side. In an interview before the opening, the chairman of the Arab League's petroleum department, Mohamed Salman, stated explicitly that he had asked Arab education ministers to include the subject of oil resources in their school curricula. To him and the other technicians who were looking ahead, the first order of business was to make the new generation of youth aware of the value and importance of oil resources in their lives.

However, the conference was not an academic seminar; it had political purposes as well. Sharp conflicts over issues came into the open between the representatives of the producer nations and the oil multinationals. But it was more than evident that, no matter how convincingly the Arab oil-producing countries could support their arguments, in the field the companies had the upper hand. To get away from this unbalanced force situation, the conference stressed the need for unity among the producing countries. At the end of its deliberations, one of its four main resolutions urged the formation of an Arab petroleum organization to coordinate Arab oil policies. This resolution stated:

> Efforts must be made to set up organizations in the oil-producing countries to plan a policy for safeguarding the sources of petroleum wealth and their sound exploitation, taking into consideration their developmental needs and the conditions prevailing in each country. Views should be exchanged between the governments of the petroleum-producing countries to discover ways of coordinating and regulating the arrangements and procedures to be adopted by each of them in oil affairs and to secure the steady arrival of petroleum on world markets.[26]

The works of the First Arab Petroleum Congress helped to publicize oil's capacity to supply new sources of income, and its potential to raise living standards and increase prosperity. But "to improve the bases of sharing profits for the benefit of the oil-producing countries," as the conference had resolved, necessitated that the Arab regimes make an effort to reconcile their political differences so as to allow the oil-producing governments to coordinate their oil policies more closely.

The Second Arab Petroleum Congress, held in Beirut 17–22 October 1960, was marked by the recent creation of OPEC. Consequently, the main issue that dominated the deliberations of the congress was the decrease in oil prices decided upon by the oil companies in August of that year. The congress concluded its meetings by adopting the following main resolutions:

1. The Congress supports the requests of the Arab Countries and their efforts to obtain some improvement of the clauses of oil concessions. It expresses the hope that Oil Companies will respond favourably to such a justified demand to assure the maintenance of a fruitful cooperation between them and the Governments, Oil Companies and consumers.
2. The Congress condemns the Oil Companies' decision to reduce crude oil prices and its derivations without the consent of the Arab producer governments. The Congress supports the position of these Governments in their refusal to accept such a reduction.
3. The Congress recommends to the Governments of Arab Countries to double their efforts to encourage, by all means, technical, economical and law studies so as to enable Arab citizens to participate in the activities of Petroleum Congresses.[27]

The Third Arab Petroleum Congress, inaugurated in Alexandria on 16 October 1961, was preceded by two major political events that had a dampening effect on its proceedings: the Iraqi-Kuwaiti crisis of June 1961 and the rupture of the Syrian-Egyptian union of September 1961. Iraq refused to attend because Kuwait was there. Syria, newly severed from its union with Egypt, was not represented because it had not yet been admitted to the Arab League. Nevertheless, the congress proceeded with its works and approved a number of important resolutions, which stressed the following points:

- The need for Arab Governments to double their efforts in order to obtain participation in the petroleum exploring and processing Companies.
- The need to train technicians and workers in view of the "Arabisation" of the Companies' personnel.
- The necessity for the Governments and Petroleum Companies to create an adequate number of technical institutes and information centres.
- The need to take the appropriate measures for oil preservation, either by a more extensive utilization or by storage in tanks for later use.[28]

The Fourth Arab Petroleum Congress, held in Beirut on 5 November 1963, was preceded by two important events: the discovery of new oilfields in Libya and the admission of Algeria to the Arab League as an independent state. The two main problems that the congress focused on were the profit sharing between the host governments and the oil companies, and Soviet competiton. The congress concluded its meetings by adopting resolutions that emphasized "getting a better share of oil revenues from foreign Companies for development purposes" and "prohibiting Israel from getting oil and its products from such countries friendly to the Arabs, and warning the E.E.C. against allowing Israel to join it."[29]

The Fifth Arab Petroleum Congress, held in Cairo 16–23 March 1965, was marked by the creation of the Palestine Liberation Organization (PLO) in 1964, growing Egyptian military involvement in the Yemeni civil war, and the intensifying disunity in Arab ranks. This congress "was of particular importance due to the recent agreement on royalties, concluded after long negotiations between the Arab Countries, members of OPEC, and the Concessionary Companies."[30] The main problems raised by the congress were: raising the prices of crude oil, finding markets for the products of the national petroleum companies, ameliorating the terms of traditional concessions, and obtaining better conditions for granting exploration permits in nonconceded areas. The congress concluded its sessions by adopting important resolutions that had great significance for future events. Two resolutions dealt with the Arab-Israeli conflict and the use of oil as a political weapon, a theme that had been neglected in previous congresses:

1. Considering that the Arabs, in their struggle for survival, cannot neglect the employment of all their efforts and weapons to protect their nationalism against any aggression,

   And being bound to preserve the rights of the Palestinian people to liberate their usurped territory, and by the resolutions taken by the two Arab Summit Conferences concerning the Creation of a Liberation Organization, and supporting the people of Palestine in their struggle,

   The Conference recommends that oil must be used, together with other economic Potentialities, as an effective weapon for the Liberation of Palestine and that the Arabs must determine their relations with other countries according to the attitude of these countries towards the Palestinian Problem.

2. The Conference recommends that the Arab Countries collectively suspend their oil deliveries to any country that boycotts an Arab Country or hurts its economic interests.

One resolution called for the creation of a petroleum organization: "The Conference recommends that all Arab Governments and Sheikhdoms take the necessary measures for the establishment of an Arab Petroleum Organization operating within the Arab League for the purpose of enforcing agreements concerning the co-ordination of Arab oil policies. This Organization would be similar to organizations working for economic unity in many other parts of the world."[31]

Growing political dissension caused the Arab oil-producing countries to shift their emphasis to OPEC as a forum in which to discuss technical matters and resolve problems. This trend gave OPEC an increasingly important role in the Middle East oil business. But Egypt, which was not an OPEC member, protested against this shift and tried unsuccessfully to push the Arab League to form an Arab petroleum organization similar to OPEC. Further, it was not long before the Arab oil-producing countries, most of whom belonged to the Arab conservative camp, realized that although OPEC presented them with a conference room in which to deal with their oil issues, the OPEC framework offered no outlet for many of the political questions its members wished to take up, "nor did OPEC provide a forum for the discussion and resolution of problems of pure politics as distinct from questions of petroleum policy."[32] This situation arose on various occasions, but made itself felt most acutely in connection with the Arab-Israeli conflict.

Still feeling the impact of the 1967 Arab-Israeli war, the Arab oil ministers, meeting in Baghdad in August 1967, recommended the formation of an Arab petroleum organization that would coordinate Arab oil policies and utilize Arab oil as an effective instrument in their foreign policy. A commission was appointed to prepare the statutes of such an organization. But not all those involved on the Arab oil industry welcomed this idea. The *Arab Oil and Gas Journal* expressed its concern that a new organization would run the risk of becoming another agency of the Arab League, whose resolutions, it said, were not carried out by anyone. It suggested that an Arab organization would furnish the oil companies with an opportunity to set off the non-Arab members of OPEC, like Iran, Indonesia, and Venezuela, against the Arab countries and might undermine OPEC by disaffecting the non-Arab countries.[33] But these points, though well taken, did not deter the conservative Arab oil-producing countries from taking the initiative and calling in January 1968 for a meeting to discuss the establishment of such an organization.

The Formation of OAPEC

On 9 January 1968, the oil ministers of Saudi Arabia, Kuwait, and Libya (under Libya's King Idris I) assembled in Beirut to sign an agreement creating the Organization of Arab Petroleum Exporting Countries. The preamble of the agreement stressed the signatories' recognition of "the role of oil as a principal and basic source of their income which they should develop and safeguard in such a way as to provide them with the greatest legitimate benefits."[34] It expressed their awareness "that oil is a wasting asset and that this fact places upon them the responsibility vis-à-vis future generations of conserving it and utilizing the wealth derived from it in economically diversified investments in production, and development projects of a long-term and fruitful nature." Furthermore, the preamble reflected their belief that "the prudent utilization of this asset is related to the role of oil in serving the economies of the consumer countries and consequently entails due consideration for the legitimate interest of these countries to obtain oil supplies for their markets on equitable terms conducive to the well-being of humanity."

The joint statement of the founding members stressed that the new organization, which would be headquartered in Kuwait, would be bound by the resolutions of the nine-member OPEC. Article 3 of the agreement stated:

> The provisions of this agreement shall not be deemed to affect those of the agreement of the Organization of Petroleum Exporting Countries (OPEC), and especially insofar as the rights and obligations of OPEC members in respect of that organization are concerned. The parties to this Agreement shall be bound by the ratified resolutions of OPEC, and must abide by them even if they are not members of OPEC.

One non-Arab member of OPEC welcomed the founding of the new organization. "The newly-created OAPEC is not in contradiction with OPEC," the Venezuelan oil minister, Dr. Jose Antonio Mayobre, stated in a press conference in Riyadh. "I believe that the new organization will strengthen OPEC since it will defend the legitimate interests of member-states and stabilize and consolidate prices," he added.[35]

Ignoring the potential use of oil as a political weapon, OAPEC declared that its principal aims were:

> the cooperation of the members in various forms of economic activity in the oil industry, the realization of the closest ties between them in this field, the determination of ways and means of safeguarding the legitimate interests of its members in this industry, individually and collectively, the unification of efforts to ensure the flow of oil to its consumption markets on equitable and reasonable terms, and the creation of a suitable climate for the capital and expertise invested in the oil industry in the member states.

In addition, the publicized objective of OAPEC was to form a bloc of Arab oil producers akin to the European Economic Community (EEC) to bolster Arab oil rights and to map out a unified Arab stand within the existing OPEC.[36] However, it was obvious that the underlying motives of the founding members were (1) to relate Arab oil supplies to oil trade policies, and (2) to separate economics from Arab politics. A well-known Western oil expert noted:

Arab petroleum organizations or one kind of another have long been advocated in the Middle East, mainly by radicals from the "oil have-not countries"; but OAPEC has neatly turned the tables. It appears to have arisen primarily from the main Arab producers' distaste for the experiment with using Arab oil as a political weapon which proved ineffective and costly last year; and also, from distaste for allowing their oil policies to be influenced directly by Arab states with hardly any stake in oil. What it may become and achieve only time will show. But its constitution, and the initial pronouncements of its member governments regarding its aims, emphasize their common interest with European consumer countries in keeping the flow of oil to Europe secure and steadily growing; and it appears anxious to seek mutual guarantees to help ensure this.[37]

The English-language Cairo daily, the *Egyptian Gazette*, had similar views on the formation of OAPEC: "It may in a degree have been originally intended as a device to protect the member countries against other Arab countries with different and more radical ideas concerning the use of oil as a means of political pressure and retaliation."[38]

This attitude, far from the spirit of the 1967 Baghdad conference, made other Arab oil-producing countries propose an Arab petroleum organization under the aegis of the Arab League with strong political overtones. The possibility that a rival organization might be set up by the progressive Arab oil-producing countries such as Algeria and Iraq (which would include in its membership other influential Arab countries, notably Egypt and Syria) with the aim of taking the lead from OAPEC on political matters, prompted the Saudi Oil Minister Yamani to make an effort to steer OAPEC more to the left. In an interview in September 1968, Yamani gave a modified political version of the purposes of the organization:

1. To keep oil activity within the organization with a view to protecting the member states from precipitate decisions and making oil a genuine weapon to serve the interests of the producing countries and the Arab countries in general;
2. To create opportunities for joint investment in the oil resources of the member states;
3. To build an economic bridge between the organization and the consuming countries so as to create an outstanding economic structure which we can utilize to expand our markets and thereby establish a stronger political centre of gravity for the states of the region.[39]

The constitution of OAPEC stipulated that its membership was limited to Arab countries whose economies are predominantly dependent on oil: "Oil should constitute the principal and basic source of its national income."

Under this membership provision, Iraq qualified to be a member.[40] It was even invited to be a founding member of the organization, but it rejected the offer, maintaining that the organization was only an "axis of reactionaries." In defining his country's position, Adib al-Jader, chairman of the Iraq National Oil Company (INOC), explained that Iraq had refused to join OAPEC because "membership was confined to countries with petroleum as the main source of revenue."[41] This arrangement, he said, had in practice excluded certain oil-exporting countries such as Algeria, and other countries likely to become oil exporters in the near future. Iraq demanded that the conditions of membership be varied in such a way as to permit the admission of all Arab petroleum-producing and -exporting countries. It was unreasonable, al-Jader argued, that the oil-exporting countries should ask Algeria to join OPEC and then prevent it from joining the Arab organization. The idea of founding such an organization was originally an Arab League idea, yet OAPEC was established after limited contacts were made among Saudi Arabia, Libya, and Kuwait, which made Iraq feel left out. Although Iraq expressed its support in principle for the establishment of such an organization, al-Jader made it clear that for the time being Iraq would cooperate with the Arab countries only within the framework of the Arab League through the Economic Unity Council, the Petroleum Experts Committee, the Arab petroleum conferences, and with all the other petroleum-exporting countries within OPEC. Al-Jader explained that Iraq would welcome a chance to join OAPEC "if the conditions were changed to permit the admission of all Arab oil-producing and exporting countries."[42]

OAPEC's Early Years

The early OAPEC meetings concentrated on setting the organization in motion. The First Ministerial Council Meeting, held in Beirut on 26 July 1968, dealt with "the basic policy of the Organization." A general conference held in Kuwait on 8 September 1968 discussed OAPEC's constitution and budget and considered Abu Dhabi's application for membership. It considered marketing Arab oil internationally and discussed ways of protecting Arab oil policies from fluctuations in world markets. In his opening speech, Kuwaiti Minister of Finance and Oil Abdel Rahman al-Atiki expressed the hope that the meeting would serve Arab oil interests, while Saudi Oil Minister Yamani called the meeting a "milestone in Arab oil history" and urged Arab oil-producing countries to join forces for the general welfare of the Arabs. Similarly, the Libyan delegate expressed his belief that the new organization would help lay down Arab oil policies on a sounder basis. In its summing-up communiqué, OAPEC announced that an agreement had been reached to appoint a secretary general, and on 24 September 1968 the Saudi Arabian oil minister was designated as acting secretary general of the organization.

Not all of the proceedings of the OAPEC meetings were disclosed. The three OAPEC members' oil ministers declined to reveal the main subjects discussed in the Second Ministerial Council Meeting, held in Kuwait on 11 January 1969. Sheikh Yamani would tell journalists only that "the current critical times in the area were reason enough not to divulge any information."[43]

On his arrival at the Third Ministerial Council Meeting, held in Tripoli on 10 March 1969, Yamani stated that the organization was working toward several goals, including the undertaking of joint projects in the interest of all Arab countries and member states in particular. "We are trying to make out of this organization an effective instrument to express our will in the oil community in a way protecting us from taking precipitate decisions," he added.[44] The brief official communiqué distributed at the end of the two-day conference stated that the conferees "discussed methods of developing and coordinating the various petroleum industries in which national companies of the three countries were engaged." Plans for a tanker fleet were discussed and several recommendations were made, but no details were given out. In April of the same year, Kuwait moved to bring Abu Dhabi into OAPEC to strengthen the organization and increase its membership.

The Libyan Adherence Question

With the advent to power of the Libyan revolutionary regime in September 1969, the OAPEC grouping was no longer limited to the Arab conservative oil states. OAPEC had then to accommodate a new, hot-tempered revolutionary regime eager to press for changes and anxious to assert itself in the Arab world. To handle the new situation, Saudi Arabia joined its Kuwaiti ally in urging other conservative Arab oil-producing countries to join OAPEC either to fill the vacancy if Libya should back out or to have numerical dominance if it opted to remain. Qatar, Abu Dhabi, and Bahrain were sounded out on OAPEC membership.

For quite some time the new Libyan regime's policy with respect to OAPEC was left to speculation. Two options were open. Libya could either (1) follow the 1968 Iraqi example and withdraw from OAPEC, thus losing potential allies in its push for higher prices from the oil companies; or (2) attend the next meeting of OAPEC and use it to propose the expansion of the organization to include the progressive Arab oil-producing countries, mainly Algeria, Iraq, and Egypt—a move that was not popular with any of its OAPEC colleagues. However, should their request be turned down, the Libyans still had the option to quit, or at least suspend their membership, and cooperate with the progressive oil states. Already the new Libyan Revolutionary Command Council "felt that the two traditional monarchical states—Saudi Arabia and Kuwait—made strange colleagues in the conference room"[45] and was moving closer to cooperation with the progressive camp.

Early in January 1970, the national oil companies of four Arab countries—Libya, Iraq, Algeria, and Egypt—agreed in Baghdad to coordinate their oil activities. At the signing ceremony, the Iraqi minister of oil and minerals expressed the hope that the agreement would "be a constructive beginning towards unifying Arab efforts in the international sphere, decreasing the power of the monopolistic oil companies that exploited our countries."[46] The Libyan head of delegations, Mustapha Kikhya, indicated that the four countries might eventually form their own petroleum grouping, which would be open to all Arab oil-producing countries "provided that they had the same goals as the founder members." Ignoring the existence of OAPEC, Kikhya expressed his hope of "developing this agreement so as to create a Pan-Arabian organization combining all Arab oil establishments."[47] However, it was no secret that the scope of activities envisaged by the new agreement did not differ much from those of OAPEC. They included the exchange of technical information, laws and regulations, contracts and related documents, and technicians, as well as the coordination of foreign marketing policy and elaboration of joint projects.

By mid-January 1970 the official stand of the Libyan government was made clear: Libya would attend the OAPEC meeting scheduled to take place in Kuwait later that month. Originally the OAPEC meeting was scheduled to be held in Tripoli, Libya, but it was postponed at the request of the Libyan government.

The long-anticipated OAPEC Fourth Ministerial Council Meeting, which was to determine the extent of future cooperation between the three member states, began in Kuwait on 26 January 1970. On the agenda were some important subjects. Saudi Oil Minister Yamani intended to bring up his proposal that governments of oil-producing countries have equity participation in foreign oil companies operating in these countries. Other subjects to be covered were the organization's future projects: the establishment of a joint tanker fleet, new refineries owned by Arab capital alone, and the building of a giant $1.5 billion drydock for the repair of tankers in the Gulf.

When the crucial two-day meeting ended, three of the world's most important oil nations were still partners, despite the fears that the new Libyan regime would withdraw from the organization. A swift restructuring of OAPEC enhanced Libya's role in the organization. The vice-president of the Libyan Oil Company, Lebanese-born Suheil Sa'adawy, was appointed to the important post of secretary general of OAPEC, replacing Yamani, who had been acting secretary general. At the same time, Kuwait, Saudi Arabia, and Libya were each given representation at lower levels in the secretariat. The final communiqué said Libya informed its fellow OAPEC members of its plans to seek an increase in the price of Libyan oil in tanks starting that week. Libya—which ranked fourth among the world's oil exporters with 160 million tons flowing overseas in 1969—was seeking to raise the posted price, then set at $2.21 per barrel. The communiqué stated that Libya wanted to bring the price of Libyan crude "to a reasonable level," and Kuwait and Saudi Arabia promised "all possible backing to achieve this aim."

In mid-February 1970, Algeria, Abu Dhabi, Bahrain, Dubai, and Qatar officially applied for membership in OAPEC and were informed that the organization's scheduled May meeting would act on their applications, almost certainly favorably.

Meanwhile, under the new Libyan leadership, OAPEC was taking a slight turn to the left. Reiterating OAPEC's "complete support" for Libya's demand that oil companies operating there raise the price of oil to bring in more revenue to the country, the new secretary general asserted, in mid-April, that "members of OAPEC could finally, if necessary, take joint action against firms refusing to respond to Libya's legitimate demands."[48] That could take the form of prohibiting, or refusing to renew, any contracts or agreements with such companies, he said. Sa'adawy urged Arab national petroleum firms to adopt an integrated policy to defend the interests of the countries that produced oil and those which consumed it. Such integration could best be achieved by encouraging companies in consuming countries to retain oil rights in Arab countries jointly with Arab national petroleum companies. This would lead to the formation of common interests between producer and consumer countries and, probably, to partnership in matters like refining and distribution.[49] In late April, and in reference to the negotiations going on between Libya and the Western companies, Sa'adawy asserted Libya's right to demand higher posted prices for its oil. "The insistence of the Revolution in Libya on securing its rights could convince foreign oil companies to change their traditional attitude of refusing any demand," he stated.[50]

The membership applications from Algeria, Qatar, Bahrain, Abu Dhabi, and Dubai were unanimously accepted by a two-hour OAPEC extraordinary session held in Kuwait on 24 May 1970. Four conservative states and one progressive were granted membership, making a total balance sheet of two progressive states—Libya and Algeria—and six conservative states—Saudi Arabia, Kuwait, Qatar, Bahrain, Abu Dhabi, and Dubai. The admission of the five new members to OAPEC was hailed by Conference Chairman Ezzedin Mabruk of Libya as a "bolstering of our efforts to coordinate Arab oil policies within and outside the Organization." He added that the increased membership would also "strengthen the organization's position vis-à-vis the oil companies operating in our countries."[51] With its new members, the status of OAPEC was greatly strengthened. The total oil production of its eight members now approached 13 million barrels a day. Together they moved 55 percent of the world's exports.[52]

With the settlement of the Libyan adherence question and the Algerian membership issue, OAPEC now could turn its attention to the promotion of its members' oil interests and the realization of mutual Arab oil projects. In consequence, the most important question on the agenda of the three-day Fifth Ministerial Council Meeting, held in Algiers on 28 June 1970, was a proposal for the creation of an Arab-owned fleet of oil tankers to compete with foreign-owned tankers, which at the time had a virtual monopoly on the shipment of oil from the Middle East and North Africa. In his opening address Libyan Oil Minister Mabruk stated that OAPEC should strive to coordinate the policies of member states so that "one day they can take full possession of their natural wealth."[53] Two days later in an interview with Algerian Radio, Algerian Industry and Energy Minister Belaid Abdessalam said that the member countries possessed all the required potential to realize common projects, but it remained to be seen whether the organization would be able to implement them.[54]

It seemed that the progressive Arab oil states had still not given up totally on the idea of forming a "progressive OAPEC" of their own when, following the closure of the OAPEC conference, the oil ministers of Algeria, Iraq, and Libya met in Algiers "to discuss further the establishment of a committee to coordinate oil policy and set up a joint fund to aid the three countries in the event of unilateral action against the oil companies." The current price negotiations of Algeria with the French government and Libya's oil-price negotiations with foreign companies were also touched upon, but it was clear that the three countries were only aligning their policies as far as their own particiular interests permitted.[55]

The Iraqi Membership Crisis

The course of OAPEC did not run smoothly for long. Shortly after the Fifth Ministerial Council Meeting, it had to face the most crucial test of its three-year span, a test that threatened to destroy it from within: the Iraqi membership crisis.

The growing influence and strength of OAPEC caused Iraq to feel left out. Its efforts to create an organization of "progressive" Arab petroleum-exporting countries had failed, and its January 1970 association agreement with Libya, Egypt, and Algeria was never institutionalized. Already encountering difficulties with IPC, Iraq hoped to enlist Arab backing, especially that of the Arab oil-producing countries, for its demands for higher revenues and increased production. OAPEC, with its economic power, could mobilize moral and political support for its members. Furthermore, with Algeria and Libya already seated as members, Iraq "hoped to turn the Organization into a gathering of 'progressives' to influence the entire Arab petroleum policy."[56]

In October 1970, the Iraqi government applied to OAPEC for membership and was informed that the next ministerial council, due to meet in December, would consider its application. But when the Sixth Ministerial Council Meeting convened in Kuwait on 27 December, it postponed action. "The candidacy of Iraq will be examined in the proceedings of the next [June 1971] session," indicated Saudi Oil Minister Yamani.[57] Till then there had been no signs that a crisis might develop over the admission application. But, for those who had some misgivings, matters came to a head in the OAPEC meeting held in Kuwait in early June 1971. Saudi Arabia used its veto privilege stipulated in the OAPEC charter—that the council would approve new members by a majority of three-quarters of the votes, "provided all the votes of the founding members are included"—to block Iraq's entry to OAPEC. This move caused the breakdown of OAPEC's Seventh Ministerial Council Meeting, which "suspended its meeting until a date to be fixed later" and led to the resignation of OAPEC's Secretary General Sa'adawy.

OAPEC's Seventh Ministerial Council Meeting broke up over three major issues: "whether to admit Iraq as an OAPEC member; how to support Algeria in its oil dispute with France; and what attitude OAPEC should take concerning the European Economic Community."[58] The *Wall Street Journal* said that Arab unity had been severely strained by the breakdown, and other sources said that the collapse was so complete that "it is doubtful if the organization can continue." The London *Guardian* commented: "The failure of OAPEC's Seventh Ministerial Council Meeting . . . could threaten political stability in the Persian Gulf. It may also mark the end of plans for joint undertakings by Arab oil-producing nations in tanker fleets, refineries and service stations." The *Kuwaiti Daily* remarked also that "the fate of the Organization hung in the balance."

Under the terms of OAPEC's charter, Iraq clearly met the required conditions for membership, chief of which was that oil be the main export and source of foreign exchange of the members. But the basic disagreement boiled down to a conflict between Arab "progressives" and "conservatives." Saudi Arabia objected to Iraq's admission because it feared that this might tip the balance of power within OAPEC in favor of the "progressives," which might eventually cause the organization to move more to the left. Furthermore, it feared that the Iraqi membership "might be exploited for political ends."

The acceptance of Iraq was endorsed by Algeria and Libya, while the other members, Kuwait and the Gulf emirates of Qatar, Abu Dhabi, Dubai, and Bahrain, remained noncommittal. However, Iraq's membership, though one of the main issues of conflict, was not the only one. The argument was intensified when Algeria and Libya insisted that Arab oil be used as a means of pressure to deter the West from supporting Israel. Saudi Arabia considered that the use of oil as a political weapon "would lead to complications with the foreign oil companies" and that "oil should be kept out of politics";[59] in support of this view, the Saudis pointed out that the original idea behind the creation of an Arab petroleum organization was to keep the oil question out of politics and to insure coordination of petroleum policy.[60]

Commenting on the breakup of the meeting, Saudi Oil Minister Yamani expressed the hope that the organization would survive "in order to implement the goals it was established for,"[61] while Libyan Oil Minister Mabruk described the outcome as "regrettable."[62]

The divisive issue of Iraq's membership remained unresolved when Libya and Algeria failed to show up for OAPEC's October 1971 meeting in Kuwait "as pressure for admitting Iraq." The two countries threatened to withdraw entirely from OAPEC "unless Iraq is admitted."[63] The Seventh Ministerial Council Meeting was postponed for the second time in five months to December 1971 in Abu Dhabi. Observers noted that "OAPEC might collapse if Saudi Arabia used its veto again."[64]

OAPEC's paralysis ended in early December when a compromise over Iraqi membership, now supported by Libya, Algeria, Kuwait, and Abu Dhabi, was reached. OAPEC members averted a crisis by unanimously agreeing to amend the organization's constitution. Requirements for membership were broadened to permit all the Arab oil-producing states to join. The new formula, submitted by Kuwait, Saudi Arabia, Libya, and Algeria, changed the membership requirements to include not only countries for whom oil constitutes the "principal and basic source" of national income, but also states for whom oil is an "important source" of national income. The organization thus became more representative of the Arab world as a whole. Under the new rules, Egypt,

Syria, and Oman, which really qualified under old rules, were admitted along with Iraq. This preserved the balance of power and counterbalanced the probable radical outlook that Iraq's membership, together with that of Libya and Algeria, would have given the organization. No other changes in the preamble, aims and powers, or organs of OAPEC were introduced.

An official communiqué issued at the end of the OAPEC conference stated that the organization would convene its next meeting in Geneva on 7 January 1972. Iraq's membership and the organization's future development plans, particularly in terms of joint oil investments, were presumably to be considered then. The Iraqi membership crisis had prevented discussions of OAPEC's long-range program and had long delayed its ambitious plans to set up a financing pool, a tanker fleet, a joint marketing board, and a large drydock at Bahrain. Commenting on the success of the Abu Dhabi meeting, Yamani said that "the Organization is reborn."[65]

But the January OAPEC meeting was delayed. It met instead in Kuwait on 4 March 1972. The opening session of the meeting approved the applications for membership of Iraq, Egypt, and Syria. The Sultanate of Oman was expected to join shortly. The meeting was described as "decisive" by the organization's restored secretary general, Sa'adawy. In an interview with the Kuwaiti daily *Al-Siyassah*, he said that the organization would prove whether it existed or not on the regional and international levels of the oil industry. He expressed hope that the council would issue a joint communiqué simultaneously in Kuwait and Brussels, headquarters of the European Common Market, in view of the importance of the European Economic Community as "the biggest consumer of Arab oil."[66]

The main issues before the conference were the establishment of an Arab tanker fleet and the construction of a drydock for ship repairs in the Gulf. Yamani explained that the two projects were then in the final stages of preparation and that the conference would discuss the establishment of an OAPEC fund to finance oil-development projects in member states and an Arab company for drilling and prospecting services. Sa'adawy later described the success of the conference as "a historic event" for the Arab oil producers.[67]

The four succeeding OAPEC ministerial council meetings (the eighth, in Kuwait on 7 May 1972; the ninth, in Kuwait on 18 November 1972; the tenth, in Damascus on 23 June 1973; and the eleventh, in Kuwait on 5 September 1973) approved the construction of a tanker fleet and the building of a supertanker drydock in Bahrain and discussed the establishment of an Arab oil-marketing company, the formation of a judicial body to arbitrate oil disputes among OAPEC member states, and the creation of a joint petroleum services company and a joint petrochemical industry.

An emergency OAPEC meeting held in Beirut on 11 June 1972 discussed ways of backing Iraq, which had nationalized the IPC facilities after IPC failed to increase production to the rate demanded by the Iraqi government. OAPEC decided to support "by all means at its disposal" the Iraqi nationalization act and pledged "to make Iraq's nationalization of IPC a success."[68] A meeting in Baghdad on 20 June 1972 of finance ministers of member states of OAPEC decided "to lend Iraq and Syria 60.6 million British pounds to help them meet foreign exchange requirements during the next three months"[69] arising from the interruption of oil pumping by IPC. The Iraqi finance minister, Amin Abd al-Karim, in his address to the conference said that the meeting embodied Arab cooperation "after the monopolistic companies faced us with various types of economic persecution, including the reduction of oil production to harm Iraq's national economy."[70] He praised OAPEC's resolution to support the Iraqi and Syrian measures. "Iraq will not forget the honorable stand taken by the sisterly countries. It will continue to strongly back the Arab nation in the various domains, particularly in liberating the national economy." The conference gave its full support to Iraq and Syria and "warned IPC's parent companies against applying sanctions to stop Iraq from selling the nationalized crude."[71]

OAPEC Reexamines Its Oil Policies

The friction between the producer governments and the oil companies gave more power to the national demand for more Arab oil coordination and more Arab control over the oil industry. The slogan "Arab oil for the Arabs," which was often repeated at the Eighth Arab Petroleum Congress in Algiers in June 1972, occurred again at the five-day conference of Arab professional trade unions, which ended in Baghdad in mid-July. Along with announcing its support for the Iraqi and Syrian nationalization moves against the Iraq Petroleum Company, the conference called upon the United Nations to protect a state's right to independence and sovereignty over its natural resources. Arab oil-producing nations were called upon to recover their national sovereignty "over the oil wealth and impose their full control over the disposal of oil resources" in the interest of Arab rights, economic and social development, the liberation of Palestine and occupied territories, and the achievement of freedom and progress for the Arab nation. Arab oil producers were also asked to reduce their production of oil "while taking into consideration its effective use as a weapon in the battle as well as the requirements of mankind."[72]

Continued U.S. support for Israel evoked many calls for economic sanctions in the Arab world, ranging from nationalization of oil installations to the imposition of a tax on U.S. companies or even a total boycott of U.S. goods.[73] Calls for action against U.S. companies because of the U.S. stance on the Arab-Israeli dispute were repeated by Commissioner General Mohammed Mahjoub of the Arab Boycott of Israel Office. At the opening session of the organization's conference in Cairo on 14 November 1972, Mahjoub proposed that the Arab states impose punitive taxes on foreign oil companies whose home countries were giving economic and military aid to Israel. The proposal was obviously a move against U.S. companies primarily, but other companies could also be affected, Mahjoub suggested. The tax would be made proportionate to the amount of aid given by the companies' home countries to Israel. The taxes would be used to finance Arab munitions plants and other arms-oriented heavy industry. Foreign oil companies, banks, and firms operating in the Arab world were making over $3 billion a year in net profits, Mahjoub asserted.[74]

During the same week, a seminar held in Baghdad entitled "Oil as a Weapon in the Struggle Against Imperialism and Israeli Aggression and as a Means for the Development of an Independent National Economy" called for direct cooperation between the producing and consuming countries, bypassing the international oil companies and sharing the profits. In his address to the opening session of the seminar, Iraqi President Ahmed Hasan al-Bakr told the participants: "The historic nationalization decision has implemented the slogan 'Arab oil for the Arabs' and we can now use Arab oil as a weapon against our imperialist enemy in all our liberation battles, particularly in our decisive battle in Palestine."

Before the year 1972 was out, the United States and the oil companies came under more fire from another influential Arab economic sector. The executive council of the International Confederation of Arab Trade Unions, meeting in December in Baghdad, adopted a resolution calling on Arab governments to boycott U.S. and West German interests in the Arab world by 1 March 1973 and to nationalize the interests of the two countries, especially oil, in the region.

By this time it was apparent that despite the oil companies' expensive drilling operations in other parts of the world, the Middle East, with nearly 60 percent of the world's proven oil reserves, would continue to be the major oil source for the industrial nations. Even nations with abundant resources like the United States, which at one time imported only 2 to 3 percent of its oil needs from the Middle East, were becoming increasingly dependent on the area to meet their rising energy needs. This had strong political implications, and there were renewed calls among the Arabs to use oil as a weapon to change U.S. Middle Eastern policy. OAPEC was put under heavy pressures by some of its members to adopt the principle of using oil as a political weapon. Some of its members who once advocated separation of oil and politics, such as Kuwait, had already changed their stands. However, Saudi Arabia resisted such a policy shift and used all its influence to prevent OAPEC from adopting such a view. But even a wealthy nation such as Saudi Arabia, whose influence in the Arab world was reaching unprecedented heights, could only endure pressure to a certain extent, and it was only a few months before Saudi Arabia aligned its policies with those of the other OAPEC members.

The year 1973 commenced with several events that had significant implications for inter-Arab oil-policy formulation. The signing of the participation agreements with the oil companies in October 1972 made OAPEC look forward to an atmosphere of mutual cooperation with the companies as well as to a role of effective coordination among member states in the economic sphere. However, as hopes for peace in the area seemed very remote, with no state showing any policy change that could result in concrete moves toward a lasting peace, the forces of radicalism in the Arab world gained additional impetus. Again, as the Arab world became increasingly agitated over the strong U.S. commitment to Israel, the use of Arab oil as a political weapon became a popular theme in Arab politics.

It was under such conditions and in this atmosphere of displeasure with the political stalemate that the Kuwaiti National Assembly met on 6 January 1978 and unanimously adopted a recommendation calling on the government to utilize Kuwait's oil resources as a political weapon in the event of renewed fighting between the Arab states and Israel. In addition, the assembly called on the government to freeze all relations with Western oil companies operating in Kuwait and to prepare the necessary legislation and decisions, taking into consideration the material and technological requirements, in case war broke out. In Egypt, the leading Cairo daily *al-Ahram* on 8 January 1973 praised the Kuwaiti recommendation, considering it "a step forward" to enable the Arab states to apply pressure on the United States to change its policy vis-à-vis the Arab-Israeli dispute. On the same day another Cairo daily, *al-Gumhuriyya*, maintained that the decision could be a catalyst of change in the present atmosphere "in which the Arabs are debarred from utilizing one of their important weapons in their battle with Israel."

The Kuwaiti National Assembly even viewed the participation agreements in a similar context. As these agreements signed by the Kuwaiti government were brought to the assembly for ratification, members of the opposition grasped the opportunity to call for an immediate 51 percent interest in the companies' operations. This, they asserted, would give Kuwait an opportunity to put pressure on the United States and other Western countries to bring about a just settlement with Israel. These views were supported by the moderate Kuwaiti *Daily News*, which said in an editorial of the time that it "wholeheartedly proposes that Arab oil-producing countries give a final ultimatum to the United States and other unfriendly Western countries that the flow of oil will be cut from them unless they change their attitude to the Arab world. The paper considers this to be a satisfactory alternative to the oil participation agreement."

Arab warning on the use of oil as a weapon was reiterated on a number of occasions, but it was left to a special OAPEC session held in early September to "attempt to draft a collective oil strategy designed to press the United States into an even-handed policy in the Middle East."[75] Arriving to attend the meeting, Yamani refused to be drawn out by questions on the use of oil as a political weapon in the Arabs' confrontation with Israel. "We believe in industrial progress in Saudi Arabia, to create a political atmosphere in the area," he said. Asked whether Saudi Arabia would restrict oil production to pressure the United States into withdrawing support for Israel, the Saudi oil minister gave a noncommittal reply: "We will produce oil according to our needs."[76]

In his public address to the opening session, Kuwaiti Minister of Finance and Oil al-Atiki made no mention of any anti-U.S. oil plans, in spite of the fact that some "Egyptian and Kuwaiti sources were leaking reports that the use of Arab oil as a weapon in the Middle East conflict was the main item on the conference agenda."[77] However, as the conference ended its meetings, it was apparent that it had reached no agreement on any draft for a common oil policy, and the issue was left off the agenda. The final statement expressed OAPEC's solidarity with Libya over its 51 percent nationalization of the major oil companies' assets. It declared that "nationalization is a legitimate and sovereign right of every country."[78]

The next OAPEC meeting, held in Kuwait following the outbreak of the fourth Arab-Israeli war, officially adopted the use of oil as a political weapon "to pressure the international community to compel Israel to relinquish Arab occupied territories."

4
The Control of Oil, 1967–1973: Participation and Nationalization

The Oil Companies Under Attack

The international political and economic realities of the late 1950s and early 1960s tended to increase the frustration of various elements in the oil equation. Though the oil-producing governments and the operating companies were often at odds, three cardinal issues, inclusive of all others, lay at the heart of the controversy. These were: (1) profitability, (2) prices, and (3) production.

The producer countries, no longer the dormant partners they had been twenty years before, started to take an acute interest in the operations of the oil companies to whom they had granted concessions.[1] They felt the implications of the world energy shift from coal to oil and wanted a greater share in the proceeds of their oil exports. These countries hoped to profit from fully integrating the producing, refining, transporting, and marketing of oil through national companies, whose entire operation would be controlled by them. Underlying this attitude was the assumption that crude-oil prices would always be low and, in consequence, profits would tend not to increase because the consumer countries would minimize their oil imports and their energy costs, and the oil companies would go along with them in this respect: "The concessionary companies belong to the oil-importing and oil-consuming countries. If the interests of the producing countries conflict with those of the consuming countries, the interests of the former are invariably sacrificed."[2]

Moreover, producer nations had begun to feel that the companies were abusing their freedom in the area of pricing by making arbitrary decisions at the expense of the host governments and without their prior knowledge. Such practices, they felt, could be halted only by having an increased say in the operation of the business. Additionally, the producer countries' conviction that the oil companies were threatening their economic development, and thus their political stability, by allowing the production of crude to rise or fall solely in accordance with commercial considerations only increased their desire to control the oil industry. Resentment against the Iraq Petroleum Company toward the end of the regime of General Abdul Karim Kassim in 1963, for example, became particularly strong on the grounds that it had not kept its promise to expand production at a certain rate. As a result, anticipated oil revenues had not risen to the levels expected.[3]

On the other hand, the multinational companies that controlled oil production outside the United States had a clear common interest in limiting output and sharing it among themselves. Uninhibited at the time by active enforcement of the U.S. antitrust laws, their worries came mainly from (1) the widespread criticism by the Arab press of their various activities, (2) the oil technocrats' impact on the masses and on government policies, and (3) the increasing pressure from the host governments for increased production, more revenues, and the implementation of participation agreements. The companies came under strong attack. They were accused of being used "as instruments in the economic warfare waged by their parent countries against the smaller states"[4] and even of being behind "attempts to carry out coups d'etat in the Arab states."[5] The Arabian-American Oil Company[6] was accused of (1) intervening in various ways to prevent the development of an articulate, organized labor movement, (2) keeping Saudi workers out of high positions and providing them with a minimum of training, (3) carrying out arbitrary dismissals, (4) preventing productive investments and the development of local industries, and (5) being responsible for the dismissal of Tariqi in 1962. The Iraq Petroleum Company was accused of (1) exploiting the discontent caused by an increase in gasoline prices in order to foment disorder and riots in Iraq and thereby force the government to take a softer line in its negotiations with the company, (2) conniving in Lebanon with local notables and politicians to the disadvantage of others, (3) bribing labor union officials, and (4) dismissing and retaining employees according to their political affiliations. Apart from the political accusations, the radical news media charged them with unscrupulous business practices, such as (1) concealing oil discoveries, (2) using false measuring instruments, (3) falsifying accounts, and (4) smuggling out oil from the producing area.

A further serious charge was that the oil companies adopted a superior attitude toward their host countries. Tariqi once sarcastically criticized the company officials' habit of referring to the industry as "this complicated oil business." He commented that "they have striven to infuse the Arabs with a sense of inferiority."[7] The ousted Algerian president,

Ahmed Ben Bella (1962–1965), once said of the oil companies that "their arrogance is reminiscent of that of the *colons*. Oil men believe that the Arab mind cannot grasp the mysteries of oil technology and the subtleties of economic science."[8] Whether these charges were true is hard to verify. However, the harm to the oil multinationals had been done and the Arab people began to feel uneasy at the presence of oil companies that extracted their wealth and left them with the "crumbs."

At times the companies offended Arab national sensibilities in their search for more profits. Their acquisition of concessions in French-occupied Algeria, which was regarded by the Arabs as tantamount to taking sides with the French government against the Algerian people, was just one example. A Saudi daily newspaper once commented: "It would be a thousand times better for [the oil companies] to make a reasonable and permanent profit and to gain the confidence of the people of the areas in which they operate than to realize fabulous but temporary profits and become the object of the hatred and animosity of their host people."[9]

The multinational oil companies managed to act, at times, as a bridge between consumer and producer governments. This go-between role tended to strengthen the companies' bargaining position with the host governments. In cases of disagreement with the producer countries, they exerted not only their own pressure but also the supporting influence of their home governments. The situation was complicated by the producer governments' dependence on oil revenues for national development and political stability; at the same time, the consumer governments had become constrained by their growing need for cheap and abundant oil imports as a result of their increasing consumption and limited local oil resources. Another complicating factor was the tremendous income that the multinationals generated for the consuming governments in the form of taxes.

The multinational oil companies resented any form of interference by the Arab oil-producing governments in their day-to-day operations in Europe and the United States. They argued that it was not practical to have the producer governments participate in the setting of oil prices, as prices often had to be changed rapidly on the basis of purely commercial considerations requiring prompt action. The companies vehemently objected to the producer governments' desire to share in the profits earned at the refining and marketing end of the business. But at the same time the companies well knew that, though they had the economic power within their grasp, the host countries had the political power. They were aware that the host countries could always go to the extreme of asserting the political sovereignty of the state should they so desire.

Negotiation or Nationalization?

In the aftermath of the 1967 June war, the Arabs embarked on a policy of wresting control of their natural resources from the Western companies. This intensified Arab effort during the period from 1967 to 1973 to control production, development, pricing, and distribution of Arab oil caused the world's oil economy to undergo drastic changes. The Arabs, who throughout the 1967 oil embargo had had an insignificant influence over their oil resources, were, by the eve of the October 1973 oil embargo, majority owners and active partners in that vital resource.

In general, the major Arab oil producers took a somewhat moderate attitude, but such an approach did not satisfy some of the hard-line Arab regimes. Consequently, two conflicting political and ideological views can be distinguished. On the one hand, the oil-producing progressive states, such as Algeria, Iraq, and later Libya, in order to keep the political initiative in the Arab world following the 1967 military defeat, took the hazardous but more popular path of nationalization, speeding the transference of control and setting the pace for the others to follow.[10] Finding the way of negotiation long, tedious, and often unrewarding, these governments were tempted to abandon it in favor of unilateral and arbitrary action that rendered meaningless all the oil concessions involved.

By contrast, the oil-producing conservatives, such as Saudi Arabia, Kuwait, and the Gulf emirates, while yielding to the Arab urge for a full takeover of their local oil installations, wanted to do so in such a way as not to offend the operating companies or damage relations with their home governments. They felt that nationalization was risky politically, economically, and technically, and they hoped that through mutual understanding the oil companies would concede to them a majority holding in the shares of the industry as part of the participation agreements. While their bargaining methods and national goals with respect to their oil resources had become more sophisticated and long range, the moderate producer nations had not carried any disagreements with their exploiting foreign oil companies to the point of direct confrontation. They sought to maximize the bargaining power of their regimes and to minimize the business middleman role of the companies without the threat of nationalization. This attitude was confirmed publicly and in private.

The Participation Option: Saudi Arabia, Kuwait, and the United Arab Emirates

Though the Arabs' struggle to control the oil industry in their countries took more aggressive forms in the years following the 1967 June war, the road had been paved long in advance. It was in 1959 that the Hendryx report brought into the open the extent of the gap between the two main adversaries and showed how tense relations between the host governments and the multinational oil companies had become.

Frank Hendryx, an American lawyer working as the legal advisor to the Saudi directorate general of petroleum and mineral affairs, presented a paper on behalf of the Saudi government to the First Arab Petroleum Congress in Cairo in April 1959. Hendryx's paper, entitled "A Sovereign Nation's Legal Ability To Make and Abide by a Petroleum Concession Contract," argued that there existed in U.S., British, and French law precedents for the unilateral alteration or nullification of parts or all of an oil concession by the oil-producing countries, either through legislation or administrative decree, "so long as their actions are taken in good faith, that is, on behalf of a substantial public interest."[11] In a dramatic challenge to the companies' views of the sanctity of oil concession agreements, the author went on to claim that should it appear that other nations similarly situated obtained greater benefits for their citizens, a unilateral contract alteration "may become, in principle, mandatory"; that the "financial interest [of a nation] must be included in the classification of matter of vital interest to a nation's citizens"; and that regardless of "any previous contractual commitment by the State not to alter the terms of an agreement, or not to alter them except under certain conditions, [these provisions] would be unavailing to prevent later alterations of the contract." Hendryx emphasized that "the purpose for which governments exist, the service of their peoples, requires that on proper occasions those governments must be released from or be able to override their contractual obligations." In fact, Hendryx intimated, there is a "moral" obligation that this be done. When queried specifically during the conference as to whether this last statement applied to arbitration clauses usually found in concession agreements, Hendryx replied: "I really did not consider this aspect of the [concession] agreement, but as the government has the right to cancel the agreement, then, I believe, it can also alter or cancel the arbitration clause."[12]

The Hendryx doctrine excited considerable debate, comment, and speculation in oil circles. Though the companies viewed it with disfavor, they did not contradict the correctness of its arguments, "which merely stated established law."[13] Presented as an official statement from the Saudi delegation, it was considered by the oil companies to present an unprecedented political provocation. Private comments by Saudi officials indicated that its primary purpose was to be a bargaining threat. The Saudis, who were in continuous negotiation with Aramco over government claims to a greater share in Aramco's profits, wanted to indicate that the Saudi government could invalidate Aramco's concession should the government decide that it was against "public interest," depriving the company of recourse to any international court or to the orderly processes of arbitration for which its concession explicitly provided.

While officials of companies not directly involved in Saudi Arabia attacked the doctrine on the grounds that it was not derived from applicable cases and was likely to deter investors, ironically the most effective rebuttal came from some Arab delegates. Libya's chief spokesman to the petroleum congress, Anis el-Qasem, asserted Libya's belief in the "sanctity of freely negotiated contracts." A United Arab Republic delegate, Dr. Mahmoud el-Ayoubi, reaffirmed his government's faith in the use of arbitration clauses, which Egyptian petroleum contracts included. The Lebanese delegation added an emphatic protest, stressing the government's reliance on recognized legal practice between it and foreign contractors.

These spontaneous Arab responses to the Hendryx theory are not difficult to interpret. The governments of the delegates who attacked the report were in dire need of the great banking institutions of the West to finance the big projects in their countries. Neither the banks nor the multinational oil companies would be willing to put up the money required or commit the necessary expertise if concession contracts did not bind each party equally or could be abrogated unilaterally.

Arab delegates expressed clearly their hope of achieving a greater share of control and participation in oil affairs. Declining the nationalization approach of Prime Minister Mossadeq of Iran, they presented their case in terms of economics and national aspirations. In their deliberations, they presented economic figures to support their case for a larger share of the profits and more say in the operations of the oil companies. In essence, the delegates sought to establish that the so-called "50-50 principle" was illusory and that only by full integration of the industry could it become a reality. Arab economists presented figures to show that total company profits exceeded Middle Eastern governments' receipts in this period by $3,330.5 million. They further asserted that there was a total profit on Middle Eastern crude oil in 1958 of about $1.60 per barrel. Of this, one-half went to the producing countries on the 50-50 basis, while the companies made another $.20 per barrel on transportation of oil, an additional "estimated" $1.00 per barrel on refining, and a possible further $2.00 per barrel on marketing— on all of which the Arabs got nothing.[14] Saudi Oil Minister Tariqi explained in a press interview that the overall Arab yearly oil revenue of some $200 million could be raised to $300 million by "full integration," according to which the companies would share not only their producing profits, but their transportation, refining, and marketing profits as well.[15]

Arguments presented by the oil companies rebutting these views and asserting that the 50-50 cut on crude-oil profits gave the producing countries a larger share than they would get by sharing the profits all the way from the well to the pump had some effect in moderating demands but did not provide any real satisfaction for the Arab nationalists' psychological need to participate more fully in the oil affairs that so profoundly affected their lives. Through fuller participation they hoped to hurdle the barrier presented by the advanced and alien industrial complex that had been erected in their midst. At about this time, the agreement by IPC to accept Iraqis on its board of directors and the appointment of two Saudi Arabians to the board of Aramco signified the companies' recognition of this need.

With the formation of OPEC in 1960, the Arab producers concentrated all their efforts within that organization to present the oil multinationals with a unified front. OPEC, however, failed to make serious progress toward this objective, and it remained to the oil-producing nations individually to deal with the oil companies to settle the issue. On their part, the multinationals resisted all such efforts; not until October 1972 were they willing to make a deal with the major Arab oil producers on the issue of participation. This softening resulted from the realization that they risked confrontation with the governments concerned. King Faisal of Saudi Arabia intervened personally to warn the oil companies that harsh measures would be adopted if they failed to accept participation voluntarily; at the same time, the heads of Kuwait, Abu Dhabi, and Qatar conveyed similar warnings. In view of this pressure, the oil companies agreed in March 1972 to 20 percent government participation and proposed to hold talks to decide on the time and method of effecting participation and to determine the compensation to be paid to the companies.

The tedious negotiations that followed lingered for some time until the producing governments expressed more firmly their desire to see a deal concluded. The problem by then had boiled down to a conflict over the rate at which the producers would advance from the initial 20 percent participation to the avowed goal of 51 percent. The Arab producers, represented by Saudi Oil Minister Yamani, wanted majority ownership by the early 1980s, while the companies hoped to delay the takeover at least until the late 1980s. At first the companies were adamant. But under pressure from the producer governments as well as from the United States, they gave in, and the participation agreement was signed in October 1972. The U.S. State Department advised against a hard line in negotiations with the oil producers because these developing countries still needed Western know-how, in marketing as well as in pumping. Besides, OPEC was thought to be a fragile thing that would fall apart at the first serious economic blow.[16]

The most significant provisions of the participation agreement, which was to become effective on 1 January 1973, were the following:

1. The initial rate of participation which was to come into effect in 1973 and remain in force to the end of 1977 was to be 25 percent of each concession, and this rate was thereafter to be raised to 30 percent on 1 January 1978, to 35 percent on 1 January 1979, to 40 percent on 1 January 1980, to 45 percent on 1 January 1981 and to 51 percent on 1 January 1982 (Article 3 and Second Supplement).

2. The companies were to be compensated for the 25 percent initial participation by a corresponding percentage of the updated book value of the installations of crude-oil production, exploration and development in the manner shown in the books used for income tax purposes in the Gulf countries, with the proviso that consideration should be given to increases in prices in order that these might be reflected in book values (Article 4).

3. The governments would effectively participate in the administration of the companies. There were, however, certain issues referred to in the Agreement as "major management issues" which needed the approval of a specified number of the shareholders, or possibly all of them. Some of these involved the sale or disposal of certain assets the values of which exceeded a specified sum, and capital expenditure and operating expenses exceeding a certain limit. The agreements covered exploration and development programmes and the establishment of new facilities, etc. (Article 6).

The agreement was signed on 20 December 1972 in Riyadh by Saudi Arabia and Abu Dhabi, and later by Kuwait and Qatar. Iraq, however, withdrew from the participation talks and announced that it would go its own way on this matter.

From the beginning, hardly anyone had been optimistic about Iraq, which had been moving closer to the Soviet Union and was thus reluctant to sign the agreement, particularly due to its concern over the cost of compensating IPC on the basis agreed to by Yamani. To adhere to the deal would have meant a payment of $400 million to IPC in compensation for the nationalized Kirkuk oilfields, but the Iraqi government, according to the Kuwaiti daily *al-Siyassah*, was willing to pay IPC only $15 million. The newspaper said that Iraq insisted on compensating the oil companies on the basis of the net book value of their investment, which it estimated at $15 million. The Yamani formula envisaged compensation on the basis of "updated book value," which took into consideration the inflation that had taken place since the investments were first made, and IPC had estimated compensation due for the nationalized assets on this basis at $400 million. In an interview with the Beirut biweekly *Le Pétrole et le Gaz Arabes* published on 1 November 1972, the Iraqi vice-president, Saddam al-Takriti, indicated on a compromising note that the Yamani formula could ease the way to an agreement on compensation with IPC. "The settlement of outstanding problems with IPC depends mainly on an agreement on compensation. For us, the only valid base for calculating compensation is the net value of investments made by the company in Iraq. The participation agreement could perhaps allow us to see the matter more clearly."

Within days of announcing the participation agreement, extensive details were published in the *Petroleum Intelligence Weekly,* and the *Economist* gave some idea of the prices the oil industry would pay for the oil it bought back. In total, the *Economist* suggested that the industry would lose about half of the profits it would have gained if it had retained ownership of the oil.[17]

The oil companies maintained that these compromises were the price to be paid to accommodate the changing times. However, part of the extra cost was passed on to the consumer in Europe and Japan, where there was a rise in the retail price per gallon. Nevertheless, the agreement was welcomed by the Commission of the European Economic Community, which announced that the price increases "would not cause any major problems for consumers if the rise in consumer prices was kept in proportion to the cost to oil companies and possible future savings were taken into account."[18] The commission was also optimistic about freight rates, which it felt were likely to fall over the next few years as a result of increases in tanker capacity.

The oil companies seemed satisfied with the deal because of the stability it offered. A spokesman for the companies described the agreement as a "milestone." A statement issued on 5 October 1972 in New York by the company negotiators said that the agreement was "comprehensive in character." The oil companies said that one of the principal aims of the negotiators was to create "a true spirit of partnership under mutually binding arrangements in each country which will endure through the remaining terms of the respective concessions, thereby assisting materially in maintaining security of oil supplies for all the consuming countries."

For the most part, the producer nations also seemed satisfied with the deal. There was an animated debate on the agreement in the Kuwaiti National Assembly during which the opposition members repeated their demands for an immediate 51 percent participation in the operations of the companies in place of the 25 percent included in the agreement. Members of the opposition wanted to use the participation issue as a bargaining chip to put pressure on the United States and other Western countries to bring about a just settlement with Israel. This attitude received support from many quarters in Kuwait. The Kuwaiti *Daily News* proposed that Arab oil-producing countries give an ultimatum to the United States and other unfriendly Western countries that their oil would be cut off unless they changed their attitude toward the Arab world. The newspaper considered that this would be "a satisfactory alternative to the participation agreement." However, the agreement was ratified without amendment when Kuwaiti Minister of Finance and Oil al-Atiki threatened to resign should the assembly reject the agreement.

In Saudi Arabia, King Faisal issued a royal decree ratifying the participation agreement. Commenting on the terms, Yamani stated that the agreement as negotiated was "more than we had dreamed of" and that if Saudi Arabia had possessed the necessary expertise to take over "direct and swift control we would not wait." The agreement was also ratified by Abu Dhabi and Qatar.[19]

OPEC also welcomed the agreement. At the end of a two-day meeting in Riyadh on 27 October 1972, OPEC issued a statement that said: "Recognizing that the draft agreement reached by Saudi Oil Minister Sheikh Ahmad Zaki Yamani secures effective participation for the states concerned, the [OPEC] conference congratulates such states and wishes them every success in implementing it." OAPEC declared that it would increase its coordinating role as the participation agreements between member states and oil companies operating on their territories were implemented.

As a result of the participation agreement, the relationship between Western oil companies and the oil-producing states underwent a major change. Both parties looked forward to a period of relative calm.

The Nationalization Option: Egypt, Algeria, Libya, and Iraq

While the conservative governments of Saudi Arabia, Kuwait, the Gulf emirates, and Libya (before the 1969 coup) attempted to increase their "take" from their respective oil industries by pressing for more participation through negotiations and bargaining, other more radical Arab states, such as Egypt, Algeria, Libya (after the 1969 coup), and Iraq opted to speed up the participation process by taking unilateral actions. These unilateral actions were taken in response to certain major political events that occurred in the states concerned, the Arab world, or on the international scene. At times, such moves were made to contain unrest within a particular state and to solidify the ruling regime, or in reaction to similar moves by another Arab leader in a bid to hold the political initiative in the Arab world.

Egypt

Since the midfifties, Egypt—perhaps because it was only a minor oil producer—was among the first Arab states to advocate more Arab control of the oil industry. It played a major role in influencing Arab oil policies in spite of the fact that its small-scale oil output was produced by foreign-owned companies, sometimes with government participation. Egyptian President Nasser became one of the most adamant Arab proponents of the idea of "Arab strength through oil." In his book *Egypt's Liberation—The Philosophy of the Revolution*, he spoke significantly about this theme, calling oil one of the three main sources of strength of the Arab world. Without making any overt threats, he referred to oil as "a sinew of material civilization without which all its machines would cease to function."[20]

In September 1956 Nasser, encouraged by the popular enthusiasm generated by his move to nationalize the Suez Canal, made a move unprecedented in Arab oil politics. He issued legislation by which an Egyptian company, the General Petroleum Authority, was set up "to associate with other bodies engaged in the oil industry." The new law contained one especially significant clause: the authority "may purchase such bodies or have them amalgamated in it or affiliated to it."[21]

Shortly after the 1956 Suez invasion, Nasser nationalized all British and French oil installations in Egypt. Radio Cairo reported on 1 November 1956 that the Egyptian ministry of industry and commerce had taken over the properties of the Shell Company of Egypt, the Anglo-Egyptian Company, and the French Petroleum Company. The Shell Company of Egypt was a marketing company jointly owned by Shell and British Petroleum, while the Anglo-Egyptian Company, registered in 1911, owned oil-bearing properties under lease from Egypt at Ras Gharib and Hurghada on the western shore of the Red Sea. It also owned jointly with Mobil Oil of Egypt, a U.S. concern, properties at the Sudr and Asl fields in the Sinai peninsula. Shell and British Petroleum each owned 31 percent, while Egypt, to whom control and management of the company had been transferred in 1951, owned only 10 percent of the shares.

The 1956 Suez intervention caused Egypt to face a severe shortage of oil, as most of its oilfields were out of production. To meet the shortage, the Egyptian government sought U.S. and Soviet help and received it. However, as relations between Britain and Egypt eased, Egypt handed back in July 1959 the sequestrated Anglo-Egyptian oilfields to the parent British concern and Shell. The agreement reached between the Egyptian government and the two major companies covered "past differences" and "future operating conditions." For their part, the Egyptians expressed hope that these fields in the future would be run "on a basis mutually profitable to the United Arab Republic and to foreign shareholders."[22]

With the close of the 1950s, Egypt assumed a leading role in Arab politics, and its role in Arab oil policies became more significant. Cairo became the focus of regional hopes for increasing Arab oil power. However, Egypt's attitude toward Arab oil had always been ambivalent. As far as the oil of other Arab producers was concerned, Egyptian oil policies were uncompromising. Egypt called upon those producers to nationalize "Arab oil" as a token of their share in the struggle against Western influence in the Arab world. Such calls were heeded by the impoverished Arab masses, who thought that an increase in oil revenues would mean improvement in their social, educational, and economic condition. However, these calls never went beyond embarrassing some of the Arab oil producers. These producers believed that Egypt spoke "out of turn" in claiming Cairo as the focal point from which to arouse public interest in oil, considering that it was last among those who had the right to call for the nationalization of "our oil." But as Arab public opinion was well-disposed toward Egypt's views on any Arab issue, other countries could hardly dispute the Egyptian claims.

At the Third Arab Petroleum Congress, held in Alexandria in December 1961, Anwar Salamah, secretary general of the Arab Federation of Petroleum Workers, suggested in a paper entitled "Government Participation in the Oil Industry and Its Effect on the Economics of the Arab States" that the Arab states should copy Egypt's example in nationalizing the oil industry in their respective territories and that the oil producers need not fear the consequences of such a step. But one year later, as joint-venture agreements proved profitable to Egypt and a number of those concessions were concluded, Nasser moderated Cairo's position, hoping that the West would feel secure enough to provide the large amounts of capital needed for new oil explorations. Thus moderation in oil affairs became the official Egyptian line. At the Fourth Arab Petroleum Congress, held in Beirut in 1963, Kamil al-Badri, chairman of the Egyptian General Petroleum Corporation, explained to Tariqi, who was advocating state sovereignty, that in joint ventures sovereignty was taken for granted. "Partnership is a practical way of ensuring that all decisions of boards of directors are taken with the full knowledge and agreement of the governments," he stated. "With 50/50 board representation, both sides could agree on costs, prices, profits, etc., 'from within.' "

After the joint ownership agreement with the Italian state-owned oil company ENI (Ente Nazionali Idrocarburi) proved profitable to Egypt, Nasser was encouraged to conclude more joint agreements with other oil multinationals. Arrangements were made with Amoco International (a subsidiary of Standard Oil of Indiana) and Phillips Petroleum in 1963. In partnership with Egyptian General Petroleum Corporation (EGPC), Amoco's oil explorations were successful, and output from the El Morgan field in the Gulf of Suez (found in 1965) began in April 1967 and continued almost unaffected throughout the June war of 1967. In April 1967, just as the El Morgan field was beginning to produce, a Cairo editor warned Iraq that "no patriot who appreciates the dimensions of the oil battle can advocate the nationalization of oil."[23] Another joint venture was made with Phillips Petroleum and the Western Desert Operating Company (WEPCO), in which EGPC was a 50 percent partner with Phillips Petroleum. In 1966 the venture produced an important oil discovery in the Western Desert, south of the El Alamein battlefield. El Alamein began production in August 1968, and its output reached a peak of more than 40,000 barrels per day, but later that output dropped sharply.

Following the 1967 June war, Nasser,

> while publicly insisting that the Arabs should stop oil supplies to the United States and Britain, had asked the American oil companies working in Egypt to continue drilling in two Egyptian oilfields. The oilfields were offshore in the Gulf of Suez, where Pan American was producing 50,000 barrels a day, and at El Alamein in the Western desert, where Phillips was producing 8,000 barrels a day. The two American companies were given assurances that their 100 or so United States citizens working on the fields would be protected against anti-American demonstrations.[24]

As a result of the 1967 hostilities, oil production continued, but exploration work that was going on before the war in Egypt's western and eastern deserts and in the Gulf of Suez area came to a complete standstill. However, established oil wells operated by Egypt were functioning normally. Within a few months, the El Morgan field alone more than offset the loss of the Sinai oilfields that fell under Israeli occupation, and it was kept functioning until the 1973 October war halted its production.

Algeria

Following the discovery of oil in Algeria in the mid-fifties, the French occupation authorities adhered to strict rules and regulations concerning prospecting and producing oil in Algeria. Under French oil law, exploration concessions were granted for periods of five years; at the end of that period, one-half of the concession area had to be surrendered to the French government for reallocation, the company being allowed to decide which areas to keep and which to surrender. Although the French government granted exploration concessions to several foreign oil companies working in association with French government and private interests, these companies were not allowed a free hand in developing oilfields that were found. This kept major U.S. oil companies away from bidding for oil rights in Algeria, and only the Royal Dutch/Shell group, British Petroleum, and a few nonmajor U.S. oil companies were left on the list of bidders. ENI stayed out to avoid offending Arab sensibilities, as it would have had to deal with the French government and thus support its claim to Algerian natural resources.[25]

Following its independence in 1961, Algeria started to assume a more dynamic role in oil policies. No longer content with a mere monetary return from the foreign companies, it pressed for government participation in the ownership and management of the concessionary oil companies. In a speech at Ouargla, Algeria, on 28 September 1964, President Ben Bella had made it clear that if Algeria were confronted with the alternatives of a high fiscal revenue without participation and a low fiscal revenue with participation, it would choose the latter. In 1965 French oil companies were placed in a privileged position whereby they paid lower royalties and repatriated a smaller proportion of their revenues from selling the oil abroad in return for agreeing to take a leading part in prospecting for new oilfields. But in the late 1960s there were frequent arguments over the terms of the agreement. The Algerians accused the French companies of not doing as much prospecting as provided for by the agreement. Consequently, the state-owned Algerian oil concern Sonatrach, which had been set up in 1963/1964, extended its activities into exploration and production.

Following the 1967 June war, the few U.S. firms that held minority interests in various Algerian ventures were assigned Algerian managers to supervise their affairs and were required to deposit all their earnings in Algerian banks. In a series of moves over a few years beginning in 1967, the Algerian government nationalized the assets of the multinational oil companies. The biggest of the nationalized companies was the Royal Dutch/Shell–owned Compagnie des Pétroles d'Algérie (CPA), which controlled 10 percent of production. Late in August 1967 Algeria nationalized the local marketing companies of Esso and Mobil. The timing coincided with the Arab summit meeting at Khartoum and was meant to impress the Arabs rather than the U.S. oil men. The move was of particular interest in that it came in response to Iraq's proposal of a three months' total ban on all Arab oil exports to Western countries supporting Israel. Algeria, though it had not voted for that proposal,[26] wanted to indicate to the Arabs that nationalizing several big U.S. firms with small Algerian interests made a more useful contribution to the cause of revolution. However, in the Sahara, U.S. oil companies went on prospecting and drilling, while the Algerian State Oil Company urged most of its twenty-five U.S. oil technicians to remain at their posts.

For quite some time Algeria's economic anchor in the crosscurrent of its East-West relations had been France, on which its oil industry, foreign trade, and secondary education system largely depended. But since the June war, many Algerian officials, concerned by the strength of the anti-Arab reaction from the French press and public that summer, started the long process of reducing such dependence with an elaborate program emphasizing self-reliance. This attitude strained French-Algerian relations and intensified the disputes between the two states.

In what appeared to be a sharp policy shift, Algeria sought membership in OPEC in April 1969. Until that time, Algeria had taken a highly independent line concerning oil production and pricing, and its sudden urge to join OPEC was greeted in OPEC circles with "surprise and puzzlement." However, it seemed that the Algerian decision was closely connected with, not to say motivated by, the dispute with France over oil and trade relations. The Algerians were preparing for negotiations with the French government over the revision of the 1965 bilateral oil and trade treaty. Once this is taken into consideration Algeria's application to join OPEC is easily understood. OPEC, with its growing strength, could prove helpful in the Algerians' bid to revise their treaty with France and in their militant campaign against the French oil companies. Algeria was admitted to OPEC in July 1969. Although Algeria took only seventh place in the OPEC league in terms of oil production, its status was heightened by the very fact that the Algerians had already obtained a substantial concession from the French oil companies and clearly showed that they intended to struggle for further concessions.

As Algeria's battle with the French oil companies intensified, its membership in OPEC proved useful. The twentieth conference of OPEC, held in Algiers on 24 June 1970, voiced the organization's full support for the "well-founded" Algerian demands. OPEC declared itself ready to "fully and actively support any appropriate measures taken by the Algerian government to safeguard its legitimate interests." Any delay in the settlement, the conference declared, might have detrimental effects on the interests of OPEC.

In February 1971, two years after it had nationalized all other oil operations in the country, Algeria took a 51 percent interest in the local assets of the French companies Compagnie Française des Pétroles (CFP) and Entreprise de Recherches et Activités Pétrolières (ERAP). It then imposed new posted prices and raised taxes retroactively. After failing in April to reach an agreement on the question of compensation for the partially nationalized French oil companies, France decided to cut off talks and end its special relationship with Algeria. It formally dismantled the close connection between its economic and political interests. The French oil companies removed their technicians, stopped the flow of crude oil from Algeria to France, and warned the world that anyone who bought what they considered to be their crude would be prosecuted in international courts.

Even the withdrawal of all French technicians did not seem to bother the Algerian government very much. Sonatrach, the Algerian state company, had already had more than five years' experience in production, refining, pipeline transport, and marketing. It was, however, more vulnerable on the distribution and marketing lines. With over half of the Algerian output of some 48 million tons going to France, the French companies seemed to be in a good bargaining position, particularly as Algeria depended heavily on oil exports for its foreign exchange. Although there were one or two minor buyers such as Brazil, the French oil embargo strengthened the oil companies' position. Any short-term gap in oil exports would be costly to Algeria, while France, which imported only about a quarter of its supplies from Algeria, had built up substantial stocks and could switch to other sources without too much difficulty.[27] At the same time, heavy pressure was put on the United States by France to freeze a deal recently signed by El Paso Gas of Texas to purchase Algerian liquefied natural gas over a twenty-five-year period. In mid-June 1971, the Nixon administration intervened in the hearings on the deal that were taking place before the Federal Power Commission (FPC), "overriding State and Defense Department views that there were no foreign-policy objections."[28]

After several weeks of strenuous negotiations, a compromise was reached on that year's hardest battle between oil companies and the host governments. Algeria agreed to pay $54 million to the French oil companies to guarantee the companies 7 million tons of crude a year at a price of around $2.75 a barrel (the going rate for the Mediterranean), and to allow it to share in the development of the Saharan oilfields on what the comapny called "economically viable" terms.[29] Even the question of back taxes, which would have wiped out any compensation, was solved.

Libya

At the time of its independence in 1951, Libya was poor in natural resources and severely limited by the climatic conditions of its portion of the Sahara Desert. The country depended almost entirely upon foreign aid and the importation of commodities necessary to the maintenance of its economy. But the discovery of oil dramatically changed the structure of the Libyan economy, and the exploitation of Libyan oil reserves began in 1956 following the passing of Royal Decree No. 25 of 1955, which laid the groundwork for awarding the first concessions.[30] The new industry provided a moderate source of capital for economic and social development, but it was fully controlled by the large multinational oil companies—both the "majors" and the "independents." The 1955 royal decree was specifically designed to attract as many foreign companies as possible to participate in exploration by giving virtual control over exploration and exploitation to the companies without regard to the country's long-term interests or needs.[31] The first year of Libya's oil industry, 1956, saw fifty-one foreign companies involved in a total of seventeen concessions. By 1967, larger companies had taken over the operations. There were forty companies at work, seventeen of them exporting oil. During the same period, the Libyan government of King Idris I (1952–1969) followed a policy of weakening and squeezing the "independents," who produced a major share of the country's oil, in support of the "majors," thus weakening its own ability to play off the various companies against one another.

The situation changed radically in September 1969 when a group of young army officers seized power from King Idris—the last of the Sanussi dynasty—while he was outside the country. The new regime, full of passionate Arab nationalist leanings, broke Libya's former close ties with the West, formed an alliance with Egypt and the Sudan, adopted a stronger Arab line toward Israel, and embarked on an oil policy aimed at exercising effective control over all aspects of the industry.[32]

For many years, Arabs had threatened to use their oil resources as a political lever. Although Egyptian President Nasser was the most prominent in advocating the use of this weapon (Algerian President Boumediene being next), it was Libyan Premier Muammar Qaddafi who, with aggressive tactics and adroit maneuvering, soon brought about the most significant changes in the international and Arab oil industry. In Qaddafi's hands, Libya's favorable bargaining position was used to whipsaw the multinational oil companies. In turn, the achievements of Libya virtually forced the rest of the OPEC countries to use Libya as a standard for their dealings with the international companies.[33]

During the early 1970s, of all producing countries Libya seemed the least inclined to nationalize. It had virtually no skilled oil men, and the new reluctance of the oil companies to train Libyans prompted Qaddafi to send them to neighboring Algeria to learn the trade. Egyptian President Nasser persistently warned Libya against overhasty nationalizations, in order to avoid economic chaos. However, the international oil situation was tempting. The closure of the Suez Canal following the June war of 1967 had increased Western Europe's energy problems because tankers had to round Africa, at considerably higher cost, rather than take the short route from the Gulf into the Mediterranean. Moreover, the Tapline pipeline, carrying oil from the Gulf to its Mediterranean terminals, had been cut by a Syrian bulldozer, making Libyan oil even more important to Western Europe, which had already changed its pattern of supplies over the previous decade toward greater reliance on North African and Middle Eastern sources of supply. These favorable conditions prepared the way for the Libyan government to move against the oil companies.

Hard on the heels of President Richard Nixon's political troubles in early July 1970 in which he took what seemed to the Arabs a position that was extremely favorable toward Israel, Libya nationalized all foreign oil-importing and -marketing interests. The move came immediately after Algeria nationalized the producing interests of four oil companies. The three major companies hit by the Libyan act were Esso (U.S.), Shell (Anglo-Dutch), and Agip (Italian). But because Libya was short of refineries, the gasoline these companies distributed and sold for Libya's domestic use was largely imported. The terminals for this incoming oil and the network of filling stations were seized, and the import and sale of all petroleum products was handled by the Libyan National Oil Corporation. Some 250 to 300 retail service stations and several oil terminals were involved in this nationalization act. Under different circumstances the change might have been made through friendly negotiations. But Qaddafi, who had insisted consistently that "if western polices moved further in Israel's favor, the oil companies might have to suffer,"[34] wanted to indicate that he was serious in his threats and meant this step as a warning to Western states to review their political stands on Arab issues.

Iraq and Algeria had both nationalized the domestic marketing of oil; Qatar and Saudi Arabia, as well as Iran and Venezuela, had formed their own marketing companies, which caused serious concern in the international oil industry. These moves further escalated the struggle of interests between the multinational oil companies and the producer countries. They occurred at a time when relationships between the companies and the producer countries were tense. Such moves were clearly meant as warnings that the nationalization of all foreign oil-producing interests was a very real possibility. In the long term, as the national oil companies of the producer countries gained experience, nationalization was inevitable. Only the "how" and "under what conditions" remained to be seen. With the Arab-Israeli conflict deeply upsetting Arab feelings in most of the oil-producing states, drastic moves by the more radical governments occurred without warning, thus disrupting international trade unpredictably.

Addressing a rally in Tobruk, Libya, on 28 March 1971 on the occasion of the first anniversary of British evacuation, Qaddafi outlined his government's oil policy:

> In the battle of oil and the destruction of international companies' monopolies in which the people won the first round, the Libyan people succeeded after liberating their will, in restoring the equivalent of 700 or 800 million dollars that the oil companies had stolen in the past from the needy poor.
>
> We are confronting oil companies with a new, unfamiliar logic, as far as these companies and the imperialist states are concerned, when we tell the states that protect these companies that their interests will be threatened. These states are aware that the revolution is capable of threatening their interest. And when we tell the oil companies that we are prepared at any time to stop the flow of oil, these companies know very well that whatever the revolutionaries say is a fact. We do not trade in words or slogans.[35]

Western policies hostile to the Arab cause prompted Qaddafi to deal another blow to the multinational oil companies in late 1971. On 7 December Libya announced the nationalization of British Petroleum "in retaliation for Britain's complicity in the Iranian occupation of three Gulf Arabian islands." BP was 48.6 percent owned by the British government, and it was the fourth largest producer in Libya, with assets "unofficially calculated at towards £75 million."[36]

Attending an OAPEC conference in Abu Dhabi, Libyan Oil Minister Mabruk denied that his country's nationalization of BP's assets would be followed by similar moves against other oil companies in the country, saying, "Our action was political and in response to the occupation of the islands." He did not think, he said, that other oil companies were threatened.[37]

By late 1972 the situation for the oil companies in Libya appeared more promising than it had for some time. Since forming the link with Egypt, which in October was tryng to buy arms in Western Europe to replace those lost after the Soviet dismissal from Egypt, the Libyan premier had taken a noticeably milder line toward the oil companies, presumably at Egypt's request. The oil companies were even hoping to get Libya to accept the Saudi participation formula rather than push for an immediate 50 percent participation, as Qaddafi had threatened to do in the past. A few months later, relations with Egypt deteriorated, and the honeymoon was over. On 30 April 1973 Libya demanded formally from all the oil companies working on Libyan soil a "100 percent control" of their local Libyan operations. The demand was passed to the Oasis Group on 30 April 1973 and to the Amoseas Group on 10 May 1973. The companies did not fully understand the Libyan demand; their negotiators arrived in Tripoli on 16 May 1973 for clarification of what "100 percent control" meant. Tough negotiations began between the government and the companies.

The companies were prepared to go along with an agreement similar to that recently reached in Iran. This would have involved placing Libyans in high executive positions, while the companies would be retained as service contractors with their economic and financial status slowly changing over a ten-year period to a pattern of 51 percent ownership by Libya.[38] But Libya did not settle for the Iranian formula of executive control and gradual equity participation. It offered compensation at net book value of the company rather than at updated book value. That went beyond the terms for participation negotiated for the Gulf states by Saudi Oil Minister Yamani the preceding autumn. The companies felt that if they gave in to the Libyan demands, the Gulf agreements might be jeopardized. On the other hand, Qaddafi would not settle for anything that would put him behind, or on an equal footing with, Yamani's agreements or Shah Pahlavi's formula. Winning all the possible economic concessions he could obtain from the companies meant that Qaddafi could maintain political power in other realms. His political goal was to establish Libya as the leading country in the Middle East oil world and himself as the major Arab leader. If he could succeed in those goals, he could force President Anwar Sadat to rethink aligning Egypt with King Faisal rather than with himself.

Libya "was in a strong negotiating position."[39] At this time, it was selling all of the oil produced by the BP fields, which had been nationalized in 1971, despite threats of legal suits by BP against the buyers of the oil. In addition, it was a certainty that, should Libya cut off oil production as a bargaining measure, Europe would face a severe oil shortage long before Libya's exchange reserves were depleted. (In 1970 the unwillingness of European governments to ration oil influenced the oil companies, supported by the U.S. government, to surrender to Libyan demands for higher oil prices.) The Libyans were shrewd negotiators. They played to the maximum

on the manifest differences between the various oil companies with a view to breaking up their common front. Clearly, in this respect the majors (notably Exxon, Mobil, Texaco, and Socal), primarily would be concerned with the possible repercussions of Libyan developments on their preponderant interests in the Gulf; the independents (like Continental, Marathon, and Occidental) with their overwhelming dependence on Libyan oil and few interests in the Gulf, would be likely to entertain any terms that would preserve their long-term guaranteed access to Libyan crude supplies.[40]

On 11 August 1973 Libya seized 51 percent of Occidental Petroleum, and on 12 August 1973 it seized the same assets of the Oasis Group, moves that undermined the 1972 participation agreements in the Gulf calling for a phased turnover to the oil-producing states by 1982. Libya's actions prompted Gulf states, including Saudi Arabia, to demand new talks for equal terms. By 13 August 1973 Occidental had acquiesced to the Libyans. The company agreed to accept $135 million for the net book value of the 51 percent and to buy back Libya's 51 percent of the oil at a price of $4.90 per barrel, a much higher price than that called for in the Gulf accords. Occidental even allowed for the differences in the grades of Gulf and Libyan oil. In accepting the Libyan action, Occidental had no intention of bearing the burden but was intending to pass it on to its customers. On 15 August 1973 Occidental notified its customers of a "cost pass on" of around $0.90 per barrel because of the Libyan action.[41] Yet another result of the Occidental agreement "was to make all the estimates of the future oil revenues of the oil-producing countries out of date. U.S. State Department estimates of these oil revenues not so long ago were based on a revenue of $3.50 per barrel for host governments in 1980. Now the $5-a-barrel mark is virtually reached and we are still in 1973."[42]

On the occasion of the fourth anniversary of the Libyan revolution on 1 September 1973, Qaddafi nationalized 51 percent of all oil interests within the boundaries of Libya that were not already controlled by the state. The companies affected were Esso, Texaco, Mobil, Royal Dutch/Shell, and Standard Oil of California. The oil companies were still formulating their response when Libya gave them thirty days to acquiesce to the nationalization, which included compensation based on net book value of the oil assets and the high price of $4.90 per barrel for the oil the companies would buy back from Libya.

Libya's tough stand was not difficult to fathom. In his 1970 confrontation with the oil companies, Qaddafi established himself, at least in the public eye, as perhaps the most important figure in the Middle East oil game. Since then, however, his position had been contested by Yamani of Saudi Arabia and Shah Pahlavi. Qaddafi, having seen his dream of union with Egypt destroyed, wanted to reestablish his dominance in oil, and this wish had been at least one reason for his early threats to the oil companies and his later uncompromising stand on nationalizing the oil assets.

The companies, for their part, preferred to defy the Libyans and so risk the "painful" outcome of nationalization of their assets, rather than sign a contract that would upset all their other agreements in the Middle East and give them little security in Libya. Furthermore, the majors knew that if they let Qaddafi win such a big concession, it would be clear to everyone that he, not Saudi Arabia's Yamani or the shah of Iran, was the pacesetter in Middle East oil bargaining. Yamani and the shah would then cause a lot of trouble in trying to reassert themselves. If Libya nationalized their assets, the majors felt that they would stand a better chance of pressuring Qaddafi by preventing most of the Libyan oil (amounting to about 800,000 barrels a day) from being sold on the Western markets. The U.S. State Department "deeply regretted" Libya's takeover of U.S. oil interests. Its spokesman, Paul Hare, refused to discuss the possibility of a boycott of Libyan oil but said that the U.S. position on the nationalization act "was clear." This position was that the United States had a right to expect that any expropriation of U.S. property "will be nondiscriminatory," that "it would be for a public purpose," and that "prompt, adequate, and effective compensation would be received from the expropriating country."[43]

For some time, the situation did not improve. The Libyans, giving themselves room to maneuver, were vague on the terms of compensation; and consumer governments, particularly Japan and West Germany, had not yet indicated whether they would support a boycott of Libyan oil. The Libyans moved into the offices of the companies involved and informed them that they must sign a commitment recognizing that 51 percent of the oil was under Libyan control before their tankers would be allowed to load Libyan oil. The Libyans secured maximum publicity from their carefully timed nationalization; however, the success of their confrontation with the companies depended heavily on what course of action the Saudis, who had tremendous world oil reserves, would take.

The Saudis were not in a comfortable position. They could replace almost immediately the Libyan output of 800,000 barrels a day that Qaddafi had threatened to cut off; to do so, however, would only play into Qaddafi's hands, because the Saudis could be easily embarrassed in the eyes of their Arab brothers if they appeared to be supporting the Western majors against an Arab nationalist. King Faisal, who had been moving his pieces in the game with great skill, did not seem to fall for the bait. In the eyes of the Arab masses, increasing production to compensate for the loss of Libyan oil could look like appeasing the West at the expense of Arab nationalism. Faisal would have liked to put Qaddafi "in his place," but not if this meant that Faisal would ultimately lose status in the Arab world. At the moment, Faisal appeared to have grasped the leadership of the Arab cause and he was unwilling to lose it in order to please the oil companies, who already appeared to have lost the ability to control their own fate.[44]

Despite Libya's deadline of 1 October 1973 by which the companies were to have agreed to the nationalization, day-to-day operations proceeded as if nothing had happened. For a few days the Libyans insisted that any tanker captains wanting to load oil must first sign a certificate recognizing that 51 percent of the oil belonged to the Libyan government. The Libyans stopped insisting after several captains refused to sign. The companies peaceably continued to lift oil. Libya's threat to sell oil directly to Western Europe, bypassing the major companies, seemed unlikely to succeed because European governments sought to prevent the Libyan leader from gaining more power, not to help him acquire it. But the Arab-Israeli war of October 1973 that was set in motion a few days later seemed to solve the Libyans' dilemma.

On the eve of the 1973 oil embargo, the condition of the Libyan oil industry was favorable for the Libyan government. Whereas in 1967 Libya's oil resources and industry had been wholly controlled by foreign (mostly U.S.) companies, by 1973 over half of the oil installations were under Libyan control. Libyan oil production, though reduced to a great extent during the period 1967–1973, provided nearly six times the revenues of 1967. The Libyan government of 1973, far more than the Sanussi monarchy (which gave only a token gesture for the 1967 embargo), was to become heavily involved in imposing the 1973 oil embargo, was more capable of seeing that it was carried out, and was in a much better position to bear the financial burden it entailed.

Iraq 1958–1973

As soon as political stability prevailed,[45] the Iraqi government of General Kassim—which took over from the Hashemite dynasty on 14 July 1958 following a bloody coup—resumed the negotiations with IPC that its royalist predecessors had begun only one week before the revolution. Various demands were put forward by the new regime. These included: (1) a more favorable profit-sharing formula, to match the 75:25 profit split pioneered in a previous concession agreement between Iran and the Italian state-owned oil corporation ENI; (2) an Iraqi shareholding interest in IPC (the company was 95 percent owned by the major oil companies, with the remaining 5 percent going to the Gulbenkian Foundation as a commission for obtaining the concession for IPC); (3) an increase in Iraqi oil production; (4) a final settlement of disputes over deductible costs; (5) better employment opportunities for Iraqis in the oil industry (though only 4 percent of all employees were not Iraqis, among the higher grades the proportion of foreigners was as high as 48 percent); and (6) relinquishment of part of the concession agreement. An agreement had been worked out on the eve of the revolution that brought Kassim to power, according to which the company agreed to surrender about 90,000 square miles covered by the original concession. The exact location of the areas to be surrendered, however, remained a difficult problem.

While prolonged negotiations failed to settle this problem, others emerged. A serious dispute arose as a result of the action taken by the Iraqi government to raise port and cargo dues at Basrah—an action that led to a decline in offtake from the southern oilfields of Iraq. Negotiations between IPC and the Iraqi government lasted for more than three years, yet no conclusive agreement was reached between the two parties on any issue or point of conflict. Throughout the negotiations, Kassim resisted the pressure of his communist allies to nationalize the oil industry. He still felt that the negotiations could be continued without resorting to that alternative. His apprehension that the oil companies might mount an economic blockade similar to the blockade of Mossadeq's Iran in 1951 was minimal compared to his fear of the formidable power of the companies' home governments and their readiness to launch an outright military intervention in the event of nationalization.

Except for occasional veiled insinuations, the Iraqi press followed the government's line in avoiding any mention of nationalization as a means of dealing with IPC. When the organ of the Iraqi Communist party, *Ittihad al-Sha'b*, argued on 1 August 1960 that the oil companies were then much weaker than in the past and that as a result Iraq need not fear the "ghost of Mossadeq," *al-Thawra*, the semiofficial newspaper, on 15 August 1960 denounced "this implied demand for nationalization." Another example of the Iraqi press's support of the official attitude came in early 1961 when thousands of workers and students staged a mass demonstration against the French occupation of Algeria. The crowds marched through the streets of Baghdad demanding the nationalization of France's share in IPC, but in its reports on the demonstration the Baghdad press and radio made no mention whatever of the nationalization demand.

With the final collapse of his three-year-long negotiations with IPC, Kassim opted for the alternative route of partial nationalization, which he had kept as a last resort. His prestige and popularity in Iraq and the Arab world had reached a low ebb, particularly when he proclaimed Kuwait to be an integral part of Iraq and threatened to annex it by force. To relieve the political pressures directed against his regime, Kassim attempted to focus public attention on several spectacular measures against the foreign enterprises in his country. By giving an early warning of unilateral action and making public his government's specific demands and the minutes of meetings with IPC, Kassim committed himself to an uncompromising policy, making it nearly impossible to make any substantial compromise to break the deadlock. Furthermore, "the majority Iraqi view is that the oil agreements now in force were concluded by a regime subordinate to Britain, and the validity of these agreements is now in question. This background of public opinion is at least as important as the specific issues under discussion as it strictly limits the Government's freedom to manoeuvre."[46]

Two months after the negotiations finally broke down in October 1961, the Iraqi government proclaimed its Law No. 80, which marked the first step on the road to nationalization. Under this law (later bypassed by the companies throughout the consecutive regimes of Abdul Salam 'Arif (1963–1966) and Abdul Rahman 'Arif (1966–1968), Iraq took back control of all areas of the country that were not actually producing oil at the time. It unilaterally cancelled IPC's rights in all of its exploration territory and in the rich North Rumaila field, which had been discovered by IPC. But IPC did not give in. As it was formally requesting that the Iraqi government accept arbitration on the points of conflict, the British and U.S. governments dispatched, in early 1962, two "cordial" notes to Kassim urging Iraq to resume negotiations with the company. At the same time British troop movements were reported in the Gulf area.

Toward the end of the Kassim era, oil production was considerably curtailed, causing great strain on the Iraqi treasury. Kassim repeatedly denounced the reduction in production as an "excessive and arbitrary economic pressure which the companies are exerting on Iraq in order to halt the rise in its people's standards of living and the country's development."[47]

With the downfall of Kassim on 8 February 1963, relations between the oil companies and the new Iraqi government improved greatly. The 'Arif government made substantial concessions in the companies' favor, such as reducing port and cargo dues at Basrah. In return, the slow decline in Iraqi oil production suddenly gave way to a substantial increase. Cordial company relations with the new regime helped convince Britain to dispatch a prompt delivery of arms to Baghdad. But an agreement worked out in 1965 between IPC and the Iraqi government that stipulated the exploitation of the relinquished lands through joint ventures was never realized, because the two-year-old regime of Abdul Rahman 'Arif never felt strong enough to ratify it.[48] In November 1967, after weeks of bargaining, a consortium headed by the French state oil company ERAP agreed to terms with the Iraq National Oil Company, under which it would explore and develop part of the IPC's expropriated (but still hotly disputed) concession. The company would act simply as a contractor, looking for oil and developing what it found. The move was a blow to IPC and the Compagnie Française des Pétroles. On 27 November 1967 a delegation of Soviets was reported by the London *Times* to have arrived in Baghdad to negotiate a similar deal.

Abdul Rahman 'Arif lasted only until July 1968, when the Iraqi Ba'thist party staged a coup. The new government accused the preceding two 'Arif regimes of squandering funds and claimed that it had inherited "a chaotic and bankrupt economy." The Ba'thist government's only resort to improve its financial standing was to ask the oil companies who controlled Iraq's main source of income to increase oil production and thus revenues. But the young regime did not feel strong enough to enter into a decisive battle with the oil companies at that early stage, particularly as oil revenues formed a high percentage of the state's budget and of development funds. Therefore, the Iraqi government had to concentrate for some time on general economic and agrarian reform. It began extensive efforts to reactivate industry and to reduce agricultural imports. Foreign trade was so directed as to conform with the development plan and to save hard currency to decrease dependency on oil revenues. Minor confrontations with the oil companies were made "in order to gain the necessary experience and information on the way to the decisive battle."[49]

In July 1969 the Ba'thist regime concluded a cooperation agreement with the Soviet Union for national exploitation of Iraqi oil.[50] The step constituted a direct challenge to the Western oil companies' interest and future in Iraq. The companies tried to appease the Ba'thist regime by increasing its share of the oil revenues. In June 1971, following two months of difficult bargaining, the oil companies signed an agreement with the Iraqi government that nearly doubled Iraqi royalties from crude-oil exports. The agreement reached with IPC applied to oil supplied at the Mediterranean terminals of Tripoli in Lebanon and Banias in Syria. The posted price of the crude was raised from $2.41 to $3.21 per barrel, retroactive to 20 March 1971. Taxes on net profits were raised from 50 percent to 55 percent, paralleling agreements reached earlier that year with Iran (for Gulf crude) and with Libya. In addition, IPC agreed to loan Iraq £10 million interest free, payments to begin in four years.[51] Although the gains to Iraq were considerable, the government failed to get the $0.10 per barrel premium it had demanded during the negotiations on the basis of the "low wax" content of the oil. Earlier that year Libya had won a $0.10 premium for the low sulfur content of its oil. But IPC was unwilling to grant Iraq the $0.10 premium because it feared it might start a series of "leapfrogging" negotiations. The Iraqi government, which had threatened nationalization when the negotiations came to a near deadlock, decided that the final offer was satisfactory and that nationalization was too risky to break off the negotiations for the sake of the $0.10 premium.[52]

The newly added revenues seemed to alleviate the government's shortage of funds for development projects and plans to exploit its natural resources. But political developments within Iraq and the Arab world, as well as on the international scene, prompted the Iraqi government to reconsider its oil policies and to take another look at the course it had shunned so far: nationalization. This policy, though sparked by a dispute with IPC over the rate of production, was actually a product of the general conditions prevailing in Iraq and the Arab world. On the whole, it was forged by the Ba'thist government to muster popular support in the face of increasingly influential opposition, chronic warfare in the north with the Kurds, isolation on the Arab front, and fear of a rising Iranian militarism on the eastern borders.

Ever since its creation in the early forties, the Ba'thist party had summed up its political philosophy in one slogan: "Unity, Freedom, and Socialism."[53] One of the main items on its political agenda was the nationalization of Arab natural resources on behalf of the Arab masses. The party also coined the slogan "Arab Oil for Arabs," so it was ironic that when the party seized power in Iraq in 1968 it made no effort to move toward nationalizing Iraqi oil assets, particulary since the government was in urgent need of the revenues the oil resources could provide. Rather, it limited its oil policies to a framework of negotiations and lapsed into a pattern of acceding to losing compromises. Although on Arab issues the Iraqi regime took radical attitudes, on internal issues it was somewhat more conservative. At a time when Algeria had taken over the French companies, Libya had nationalized British Petroleum, and both Nigeria and Venezuela had taken over more than 20 percent of the operating companies, Iraq was throwing in its lot with Saudi Arabia (presumably its "arch political enemy"), Kuwait, and the Gulf emirates to get from the companies a formula of a decade-long transition to a 51 percent majority interest. Many observers felt that such an attitude would not last. It was obvious that the tension between a radical socialist party in power and a foreign-owned Western company with huge financial power and political backing that was using the oil-production rate to extract political and economic concessions would one day come to a breaking point. The Iraqi regime's new nationalization policy should be seen against such a background. It was merely a matter of time and the proper objective circumstances.

Domestically the Ba'thist party was working hard on economic development projects. Its 1971/1972 budget called for a 17 percent increase in spending on these projects. The total budget was put at $2.78 billion, and the projected revenues were estimated at $2.66 billion, to be supplemented by $1.5 million in cash revenues held by state companies.[54] The June 1971 agreement with IPC increased government revenues from oil by 81 percent, from $507 million in 1970 to $914 million in 1971. That was expected to rise to $1,039 million in 1974 when, under the same accord, production in the southern fields was to be increased.[55]

This accord seemed to give the Ba'thist regime a degree of financial, if not political, stability.

Within the Ba'thist party the power struggle continued. The winter of 1971 witnessed the removal of key Ba'thist party members from their posts, while the summer of that year witnessed trials of high Iraqi officials charged with "treason." Widespread purges directed against political opponents helped to isolate the regime and to decrease its popular support. To a great extent these purges caused other political forces in Iraq to reject governmental offers of forming a "coalition."

In the north, where the Kurds had enjoyed a majority, the struggle for administrative autonomy had continued on and off ever since the establishment of the British mandate in Iraq.[56] Until the 1970 armistice agreement, which laid down a three-year deadline for autonomy, the Kurdish Democratic party, led by Mulla Mustafa el-Barzani, had waged a full-scale guerrilla war for nearly ten years. However, the slow implementation of the March 1970 agreement augmented dissent among the Kurds and a collision seemed imminent. The Ba'thist regime felt that the Kurdish political unrest was incited by subversive agitators (Iran, the United States, and Israel). The Kurds, for their part, distrusted Ba'thist intentions and feared that the Iraqi government was stalling in order to gain time and eventually to liquidate their movement. The "deep regret" expressed by the Ba'thist party over the attempt on the life of the Kurdish leader el-Barzani in September 1971 did not convince the Kurds that the government's hands were clean. Reported skirmishes between Iraqi troops and Kurdish rebels indicated that Iraq was on the brink of a new Kurdish war.

On the regional front, the Ba'thist regime had been isolating itself within the Arab world. Ever since the Royal Iraqi government refused to sign an armistice agreement with Israel in 1949, Iraq had nursed its reputation of unflinching opposition to any compromise over the Palestine problem. It rejected the 22 November 1967 UN Security Council Resolution 242,[57] denounced the Geneva talks in toto, and rejected all peace initiatives. Mutual dislike between the Ba'thist regimes in Baghdad and Damascus had added zest to a rivalry almost as old as recorded history between the two river civilizations of Syria and Iraq for hegemony over the region.

Moreover, Iraq's cooperation with the Soviet Union had incurred Qaddafi's anger, as the Libyan leader viewed entering a treaty with the Soviet Union by an Arab state as infringing upon Arab sovereignty. Algeria had for some time aligned itself with Egypt concerning political solutions to the Palestine conflict. The Palestine Liberation Organization was still bitter over the role played by the Iraqi regime in the September 1970 clashes with Jordan, when Iraq, which earlier had been promising the PLO full military support, had refused to get involved when fighting broke out, but supplied military and medical aid to the Jordanian army.

Iraq's efforts to start a dialogue with Syria, Libya, Egypt, and the PLO were rebuffed. With its non-Arab neighbors it fared equally badly. Along its eastern borders, the Ba'thist party was worried about a growing Iranian militarism. Massive Iranian budget increases "for defensive purposes" inspired this alarm. Iranian occupation of three Arab islands, strategically located near the entrance of Iraq's only outlet to the Indian Ocean, posed a military threat as well as a political challenge that the Iraqis made an effort to ignore. They lowered their guns and let the Iranians take the islands "peacefully."

In retrospect, one can easily grasp the staunch Iraqi stand when the crisis with IPC erupted in mid-1972. The state newspaper *al-Thawra* reflected this mood when it wrote on 28 May 1972: "We will not hesitate when the decisive moment arrives. . . . The monopolistic companies would be mistaken if they thought that we were engaged in threats and propaganda. We do not want a complete rift with the companies, but if they do not respond to our demands, a complete rift it will be." Previously, the eleven-year-old dispute with IPC had been settled through negotiations and compromise. Neither the present nor the previous regimes had felt strong enough for a direct confrontation with IPC. The relations between the Iraqi government and IPC deteriorated more when, in September 1971, Vice-President Salah Ammash, the initiator of the strategy of limited reconciliation with IPC that led to the settlement of a long-standing dispute, was removed from office. His absence helped to widen the communications gap between the Iraqi government and IPC.

A drastic fall in oil output from the Kirkuk region precipitated a major crisis for the government in June 1972. Through February, oil production had been running at full capacity, but it fell nearly 50 percent in March. As a result, the government estimated losses at $86 million; if the reduction continued at that rate, total loss for 1972 could reach $312 million, almost one-third of the government's budget of $1,040 million.[58] This loss of revenue caused great disturbances within the government and, combined with the other forces acting against the regime, posed a serious threat. Development programs would be held up and vitally needed hard currency would be spent. The Iraqi government felt that the production cut was a political move taken to force it to agree to IPC's terms on unresolved outstanding issues, and further, "to humiliate it, and even bring it down."[59] Negotiations thus broke down.

IPC, well aware of the regime's political difficulties, felt that this was the most suitable time to press its demands. It claimed that its cutback was "purely economic," arguing that production from the southern fields of Iraq, which was shipped out through the Gulf, was still at full capacity and that only the Kirkuk oil piped to the Mediterranean had been affected. IPC held that the reason for the cutback was that the price agreements of 1971 had grossly overpriced Mediterranean crude in general, and Iraqi crude in particular. Thus, oil shipped from the Gulf around Africa arrived in Europe with a $0.24 per barrel advantage over Kirkuk oil. In addition, the company argued, a mild winter and an industrial slowdown in Europe had slowed demand. Tanker rates had gone down and over 100 tankers had been laid up.

Rebuttals of IPC's claims were voiced most distinctly by OPEC's secretary general, Dr. Pachachi. He responded that

> a drastic cut of that magnitude is not usual in the oil industry and cannot be attributed to commercial considerations or market necessities. It is clear beyond any reasonable doubt that the company's production figures reflect a deliberate and premeditated measure, and a high-level managerial policy decision aimed at punishing Iraq for its independent national oil policy and at exerting pressure to hinder implementation of the development programmes.[60]

In addition, Pachachi noted that "(1) production in Nigeria increased in the same period as the fall in freight rates; (2) freight rates started to decline long before IPC cut production; and (3) Aramco did not reduce its Mediterranean offtake from Sidon (Lebanon) by anything comparable to IPC's cut."

Strengthened by support from OPEC and the Arabs, and having taken two communist ministers into the cabinet to insure Soviet support, the Ba'thist party issued an ultimatum to IPC threatening "all legal measures . . . deemed necessary." The IPC negotiating team offered to raise June production from the northern fields to nearly 1 million barrels a day to avoid a major confrontation. That was short of the 1.2 million barrels on which the Iraqis were insisting, but it was a long way up from the 694,000 barrels a day produced from the fields during March and April.[61] Had the volume of production been the only issue, Iraq might have been satisfied that it had won a large enough victory on this point. On its side, IPC believed that it could stave off the threat of nationalization by offering more money to a regime that badly needed it; but more was at stake for the Ba'thist regime. The regime sensed that with the erosion of time and the pressure of seemingly endless confrontations, the major oil companies no longer presented the united front that they once had. Further, the regime felt itself capable of running the production side of the nationalized oilfields. Hence, the Ba'thist regime embarked on the road to nationalization.

On 1 June 1972 the Iraqi Revolutionary Command Council unilaterally issued a resolution nationalizing the operations of IPC's Kirkuk oilfields according to the new Law No. 69. This move gave the Iraqi government control of 65 percent of the oil-producing sector of the national economy.[62] The main points of the announcement were:

1. Compensation was to be paid to IPC.
2. A state company, the Iraqi Company for Oil Operations (ICOO), would take over the assets and rights of IPC.
3. Iraqi nationals working for IPC were to remain at their jobs.
4. The government offered to enter into negotiations with the French interests in IPC (CFP, with 23.75 percent of IPC).[63]

The nationalization decision did not include the Basrah Petroleum Company, which was a valuable source of the hard currency needed to enable the government to stand up to the pressures of the IPC oil companies, and force the companies to accept the nationalization act and to acknowledge Law No. 80.

The Iraqi nationalization measure received immediate moral and financial support from OAPEC, which made the decision to "back it by all means at its disposal." The move also received approval from a meeting of the eleven-nation OPEC. The Soviet Union, which had been encouraging Arab oil nationalizations and Arab self-reliance in oil, stepped up its efforts to make the Iraqi nationalization act succeed. With their sudden decline of influence in Egypt, and Syria's refusal to sign a formal treaty of alliance despite its heavy reliance on Soviet military aid, the Soviets had focused on Iraq and on Soviet-Iraqi relations.

This Soviet Middle Eastern oil involvement alarmed the United States, which felt the necessity of finding a suitable compromise between Iraq and IPC that would send the Soviets elsewhere to pursue their active new overseas oil policies. Speaking in Algiers on 4 June 1972, a few hours after the Eighth Arab Petroleum Congress sent off a message of total support to Iraq, James E. Akins, director of the U.S. Office of Fuel and Energy, said optimistically that the nationalization of IPC "need not necessarily be an unmitigated disaster." The old oil concessions, he said, "were not written by divine will on tablets of stone, and I am not saying they couldn't or shouldn't be changed." Perhaps equally optimistically, Akins was sure that "arrangements [would] be worked out to benefit to both sides."[64]

IPC remained remarkably quiet. Its lawyers had worked out contingency plans but the company was reluctant to put these plans into effect. IPC obviously had decided to do nothing that would cause the situation to deteriorate further. Mediation efforts were already in progress.

As a result of Saudi Oil Minister Yamani's private efforts, OPEC, at IPC's request, accepted the role of mediator. Two preconditions for mediation set at OPEC's 10 June conference were already accepted by IPC: "(1) any mediation would be in the framework of Iraq's June 1st nationalization act; and (2) while mediation was in progress the companies should take no legal action or embargo, to hamper the flow of oil from Iraq's northern oil fields."[65] IPC's reluctance to take legal measures againt Iraq was a clear indication of the alarm with which the oil companies viewed the growing strength of the producing governments, of OPEC, and of OAPEC. OAPEC at the time was holding an emergency meeting in Beirut to discuss participation agreements and total nationalization.

As a result of its nationalization act, Iraq stood to lose nearly $200 million if it did not export 57 million tons of oil from the northern oilfield. This constituted most of Iraq's hard currency revenues, which came from IPC's sales to Western customers. As a result, Iraq was obliged to ask all its creditors and trading partners to accept payment for goods and services in crude oil. Furthermore, it was faced with the problem of marketing its nationalized oil, which was now offered at reduced prices with immediate delivery. The Soviets quietly tried to help Iraq solve its oil problems. However, despite their growing oil needs, the Soviets were not yet able to take enough Iraqi oil to help Baghdad significantly. Eastern Europe, including East Germany and Bulgaria (in addition to the Soviet Union), started to buy Iraqi nationalized oil. But Iraq's opportunity to break the united front of the companies materialized when it was able in mid-June to reach an agreement with the French government concerning the 23.75 percent French holding in the field. France agreed to buy from the nationalized Kirkuk field an amount of oil equal to its share in the field when it was operated by IPC. The 23.75 percent ceiling made it difficult for the other IPC members to take legal action against the sale on the grounds that the oil was not Iraq's to sell. The Soviets encouraged Iraq to proceed with the deal because it guaranteed Iraq a major source of the hard currency that Moscow could not supply.[66]

Overshadowed by the Israeli downing of a civilian Libyan airliner and the Black September group's operation in Khartoum, Iraq signed with IPC in late February 1973 an agreement that settled their long dispute and stipulated the terms of the nationalization of IPC's Kirkuk fields. Under the new agreement, IPC accepted Iraq's Law No. 80, issued in 1961, which deprived the consortiums of 99.51 percent of their concession areas and restricted IPC to the then-producing fields. IPC also recognized the nationalization of the northern fields, thereby freeing the state-owned Iraq National Oil Company, which then was developing the field with Soviet financial and technical help, to sell oil produced from these areas to Western buyers without fear of legal countermeasures by IPC. In return, Iraq was to pay the consortium $350 million and permit IPC member companies to lift crude worth $320 million as compensation.

IPC's softening in its negotiations with Iraq can be seen, in part, as a sign of the company's inability to assert what it might consider its legal rights by foreign intervention or a military coup. The company had no other choice but to go along with the U.S. and British foreign-policy planners who were eager that a settlement be reached as early as possible to extract Iraq from Soviet influence, which had risen alarmingly. Thus, the settlement can be interpreted as a Western effort to decrease

> Iraq's dependence on the Soviet bloc in the petroleum and economic spheres. So long as Iraq was in confrontation with the western oil companies, it had no alternative but to turn mainly (with the exception of some help from countries like France and Italy) to the Soviet bloc for assistance in oil exploration, development, and marketing. Now the Iraqis have the entire world to choose from in selecting customers, contractors, and partners for future oil ventures. . . . Nevertheless, the companies have still managed to salvage something worth having. Apart from the compensation for 15 million tons of oil for the IPC nationalization—worth over $300 million— they have held on to their rights in the BPC (Basrah) fields where production capacity will be more than doubled to reach 80 million tons per year (1.6 million barrels per day) in 1976, thereby making up almost all that was lost in the north. This will be all the more attractive in that the BPC expansion will probably be the cheapest in the whole Middle East in terms of capital investment per unit of capacity.[67]

On 7 October 1973, one day following the eruption of hostilities between the Arabs and Israel, the shares held by the two U.S. companies, Standard Oil of New Jersey (Exxon) and Mobil Oil Corporation, which amounted to 23.75 percent of the total shares of Basrah Petroleum Company, were nationalized according to Law No. 70 of 1973 and were attached to the Iraq National Oil Company. The step was taken "as a punitive measure for the U.S.'s stand towards the Arabs,"[68] and "in retaliation for Israeli attacks on Egypt and Syria."[69]

On 21 October 1973, Iraq (which had not concurred in OAPEC's October 17 cutback decision) announced nationalization of the 60 percent Dutch holding in Shell's 23.75 percent interest in the Basrah Petroleum Company as a "punitive measure against the Netherlands for its hostile stand towards the Arab nation."[70] The ownership was transferred to the Iraq National Oil Company.

On 20 December 1973, the Gulbenkian Foundation's 5 percent share was nationalized according to Law No. 101 of 1973, giving the Iraq National Oil Company a total ownership of 43 percent of the Basrah Petroleum Company's shares.

Iraq, which only a few years earlier had had its oil production under the exclusive monopoly of IPC for forty-six years, was by the end of 1973 in full control of 85 percent of its oil production. It ranked among the ten largest oil producers in the world—its North Rumaila oilfield being the sixth largest in the world.

In the final analysis, no matter which course, participation or nationalization, was taken to increase Arab power and influence in the oil industry, one fact remains clear: By October 1973 the Arabs had more to say about this vital energy source than they had had in June 1967. Thus, the decision of the Arab oil ministers on 17 October 1973 to reduce or halt Arab oil exports to countries "unfriendly to the Arab cause" or "to those supporting Israel to hold on to its territorial conquests" carried, in theory and practice, much weightier implications than that of its unfortunate predecessor of 5 June 1967.

5

The Shift from the Nasser Era to the Faisal Era, 1967–1973

The Saudi Predicament

Since his accession to the throne in 1964, King Faisal had distinguished himself from those Arab leaders who employ fiery rhetoric and empty threats. He seldom spoke in public, and even when he did he gave only a hint of the direction his thoughts were taking.[1] Until 1973 the Saudi monarch pursued a strongly pro-Western foreign policy. This policy was based on four fundamental principles:

- to prevent radicals and nationalist incursion in the Arabian peninsula;
- to prevent communism from spreading its influence in the peninsula;
- to maintain friendly relations with the industrialized non-communist world; and
- to support Islamic movements to promote solidarity among Muslim countries.[2]

On a number of occasions Faisal reiterated his views that: (1) foreign ideologies do not serve the interests of the Arab nation and Islam; (2) communism is Islam's worst enemy; and (3) political radicalism in the Gulf is supported by foreign ideologies.[3]

As far as his country's oil was concerned, Faisal was the staunchest supporter of the dictum that oil and politics do not mix, and as a result Saudi Arabia adopted the policy that "a commercial oil operation should be divorced from political considerations."[4]

In spite of Saudi Arabia's traditional Arab position on the Palestine question, Saudi monarchs prior to October 1973 had kept oil economics and Arab politics apart. The three Arab-Israeli wars of 1946–1948, 1956, and 1967 did not adversely influence the volume of petroleum production in Saudi Arabia. The closing of the Suez Canal in 1956 and 1967 did affect production, but the adverse effect was short-lived. Oil production continued to increase.[5] This Saudi policy of dissociating oil from politics calmed Western fears that oil might be used as a political lever. Other oil-producing countries' attitudes were important, but Saudi Arabia alone had the oil reserves to expand production to the extent the Western countries needed.[6] Furthermore, Saudi Arabia's stance was reflected in that of the other Gulf Arab oil-producing emirates, which followed the Saudi lead.

The bitter defeat of 1967 in the war with Israel was a watershed in modern Arab history. It struck deeper into the life and political convictions of every Arab than any other recent political event. To many, the dimensions of the defeat were incomprehensible. To this very day it is impossible to convey to the non-Arab world the depth of the shock produced by the swift Israeli victory on 5 June 1967. At the time, even Nasser's public admission on Radio Cairo and on television that the battle had been lost failed to convince multitudes of the people that a miracle would not occur. It took the Arab people time to realize that Nasser had been defeated and—worse—that his army had not put up a fight. Once the message was received, "an intense wave of self-criticism" began.[7]

The June defeat diffused the two-pole Arab political structure, with Cairo as the capital of Arab forces of nationalism, pan-Arabism, and "revolution," and Riyadh heading the much weaker forces of traditionalism and pro-Western conservatism. The defeat challenged Egyptian leadership of the Arab world. It undermined Nasser's power and image, which had been strengthened by his political successes at international conferences such as the 1955 Bandung Conference, where he gained prestige in the eyes of the Arab masses as a champion of nonalignment, and by his defiance of foreign powers in the nationalization of the Suez Canal. Nasser's close associations with leading world political figures, his championing of the cause of revolution and national independence, and his militant stands against Israel and pro-Western Arab regimes had added to his prestige. The 1967 defeat cost Nasser, outside Egypt, his supreme authority as a revolutionary torchbearer. More importantly, it brought the western and eastern halves of the Arab world closer together. Nasser was forced to accommodate himself to a more even distribution of power among the other Arab heads of state. For the Saudi monarch, this concession was a major breakthrough. It gave Faisal the opportunity to make Saudi Arabia into a focus for Arabs who looked to "evolution rather than revolution" to shape their future.[8] This made Saudi Arabia the main stabilizing influence in a highly volatile area. By November 1967 the Saudis, like many Arab moderates, began to shift their Palestinian policy from an "elimination of Israel" to a "containment of Israel" approach.[9]

But it was not until the death of Nasser in September 1970 that the Saudi monarch began to assume a dominant role in Arab affairs. Nasser's death left a huge power vacuum in Arab politics. It greatly dissolved what the military defeat, the Arab summit meetings, and inter-Arab solidarity could only soften, namely, the polarization of "revolutionary" and "nonrevolutionary" Arab states. Moreover, it mitigated the revolutionary polycentrism that Nasser's charismatic leadership had created.[10] This new political reality, emerging after Nasser's death, prompted Faisal to fill the vacuum. His hope of leading the Arab world on what he believed was the proper track seemed closer to realization. He had always had a special interest in proving that "moderation" was the wiser and more fruitful course of action in pursuing Arab political and economic objectives. He held the conviction that Arab unity could never have any real meaning, could not even exist, unless cemented with Islam; it logically followed that the birthplace of Islam—Saudi Arabia—should be at the center of Arab unity, and that the duty and responsibility of leading the Arabs should rightly fall on the Saudi monarch's shoulders.

But to yearn is one thing, to achieve is another. At the least, success required direct involvement in inter-Arab politics, particularly in the extremely delicate and controversial Palestinian issue, and the use of Saudi wealth and resources in the Arabs' struggle against Israel. Central to this struggle was the need to procure Israeli withdrawal from occupied Arab territories, in particular from Jerusalem.[11] If that objective should be achieved, Faisal would not only succeed Nasser in Arab leadership, but would also procure an Islamic prominence that could deter for a long time any aggressive act against Saudi Arabia from such rival neighbors as Iran.

From an impression fostered by Aramco executives and encouraged by the U.S. State Department, the Saudi monarch believed that his good relations with Washington would convince the United States to put pressure on Israel to withdraw in exchange for a more permanent political settlement. The project seemed feasible, particularly because U.S. diplomacy before the death of Nasser had been moving in that direction, and U.S. declarations maintained that the Middle East was of "highest priority." But Nasser's death and the success of Jordan's King Hussein in ousting the Palestinian commando movement changed the U.S. Middle Eastern equation. The United States lost its desire for a political settlement in the area because the situation was de facto favorable. President Nixon, who could have played a dynamic, effective role, became more and more distracted by presidential elections, Vietnam, and, later, Watergate. On its part, "Israel believed that time was on its side and that there was no need for a change or shift in its posture."[12] Thus, to the Israelis any concessions appeared superfluous. They felt far too confident to yield to any pressure, especially with a U.S. president worried about his reelection chances.

Convinced that Washington held the key to the recovery of lost Arab territory, Faisal moved to exert pressure on the United States to reevaluate its Middle East policies. For this strategy to be successful, the Saudi monarch needed to coordinate his efforts with other Arab leaders, particularly the new Egyptian president, Anwar Sadat. Consequently, the relations between Riyadh and Cairo became more friendly.

The Saudi-Egyptian Axis: The Politics of Convergence

From the beginning, the choice of Anwar Sadat to succeed Nasser was accepted as a suitable temporary compromise by all the factions vying for power in Egypt. It was felt that an intermediate transitional period was needed before the country could stabilize after the loss of Nasser. Sadat was an unknown quantity, and when he took over "few thought he would be more than a stop-gap leader."[13] Sadat's early months in power were characterized by his attempts to control the Egyptian bureaucracy and the growth of different axes of power from the remnants of the Nasserite regime. Growing opposition to his leadership prompted Sadat to take strict measures against what he called the "centers of power," and in May 1971 Vice-President Ali Sabri and five high-ranking officials were arrested and charged with conspiracy. Although this move consolidated Sadat's position, it did not solve the internal political problems caused by Egypt's deteriorating economic situation.

Outside Egypt, Sadat's image was shaky. Sadat was constantly worried by the efforts of Libyan leader Qaddafi to assume Arab leadership and by increasing pressure to effect a Libyan-Egyptian merger. Sadat looked around for support and Saudi Arabia seemed the best potential ally. On his part, Faisal knew that his position would be strengthened if he could pry Egypt away from the ambitious Qaddafi.

In June 1971 Faisal paid a visit to Cairo, where he was received warmly both publicly and privately. The joint communiqué issued after the ten-day visit indicated an amount of good will between the two countries that had been unknown in the Nasser years. Faisal referred to Egypt as the "citadel of steadfastness" and urged support for Egypt, an indication that Saudi Arabia was intending to continue its subsidies and possibly to increase them. Sadat, with his Muslim Brotherhood background,[14] went farther than Nasser ever would have gone in espousing Faisal's Islamic orientation. Jerusalem was mentioned first on the list of lands to be liberated. Socialism was never mentioned, and Islam was referred to as "the religion of social justice." The Arab press, with the exception of Iraq, hailed Faisal's visit as the opening of a new era in Arab unity and internal relations. The visit was viewed as a signal of increased Saudi commitment to Arab affairs and, in particular, to the Palestinian question. The joint communiqué affirmed that there would be no lasting peace in the Middle East unless the Palestinian people regained their usurped rights. Some observers cautiously noted that the talks also established a balanced basis for possible future cooperation.[15] The visit, with its political and financial outcome, bestowed on Sadat the moral support he urgently needed to bolster his shaky regime.

Domestic unrest caused Sadat to loosen some of his internal governmental controls and to raise his tone against both the United States and Israel to gain public support for his regime. But his threats and speeches were not taken seriously by either the Egyptian public or foreign observers. The climax was when Sadat asserted that 1971 was the "year of decisiveness," and that year passed without any show of force to end the Israeli occupation. Sadat's explanations of why the war of liberation had not been launched became the subject of numerous witticisms.

Egyptian public doubts about Sadat's expectations and future plans were reflected in continuous demonstrations. These climaxed in unprecedented student occupations of universities and the distribution of daily pamphlets attacking Sadat's internal and external policies and demanding more support for the Palestinian resistance movement. In response, Sadat raised the tone of his rhetoric against Israel, declaring his readiness "to pay a million lives as the price of this battle."[16] But despite this show of confidence, Sadat faced increasing domestic opposition, which he feared might lead to his ouster before he could fulfill his promise to liberalize Egyptian society and to liberate the Israeli-occupied territories—the two factors he hoped would distinguish his regime from that of Nasser.

By mid-1972, the state of "no-peace, no-war" had made Egyptians more restless. They felt that this condition must end, as it hurt Egypt and benefited Israel. Voicing Egyptian frustration, *al-Ahram*'s influential editor Haykal went so far as to call the state of affairs "an historical crime" (16 June 1972). Many blamed the situation on the presence of Soviet technicians in Egypt. Some argued that as long as the Soviets remained in Egypt, their presence would be an obstacle either to a political settlement or to war. This led the Egyptian opposition to launch a campaign to end Egyptian dependence on the Soviet Union for military and economic assistance. In May 1972 Sadat rejected a petition written by prominent Egyptians to end the Soviet presence in Egypt. In July, however, he took the world by surprise when he announced that the functions of Soviet military advisors in Egypt were terminated.[17] Officials in Cairo referred to the new stage of Soviet-Egyptian relations as "an objective pause with a friend." The pro-Moscow Lebanese daily *al-Nida* commented on 20 July 1972: "The struggle reached a climax when Lt. General Sadek, who is known for his hostility to the Soviet Union, called on Sadat at the head of a military delegation. Sadat was asked to make a decision for removal of Soviet advisers from Egypt and to reconsider the foundations of Soviet-Egyptian relations. The request was accompanied by a threat of interference in the political affairs of Egypt." Although Saudi Arabia made no public statements, there was no doubt that the news of Sadat's decision was received with much satisfaction.

In early 1973 Sadat's claim that the reshuffling of his cabinet ministers of 27 March 1973 was designed for "total confrontation" with Israel was dismissed by international press observers, who noted that Sadat was "intent on winning over the middle classes, who, though initially attracted by promises of liberalizing measures and the expressed desire to reach a peaceful settlement with Israel, were progressively disenchanted by Sadat's inability to get Egypt out of a corner."[18] But a minority of foreign observers did not dismiss Egypt's military threats in May as they had done on previous rounds. It seemed that as Sadat had played out his domestic options, he might feel forced, despite Israel's military superiority, to reestablish his credibility as a leader through some sort of military action. "It seems that nothing short of big-power intervention to impose a political settlement will now prevent him from choosing war as a final throw," wrote Tom Little in the *Jerusalem Post* on 4 May 1973. "There is no one else to blame if his already threadbare credibility is finally torn to shreds by another fruitless year of empty talk."

The more optimistic viewpoint was that Sadat's steps to prepare for fighting were intended to safeguard his domestic flank and give urgency to his diplomatic offensive in the United Nations and Europe. Arab military capability, compared to Israel's, was dismissed as a hopeless final alternative for Sadat. One of the main arguments was that Sadat might be stalling for time to see the effect of the energy shortage on U.S. foreign policy. By then, the Saudis had been warning the United States that Saudi oil production would not be expanded to meet U.S. demand unless the United States modified its Middle East policies.[19] Moreover, it seems that Saudi Arabia had assured Egypt that Saudi crude would be cut off if hostilities resumed.[20] This appeared to have some effect on the United States. The U.S. State Department reported on 2 May that financial aid to Arab states, notably Jordan and Saudi Arabia, would be increased and aid to Israel decreased. Although that decision hardly affected the political stagnation, it was an indication that the Arabs, particularly the Saudis, still carried some winning cards, and Sadat had until October to watch the U.S.-Saudi game.

Meanwhile Egyptian pressure on the Soviet Union and the United States increased. Cautious criticisms of Soviet support of the ceasefire were launched in the Egyptian press. Pressure on the United States took a more concrete form. The Egyptian media stepped up their campaigns against U.S. interests in the area, calling upon the oil-producing countries to exert economic pressure on the United States. On 30 April 1973 the Egyptian weekly *Roz al-Yusuf* warned that if the Arab oil-producing governments did not respond to the Egyptian demands, Arab workers might do it for them. Cairo issued a call to Arab workers to express their solidarity by boycotting U.S. interests for twenty-four hours on 15 May 1973, the anniversary of the establishment of the State of Israel. An agreement was reached with the Cairo-based Federation of Arab Workers to stop the pumping of oil for one hour on that day as a demonstrative gesture. Furthermore, the question of economic pressure was discussed in the talks held by the Egyptian minister of war, General Ahmed Ismail Ali, during his late April tour of Arab capitals, especially in Saudi Arabia and Kuwait.

To invest his warnings with greater credibility, Sadat intensified his preparations for war. The Egyptian media played up Sadat's statements that "the night won't last much longer" and that "Egypt will be engaged in war sooner than it is generally believed." It took four days of deliberations for the Egyptian National Assembly to approve the government's program; its final statement reasserted that Egypt had no other course but war.

Egyptian war drums were not only meant to encourage the United States and the Soviet Union to break the impasse with Israel. They were also directed at pro-Western Arab countries in hopes of persuading them to use their influence and friendship with the West to change the status quo. Although the sounds were hardly heard in Washington and Moscow, they were seriously considered in Saudi Arabia and Kuwait, where memories of the 1967 "involuntary" involvement in Arab militant affairs were still fresh.

Arab-Saudi Linkage: Pressure to Employ the Oil Weapon

For quite some time following Nasser's death, Faisal felt the pressures of assuming Arab leadership. It became obvious that unless he kept moving forward, and at a quicker pace, he had no chance of maintaining a dominant political role in Arab leadership circles. As clouds loomed on the Arab political horizon with the growing Arab frustration over U.S. policy in the Middle East, Saudi Arabia came under increasing pressure to make, at the very least, a declaration of intent to use its oil as a political weapon.

In Egypt, the Cairo daily *al-Gumhuriyya* wrote on 21 July 1972, "the world is telling us that it cannot do without our oil, but we do not bother to make oil a weapon in our hands." In a commentary on Cairo Radio on 29 July 1972 it was suggested that Arabs reconsider the oil concessions granted to U.S. firms, that taxes on U.S. oil profits be increased, and that the rate of production be deliberately restricted to damage the U.S. economy. Moreover, President Sadat, in an interview with *Newsweek* on 31 July 1972, warned the United States that its interests in the Arab world "will shortly become part of the battle for the recovery of our land." In an answer to a question about a possible Arab oil boycott, he said that he had never asked for a boycott, "but I have spoken about U.S. interests in the area." On 9 April 1973 *Newsweek* published another interview with President Sadat in which he asserted that the "oil weapon" would be used in any future Arab-Israeli war.[21]

In Kuwait, the Kuwaiti ruler pledged on 13 March 1973 that "his country would use its oil wealth as a weapon when the 'zero hour' for the Arab battle against Israel came."[22] In Libya, a stern warning that if the Middle East crisis deteriorated further, oil would be used as a weapon by the Arabs was voiced by Colonel Qaddafi. Speaking at a press conference on 13 May 1973, Qaddafi said: "If the situation deteriorates, the day will come when oil will be used as the ultimate weapon in the battle. If the Arab governments do not do this, the Arab peoples will take the initiative and do it. All estimates foresee a growing need for oil in the consuming countries, and oil will not lose importance in the future. The world—and above all the United States—needs more oil every year."[23]

Two days later Libya joined three other Arab states—Kuwait, Iraq, and Algeria—in suspending oil production for a twenty-four-hour period as a protest on the twenty-fifth anniversary of the founding of the State of Israel. The Libyan minister of information, Abu Zaid Durdah, explained in a newspaper interview that this action was taken in accordance with a decision of the conference of Arab professional trade unions held in Cairo at the beginning of the month. Commenting on the possibility of using oil as a weapon, Durdah said:

We consider that everything at present being written about oil and the supposed energy shortage in the U.S. is a propaganda campaign put together with the precise aim of preparing international opinion for a subsequent justification for aggressive actions which Washington is currently preparing against the Arab nation, either directly or indirectly, via its agents in Iran, occupied Palestine and Ethiopia, and using some Arab heads of state. . . .

We therefore think it is our duty to draw the attention of the peoples of Europe to the fact that the U.S. is in fact working to lead Europe towards economic catastrophe. It is thus their duty to realize this fact and turn to the Arab countries with a new spirit and to open a new chapter in Arab-European relations based on a cooperation founded on equality and respect for mutual sovereignty.[24]

As a result of continued political pressures caused by the lack of concrete progress in peace negotiations and other factors (such as the U.S. rebuff in September 1972 of a Saudi proposal for a special commercial oil agreement between the United States and Saudi Arabia), Saudi Arabia made, in April 1973, its first public statement linking the flow of oil to the United States with the Nixon administration's Middle East policy. In an interview with the *Washington Post* published on 19 April 1973, Saudi Oil Minister Yamani made it clear that Saudi Arabia would not significantly expand its present oil production unless the United States changed its pro-Israeli stance in the Middle East. The newspaper quoted Yamani as saying that Saudi Arabian fulfillment of its plan to increase production from its present level of 7.2 million barrels daily to 20 million barrels daily by 1980 was still a "good possibility," provided the United States "creates the right political atmosphere," with special reference to U.S. policy toward Israel. The *Post* report continued: "Yamani said that Saudi Arabia was already getting more money from oil than its small economy could absorb. 'If we consider only local interests,' he said, 'then we shouldn't produce more, maybe even less.'" Yamani's message was clear: "The Saudis are increasingly frustrated over the lack of American responsiveness to their efforts to establish a basic, long-term political and economic understanding." The same message was related to Frank Jungers, president of Aramco in Saudi Arabia, by King Faisal's close advisor Kamal Adham:

The Saudis, [Adham] said, in spite of their problems with the Egyptians, could not stand alone when hostilities broke out: they had expected that after President Sadat had expelled the Russians from Egypt, the Americans would have persuaded the Israelis to negotiate with the Arabs. Adham was sure that Sadat, a courageous and far-sighted man, would have to "embark on some sort of hostilities" in order to marshal American opinion to press for a Middle East settlement.[25]

The Saudi initiative in Washington was received in the Arab world with extreme enthusiasm. In Cairo, the daily *al-Akhbar* commented on 24 April 1973:

Mr. Yamani's message to the United States, which comes at a time when America is going through an acute energy crisis, is a warning shot to the U.S. government because of its continued backing of Israel and its hostile stand toward the Arab nation. It means to say that the United States should not expect any help from the Arabs in facing up to its energy crisis. The real import of this warning is that it has come in spite of desperate U.S. attempts to intimidate the Arabs and prevent them from utilizing their oil weapon in the battle of destiny with the Zionist foe and those who back him. But these attempts have failed and the Saudi warning has now come introducing the use of oil in the battle.

But this warning should be only the first step to be followed by others . . . if the United States fails to change its policy of unlimited military support for Israel and its expansionist aims in the Arab homeland.

The Kuwaiti weekly *al-Risalah* observed on 22 April 1973 that the warning issued by Yamani was a precedent with far-reaching implications, for it signaled a change in Saudi policy not to use oil as a political weapon as enunciated at the Khartoum conference of 1967. The paper went on to say that Saudi Arabia, aware as it was of the U.S. dire need of crude oil, had found the time opportune to use oil as a weapon to pressure the United States to change its stance vis-à-vis the Arab-Israeli conflict: "We welcome this new stand of the Kingdom of Saudi Arabia and urge most strongly that all the oil-producing countries combine in issuing a unified warning that Arab oil will be denied not just to the United States but to any country which assists Israel, whether overtly or covertly."

At the same time, the Saudi warning to the United States received a warm endorsement from Yasser Arafat, chairman of the Palestine Liberation Organization, who was quoted as saying: "This is an important change that makes us optimistic about the future of the battle of liberation."[26]

Saudi Politics and Arab Radicalism

The Saudi monarch entertained no hopes that the United States would abandon Israel or even stop supplying it with arms, but he obviously wanted a concession with which to impress the rest of the Arab world. He felt that unless he delivered something tangible to the Arab masses he would not be able to face the growing tide of radicalism caused by the humiliation and frustration building in the Arab world. Faisal knew that the Arab masses did not need any more Nassers to stir their latent potential for violence and revolt. He feared that, sooner or later, he could no longer count on the freedom from significant pressure from militant Arab groups or regimes that he had been enjoying since the

1967 June war. Furthermore, Faisal had only to remember the attempted coup in the summer of 1969 by Saudi Air Force officers to emphasize the volatility of the situation. Though military coups in Saudi Arabia had been unsuccessful so far, there were no guarantees that future attempts might not succeed.

It had been a long time since the Khartoum conference of 1967, when Saudi Arabia agreed to join other Arab oil states to give financial aid to Egypt to help it overcome the 1967 defeat and loss of income from Suez. Egypt, in return, had agreed to pull its army out of Yemen. The growing radical tide within the Arab world no longer needed subversive incentives from Cairo or Damascus to keep the indigenous revolutions alive. Faisal had only to look south to Oman, where one of the world's nearly forgotten conflicts had been smoldering since 1965, in a remote and rugged area, between British-led Omani troops and leftist insurgents.[27] Jet fighters, artillery, Saudi financial aid, Iranian military assistance, and the most sophisticated Western anti-guerrilla war techniques had not yet succeeded in destroying the troops of the People's Front for the Liberation of Oman. In North Yemen, foreign intervention, incompetent administration, tribal quarreling, and political instability had reached the point where the country could at any moment fall into the hands of any revolutionary group that mastered the situation. In South Yemen, conciliation between the Islamic conservative-autocratic regime in Saudi Arabia and the "scientific socialist" South Yemeni regime seemed difficult to attain. Saudi efforts to undermine the South Yemeni radicals by supporting opposition elements and providing mercenaries to the military operations of the hostile North Yemen Republic met with failure. On the contrary, the ruling faction of the Progressive Revolutionary party of South Yemen became more radicalized, and its hold on power more secure. In June 1969 an extreme leftist faction seized power and closed off all avenues of negotiation with Saudi Arabia. The new regime succeeded in suppressing all pro-Saudi subversive elements.[28]

A new line of operations against Western economic targets by Palestinian commandos had been initiated during the last few years by the Black September Organization. On 6 February 1972, Black September blew up assembly units of the Strenver electronics plant in Hamburg, West Germany, and a natural gas pumping station and pipeline in Rotterdam, the Netherlands. On 5 August 1972 it destroyed five oil tanks in Trieste, Italy. The organization declared to the Palestine News Agency on 5 August 1972 that it would "continue to strike at imperialist interests wherever they are found." Early in 1973 the group attacked the Saudi Embassy in Khartoum, Sudan, killing three diplomats.

The sabotage of Tapline on 22 January 1973 was indicative of the times. It was not the first time that an explosion had interrupted the flow of Saudi oil to the Mediterranean. In 1969 the pipeline had been sabotaged by Palestinian guerrillas and closed for 110 days, and the flow was interrupted for short periods in 1971 by explosions in sections of the pipe in Syria, Jordan, and Lebanon. However, it was the first time that such an explosion had occurred on Saudi territory. The sabotage itself carried strong political implications as it was a reminder of the vulnerability of oil installations, but the fact that it happened on Saudi territory gave the incident more significance. To the Saudis, it warned of the difficulties that were to come should they fail to use their oil leverage in the efforts to apply pressure for an Israeli withdrawal from the Arab territories occupied in 1967. The Saudis asserted, however, that this kind of pressure would not make them yield. Consequently, the Saudi position dissociating oil from politics was reiterated by the Saudi minister of foreign affairs, Omar al-Saqqaf, who stated in early February 1973 that Saudi Arabia would not cut off oil to the West or use oil as a political weapon. Instead, he said, Saudi Arabia wanted to use this vital resource to develop the country and build its armed forces. The Saudi minister added that, although the oil weapon could be used against one's enemies, it was a double-edged weapon that could also hurt the country that used it as well as its friends.

Explosions at one of Aramco's largest Saudi refineries on 5 and 16 August 1973 were hardly mentioned and never explained either by the Saudi government or in the press, but they clearly indicated that unless the oil-producing states exercised the oil weapon, militant Arabs might turn from hijacking planes or kidnapping hostages to blocking the flow of oil and sabotaging oil installations, which are easily damaged and take long to be repaired.[29] Nevertheless, the threat of radical action against Saudi Arabia or its oil installations failed to coerce the cautious Saudi monarch to make any commitments to the Arab world on the use of oil as a political weapon. To the contrary, he made attempts to explain to the Arab masses the Saudi rationalization for dissociating politics and oil. In an interview with the Lebanese weekly *al-Hawadeth* published on 30 August 1973, Faisal expressed the belief that there were "attempts to make the Arabs fall under the illusion that cutting [the United States'] oil is the only way this oil can be used as a weapon in the battle." He reportedly asked: "Where would we get the money if we cut off the oil not only for supporting our country but also for providing assistance to our brothers on the Israeli front lines?"

Faisal's son, Prince Saud, was quoted in the same article as saying: "Against whom do we want to use the oil weapon? Arab talk about a boycott gives the impression that we are threatening the entire world, while it is understood that our purpose is to bring pressure to bear on America." Furthermore, Prince Saud cautioned that in the event of an oil embargo "the United States would be the last country to be hurt, because the United States will not become dependent on Arab oil before the late seventies." And he added: "Arab oil has not yet begun to flow to the United States' refineries because the American oil-import restrictions were only lifted recently."

U.S.-Saudi Linkage: Pressure to Readjust Mideast Policy

To the West, the tense international oil situation in 1973 boiled down to one question: "Are the Arab oil producers, especially Saudi Arabia, friendly and cooperative?" Until the beginning of 1973 the West had had no cause for serious concern. Only a few months earlier, Saudi Oil Minister Yamani had proposed a special commercial oil agreement between Saudi Arabia and the United States. While many Arab states had stepped up their threats to U.S. interests in the area, Saudi Arabia offered to guarantee a continuous flow of oil to the United States in return for lifting the duties on the oil and granting the right to invest Saudi oil revenues in the U.S. oil industry.[30] Yamáni, in an address to the Middle East Institute's twenty-sixth annual conference, held in Washington on 30 September 1972, explained that such an agreement would insure the supply of crude oil to meet the U.S. demand for foreign oil, which was expected to soar from 4.6 to 12 or 13 million barrels per day by 1980.[31] Yamani, who was then negotiating participation agreements with the oil companies, wanted to reassure the oil companies and the U.S. government of Saudi goodwill toward the West. He wanted to indicate that the United States, and by implication, other major oil-consuming countries, had no need to worry about the security of future supplies. If Saudi Arabia were allowed to make substantial investments in the U.S. oil industry, the United States would then have Arab funds at its disposal "as a hostage." For its part, Saudi Arabia would profit from its surplus revenue. Without access to profitable investment opportunities, it might be forced to limit production. But Western efforts were still required to persuade Saudi Arabia to pump more oil out of the ground than its own national interest would incline it to do.

By the end of 1972, King Faisal was still insisting that his country's policy was that oil and politics should not be mixed; he let his oil minister announce that Saudi Arabia would meet the world's needs by expanding its production from 8 to 20 million barrels a day by 1980.

It was the hope of the Saudi monarch that the United States would use its influence to persuade Israel to yield territory it had held since June 1967. In the April 1973 issue of *Foreign Affairs*, James E. Akins of the U.S. Office of Fuel and Energy noted that to every visitor the Saudi monarch insisted that "the United States policy in the Middle East, which [Faisal] characterizes as pro-Israel, will ultimately drive all Arabs into the communist camp." In late April 1973, Yamani told the U.S. secretary of state, William Rogers, that unless the United States did something about the Mideast situation, Saudi Arabia might find it difficult to increase its oil production or even to maintain its present output.[32] On 3 May 1973 Faisal confided to Aramco President Jungers that only in Saudi Arabia were U.S. interests relatively safe, but that even in his kingdom it "would be more and more difficult to hold off the tide of opinion."[33] Furthermore, in his meetings with the executives of Aramco in August 1973, the king made it clear that his plans for a mammoth expansion program depended on whether the U.S. government showed more sympathy for the Arab position and demonstrated greater readiness to pressure the Israeli government to withdraw from the bulk of the Arab territories occupied in the 1967 war. He reiterated this position to the U.S. public through the U.S. mass media. On 31 August 1973 NBC quoted the Saudi monarch as saying that his country did not want "to place any restrictions on our oil exports to the United States, but America's complete support of Zionism against the Arabs makes it extremely difficult for us to continue to supply the U.S. petroleum needs and even to maintain our friendly relations."[34] In its issue of 10 September 1973, *Newsweek* quoted Faisal as saying that "cooperation requires action on both sides: not sacrifices on one side and negative, if not hostile, attitudes on the other side." All these messages were directed at Washington. The Saudi king, in essence, was telling the U.S. government that although he valued his friendship with the United States, that friendship would be affected by continued, total Western support of Israel.

Resolution 242, unanimously passed by the UN Security Council on 22 November 1967, called on the Arab states to recognize Israel in return for Israel's withdrawal from Arab territories occupied in 1967. Although Faisal was never enthusiastic about the resolution, as it made no specific reference to Jerusalem, he was ready to put the weight of his oil power behind the resolution for two reasons: first, to align Saudi policy with Egyptian policy, which accepted the resolution as a basis for any future negotiations with Israel, and second, to provide maneuvering room for himself and for the United States. Precisely because the resolution was vague, it was generally acceptable.

The predicament of U.S. Mideast policy was complex and deep-rooted. Exxon's former Middle East negotiator Howard Page expressed the contradiction in U.S. foreign policy when he said, "Our economic policy was ensuring that we became increasingly dependent on Middle East oil, while our foreign policy was ensuring that the oil would be cut off."[35] Furthermore, the United States did not want to shift its Mideast policy, even a little, if it appeared to be doing so under duress. Some U.S. officials, such as Secretary of the Treasury George Schultz, publicly attacked the oil-producing countries, asserting that these countries "do not have America by the throat." U.S. officials talked, though without concrete planning, about decreasing dependence on foreign oil and developing alternative sources of energy. President Nixon asserted that the United States "could avoid dependence on the Middle East oil" by increasing production of coal, stepping up nuclear power development, and speeding up completion of the Alaska pipeline, as well as by deregulating natural gas prices and relaxing clean-air standards. In 1973 the Nixon administration eased restrictions on the importation of foreign oil and consented to increases in domestic prices of gasoline and heating fuels.

To the rest of the world, it was obvious that Nixon and his energy advisors could muse about developing alternative sources of energy but that in the short run there was little that could be done. Real U.S. dependence on Arab oil was to begin in 1975 and 1976, and was expected to last until the United States started to produce, probably sometime in the 1980s, a large-scale substitute for oil that would gradually decrease its dependence on Arab oil. The London *Financial Times* observed that "President Nixon's warning to the Arabs that the United States may forsake oil for alternative sources of energy had a hollow ring to it. In the immediate future, the United States' ability to ensure adequate supplies of oil will depend to a large extent on the success of its diplomatic strategy in the Middle East."[36]

President Nixon announced in March 1973 that he was drafting a proposal to encourage the oil-importing countries to act collectively in their dealings with the oil-producing countries. This infuriated the Saudis. If the United States and its allies exerted pressure, Yamani warned publicly, the West could forget about Saudi Arabia's raising its future oil production to suit the West's needs. Saudi Arabia needed only the income provided by the production of 6 million barrels a day.

The assertion of the United States that this growing dependence on Middle East oil would not influence its policy toward the region hardened attitudes in the Arab world. Speaking to the press on 19 May 1973, the U.S. ambassador to the United Nations, John Scali, stated that "oil or the lack of it will not be an issue in U.S. policy in the Middle East." Scali's statement was made after a meeting in New York with Israeli Foreign Minister Abba Eban, who had told a press conference in Miami earlier in the week, on 16 May 1973, that "there is no reality in the idea that the Arab governments will deny the sale of their oil on political grounds, just as they've never done it in the past. The oil-buying countries have alternative places in which to buy. The Arab states have no alternative but to sell their oil because they have no other resources at all."

The hint of Senator William Fulbright, chairman of the Senate Foreign Relations Committee, that present U.S. policy could result in an oil embargo against the United States, and that the resulting energy crisis might cause the United States to contemplate military intervention in the area via its "militarily potent surrogates" Iran and Israel, put the Arab oil producers on the alert. This was the first time that a U.S. official publicly referred to the possibility of using force against the Arab oil producers. Although the next day, 22 May 1973, the U.S. Department of State dissociated itself from Senator Fulbright's comments,[37] the statement provoked a wave of anti-U.S. sentiments in the Arab world and promoted solidarity among the members of OAPEC.

Anti-U.S. feelings in the Arab world were intensified when the United States on 26 July 1973 vetoed a UN Security Council draft resolution that expressed "serious concern" at Israel's lack of cooperation with UN Middle East peace efforts, "strongly deplored" Israel's continuing occupation of Arab territories, and reaffirmed Resolution 242 of 1967. The resolution, which received thirteen affirmative votes with China abstaining, was defeated as a result of the U.S. veto.

The Saudis began to react to U.S. Middle East policy. At the September 1973 meeting of OPEC in Vienna, Saudi Arabia led the assault on the Tehran price agreement of 1971. This step meant that Saudi Arabia would not oppose price hikes. For the first time, the Saudis took a line considered "disruptive" to U.S. interests. Western observers saw the Saudi move as a response to President Nixon's threats.

Nevertheless, and despite the fact that Yamani was still warning of a production freeze, King Faisal kept projecting a friendly image to the West. However, he was beginning to feel that as a result of his vehement opposition to communism and radicalism, his friendship with the West was taken too much for granted. By early October it was clear that Saudi Arabia was preparing to back up its threat if the United States would not put pressure on Israel to withdraw from Arab territories it had occupied in 1967. Should the oil weapon be used, however, Faisal advocated its use as a weapon of persuasion; he preferred a gradual approach, freezing the production level or limiting its rate of growth rather than imposing an immediate cutoff. However, major events soon shook the Middle East that changed the picture radically.

6
The Leverage of Oil, 1973/1974

The Great "Energy Crisis" Debate

By the late sixties and early seventies, scholars and oil experts in the United States were divided into two schools of thought about the possibility of an Arab oil embargo and its potential to cause an oil shortage. The dominant school argued that there was no supply shortage and that future supply would probably match demand. With the 1967 oil embargo experience fresh in their minds, these experts maintained that the oil weapon was ineffective and that oil imports could safely be increased, as "the Arabs can't drink their oil." The leading figure in this school was Massachusetts Institute of Technology economist Morris A. Adelman, who in his 1972 article "Is the Oil Shortgage Real?" in *Foreign Policy* asserted that there was "absolutely no basis to fear an acute oil scarcity over the next 15 years."[1] Adelman argued that the "world 'energy crisis' or 'energy shortage' is a fiction. But belief in the fiction is a fact."[2] He continued: "There is no more basis for fears of acute oil scarcity in the next 15 years than there was 15 years ago— and the fears were strong in 1957. The myth that rising imports (of the United States) will 'turn the market around' is only the latest version of the myth that rising imports (of Europe and Japan) would 'dry out the surplus in 1957–70.' "[3]

Adelman rejected the arguments of James Akins, director of the U.S. Office of Fuel and Energy, that a "supply crisis" could be caused by even one Arab nation stopping oil production. He stated categorically:

Such a "crisis" is a fantasy. Five Arab countries produce an aggregate of one MBD [million barrels per day]; they would never be missed. In 1951, Iran, producing nearly 40 percent of Persian Gulf output, shut down; yet 1951 Persian Gulf output actually rose. No Arab or non-Arab country is nearly that important today. In the winter of 1966-67, Iraq—about 10 percent then as now—shut down, and there was not even a ripple on the stream.

If any proof were needed that an Arab boycott will hurt only the Arabs and soon collapse, the 1967 experience should suffice.[4]

Adelman concluded: "Oil supply is threatened by one and only one danger: a concerted shutdown by the OPEC nations. No single nation can do any harm."[5]

In mid-September 1973 Adelman appeared on the television program "Firing Line," where he was introduced by the program's host, William F. Buckley, Jr., in the following fashion:

We have here the rarest bird in America, a responsible economist who believes that the energy crisis is substantially a phony. He is Professor Morris Adelman of M.I.T., whose thesis is that the supplies of oil are sufficient for any predictable need, that no single country has in fact the leverage to deny us the oil we want and that the best thing to do under the circumstances is to decartelize the situation surrounding the Persian Gulf.[6]

In response to a question by Buckley as to why Adelman thought Americans "have no reason to take seriously the recent threat of King Faisal to deny us oil," Adelman stated: "If we choose to take it seriously, it becomes serious." Then Adelman proceeded to say: "If [Faisal] thinks that we are scared, then he's well advised to keep brandishing the weapon. If he sees that we are not scared—and in a recent interview both the King and Prince Saud al Faisal seemed to be suspecting that we were not panicking—then the best thing for him to do is either to fall silent or else make some gesture to save face." The following exchange then ensued:

Mr. Buckley: Well, you have said, "Let him go ahead and stop selling oil and let's see what happens." Your point is that it's an empty fuse, is it?

Mr. Adelman: It's an empty fuse unless our government treats it as being important; and if we do, and if past experience is a guide, we'll have perhaps Mr. Kissinger and our new ambassador to Saudi Arabia making secret or open flights. The greatest oil agreement in world history will be announced and it will be for some 10 years, and it may last as many months if it be fair weather, and then we'll be back about where we are now.

Other proponents of the "no crisis" school found support for their position within the U.S. administration. Anthony Sampson wrote for the London *Observer:*

Adelman, like many other oil experts at the time, was confident that an Arab embargo could not be sustained, as the attempt in 1967 had indicated, and his view was supported by a special task force on oil imports headed by George Schultz (late Secretary of the Treasury), which had reported in 1970. The report was skeptical about an Arab shutdown and was complacent that imports could safely be increased.[7]

Writing in the *New York Times* on 20 May 1973, William D. Smith summed up the main thesis of this school:

A considerable body of opinion in diplomatic and academic circles maintains that the Arabs do not yet and may never have the strength to mount a long-term oil embargo on the United States. They note that Iran, a non-Arab state, is a major oil producer and unlikely to go along with an embargo. In addition, Europe and Japan might be able to shift some of their imports to the United States in case of embargo.

These arguments dominated U.S. thinking,[8] and as Joseph S. Szyliowicz showed: "There was a near consensus prior to the October war that the Arab oil producers would not impose an embargo."[9] Similarly, U.S. energy policymakers undervalued the significance of Arab oil, judging that if Arab producers reduced their oil production other non-Arab OPEC members would raise theirs to prevent an oil shortage. Much hope was invested in Iran, whose foreign minister on 25 April 1973 assured the United States that in the event of such a boycott, Iran was prepared to increase oil production to meet U.S. needs. This assurance seemed credible because Iran was one of the world's largest producers of oil. In May 1973 the *Middle East Intelligence Survey* observed:

This, along with Iran's growing military muscle, makes it unlikely that any of the Arab oil producers will carry out their threats. No doubt Deputy Secretary of State Kenneth Rush had these realities in mind when he stated firmly after the meeting of Middle East U.S. Ambassadors in Tehran, on April 24, that the U.S. had no intention of altering her foreign policy in the face of a threatened oil boycott.[10]

On the other hand, there were only a few experts who argued that an Arab oil embargo was possible and that an oil shortage would probably follow. The main proponent of this school was James Akins, "one of the few that took Arab threats to impose an embargo seriously."[11] In an article entitled "The Oil Crisis: This Time the Wolf Is Here," published in *Foreign Affairs* in April 1973, Akins wrote:

A collective Arab boycott is not the only conceivable political threat. Until now the world has enjoyed the luxury of considerable surplus production capacity, relative to total demand. Now that has changed. The United States now has no spare capacity and within the next few years, assuming other producer governments and companies do not invest in huge added capacity, the production of any one of seven countries—Saudi Arabia, Iran, Iraq, the Federation of Arab Emirates, Kuwait, Libya or Venezuela—will be larger than the combined spare capacity of the rest of the world. In other words, the loss of the production of any one of these countries could cause a temporary but significant world oil shortage; the loss of any two could cause a crisis and quite possibly a panic among the consumers.

No, the threat to use oil as a political weapon must be taken seriously. The vulnerability of the advanced countries is too great and too plainly evident—and is about to extend to the United States.[12]

The thrust of Akins's article was that "the oil crisis is a reality that compels urgent action."[13] But his views went unheeded as he was "discounted by his superiors as a committed Arabist."[14]

The Embargo: An Agony of Decisionmaking

With the outbreak of Arab-Israeli hostilities on 6 October 1973, the use of Arab oil as a political weapon immediately suggested itself. Less than twenty-four hours after the fighting started the executive committee of the PLO called for an immediate halt to the pumping of all Arab oil to the West.[15] The Iraqi government responded on the same day by nationalizing the interests of two U.S. companies, Exxon and Mobil, in the Basrah Petroleum Company.[16] However, Iraq dissociated itself from Arab collective action. Charles Doran in *Myth, Oil, and Politics* (1977), commented: "One suspects that Iraq's own commercial ambitions actually overshadowed its disenchantment with the commonly accepted Arab strategy for dealing with the Israeli issue. Although Iraq's stubborn autonomy probably did not undermine the joint strategic effort of the Arab governments, it served to call the effectiveness of the strategy into question."[17]

According to the *Middle East Monitor*, King Faisal sent a message to Secretary of State Henry Kissinger immediately following the outbreak of hostilities, calling on the United States to "force Israel to pull out of Arab lands and to restore the rights of the Palestinian people in their land."[18] Joining other Arab states who either sent or announced that they would be sending troops to the front (including Tunisia), Saudi Arabia announced that it had put its armed forces on alert, but ignored the use of oil-production cuts as a weapon.

Ironically, it was Israeli military operations that caused the first cutback in Arab oil production. Israeli air and sea raids considerably damaged the loading facilities of two of the four east Mediterranean terminals, Banias and Tartus, in Syria. A third terminal, Sidon in Lebanon, remained open, but its proximity to the hostilities zone kept oil tankers away. As a result, output from Saudi Arabia and Iraq was greatly reduced before any cutback decision on the Arab side was actually made.[19] Israel also suspended operations at the Ashkelon terminal as of 6 October 1973, thus halting a potential 500,000 barrels per day of oil exports.[20]

During the early days of the October war, it was apparent that the conservative oil-producing states were hesitant to impose an oil embargo on the West.[21] They hoped that the situation would not reach the stage where it would be necessary to make cutbacks. However, the insistence of Egypt, Syria, Algeria, and Libya, coupled with the militant mood that prevailed in the Arab world during the war, forced them to reconsider, and oil was brought into the center of Arab war politics.

Amidst the warnings issued in the various Arab oil-producing countries, Kuwait announced on 9 October that OAPEC would meet in Kuwait to discuss "the role of oil in the light of current developments."[22] This move, encouraged by Saudi Arabia, was seen as an effort on the part of the Gulf states to gain time as they escalated their diplomatic efforts in the United States. The official U.S. announcement that it had started a massive airlift of military equipment to Israel made their position more difficult. But when Radio Baghdad on 16 October began denouncing Saudi Arabia as a reactionary monarchy, the Gulf states had no doubt that if they held back, Egypt, Syria, Libya, Algeria, and Iraq would launch a barrage of hostile propaganda against them that would greatly strengthen the guerrilla movements in the Gulf.

At the same time, Sadat's growth in popularity and stature in the Arab world as a result of his military initiative against Israel reached an unprecedented climax that worried Faisal. The Saudi monarch feared that if the war terminated without his country's effective participation, it would reflect badly on his image and on his country's credibility. Despite early rebuffs, he still had faith in the United States. Consequently, on 17 October, the Saudis headed a delegation of four Arab diplomats who met with President Nixon and proposed a peace plan. They urged the United States to participate directly in mediating the conflict. On the same day, ten Arab oil-producing countries met in Kuwait and issued a communiqué[23] indicating that oil production would be reduced by 5 percent of the September 1973 level of output in each Arab oil-exporting country, with a similar reduction to be applied each successive month until the total evacuation of Israeli forces from all Arab territory occupied during the June 1967 war was completed and until the rights of the Palestinian people were restored.[24]

The unfruitful meeting with President Nixon and increasing pressure from other Arab countries prompted the Saudi monarch to increase his pressure on the West. On the same day that Abu Dhabi announced it was halting all its oil exports to the United States, Saudi Arabia declared that it was immediately cutting its oil production by 10 percent "to pressure the United States into stopping support for Israel."[25] In its announcement, the Saudi government warned that all oil exports to the United States would be cut if the United States continued to aid the Israeli forces. One Western observer noted that "Faisal must have had very mixed feelings about the 1973 oil embargo, but he decided that his own convictions and his whole credibility with the Arab world, to say nothing of the danger of internal trouble, assassination, and sabotage by Palestinian terrorists, left him no alternative but to join in."[26]

Nixon's response to the Saudi warning was to ask the U.S. Congress on 19 October for $2.2 billion in emergency aid to Israel. This escalation prompted Libya to order an immediate cutoff of all its exports to the United States and to raise the price of oil from $4.90 to $8.92 per barrel. On 20 October Saudi Arabia delivered its long-delayed response to the U.S. move by announcing a decision to halt all oil exports to the United States.[27] In the London *Observer*, Sampson described how the Saudis went about implementing their decision:

> In Riyadh, Yamani and other Saudi ministers summoned Jungers of Aramco to discuss the enforcement of the embargo: the Saudis (Jungers noted) appeared glum and disillusioned with the U.S. They had already worked out the embargo in some detail, and they insisted that apart from the 10 percent cutback, Aramco must also subtract all shipments to the U.S., including shipments to the military. Aramco would have to police the whole complex operation, and any deviations from the ground rules would be harshly dealt with.[28]

On 21 October Kuwait, Qatar, Bahrain, and Dubai followed the example of the Saudis by imposing a total embargo on oil exports to the United States. They announced that they would act similarly against any other country that supported Israel.[29] Two days later, on 23 October, Kuwait, which had ordered an immediate 10 percent cut in production two days earlier, embargoed oil shipments to the Netherlands for "its hostile attitude towards Arab rights and its pro-Israeli bias."[30] Oil exports to that country were also curtailed by Abu Dhabi on 23 October, by Qatar on 24 October, by Oman on 25 October, by Libya on 30 October, and by Saudi Arabia on 2 November. However, the embargo did not cover oil shipped to Rotterdam to be refined and reexported to nonembargoed countries.

By the beginning of November, oil production had already been cut back by at least 25 percent in Kuwait, 10 percent in Saudi Arabia, Algeria, and Qatar, and by at least 5 percent in Libya, Bahrain, Dubai, and Oman. Before the embargo went into effect, total U.S. imports of Arab oil averaged around 1.8 or 1.9 million barrels per day, equivalent to 28 percent of aggregate U.S. imports and 10 percent of total U.S. oil consumption.[31] Dutch imports of Arab oil, on the other hand, had reached 1.47 million barrels per day, or 71 percent of overall Dutch imports.[32]

On 4 November 1973 the Arab oil ministers held their second meeting in Kuwait to consider how their embargo decision had been implemented and to evaluate its results. In their deliberations, they determined that in order to accelerate the process of reaching a political settlement for the Arab-Israeli conflict,

> they would raise the oil-production curb to 25 percent below the September 1973 level, including the volumes deducted as a result of cutting off oil supplies to the U.S. and the Dutch market. After that, the reduction will continue in December by 5 percent of November production. The reduction will not affect the share which every friendly state has been importing from each Arab oil-exporting country during the first 9 months of the current year.[33]

At this time Saudi Arabia had already experienced a staggering 31.7 percent drop in production and Kuwait 25 to 30 percent. As a result of the decision, there was a total reduction of about 2.8 million barrels a day, or some 28.5 percent below the September average. In addition, the meeting decided to send the Algerian energy minister and the Saudi oil minister to Western capitals "to explain the Arab point of view regarding the oil-production cutback measures."

In Europe, the development of a less hostile attitude toward the Arabs, and in the United States, increasing efforts to reach a political settlement in the Middle East, prompted the third Vienna OAPEC meeting of 18 November 1973. The OAPEC countries decided not to implement the 5 percent reduction for the month of December with respect to European countries. This move was taken in "appreciation of the political stand taken by the Common Market countries in their communiqué of November 1973 regarding the Middle East crisis."[34] Nevertheless, with the exception of Iraq, OAPEC decided to continue the embargo against the United States and Holland.

In a news conference held in Washington on 21 November 1973, Secretary of State Kissinger warned that retaliatory action would be taken "with enormous reluctance" by the United States if the Arab oil embargo continued "unreasonably and indefinitely." Regarding the Middle East peace agreement, Kissinger added that Israel would have to give up territories occupied since 1967, but that permanent boundaries would be negotiable and would have to "have an element of security arrangements," including possible "outside guarantees." Settlement of the Palestinian problem and of the status of Jerusalem would also have to be part of any pact, he asserted.[35] Responding to the U.S. position two days later, Israeli Defense Minister Dayan maintained that Israel must retain its former Arab territories for "security reasons." He stated that Secretary Kissinger's suggestion that Israel withdraw in return for security guarantees could only supplement "defensible borders, not substitute for them."

The Sixth Arab Summit Conference, held in Algiers on 28 November 1973, decided to include Portugal, Rhodesia, and South Africa on the list of embargoed nations. The conference, though determined to intensify application of the oil weapon, decided to exempt Japan and the Philippines from the 5 percent oil-export cut scheduled for December 1973. It qualified the progressive monthly reduction formula by adopting a ceiling for reductions in production "to the extent that reduction in income should not exceed one quarter on the basis of the 1972 income level of each producing country." Considering that oil prices (excluding dollar depreciation adjustments) had risen by 70 percent since 1972, this ceiling meant that oil-producing Arab states could in fact reduce output to some 45 percent of the 1972 level before reaching the minimum 75 percent of the 1972 revenue level.[36] Consuming countries were classified in three categories: (1) "friendly," (2) "neutral," or (3) "supporting the enemy." The classification was to be applied and reviewed by a committee of the ministers of foreign affairs and oil of the Arab oil-producing states. Any neutral country reclassified as friendly would receive the same quantities of oil that it had imported in 1972, while reexport of oil from any country to a hostile state was to be guarded against. The conference endorsed "political efforts" toward a peace agreement conditional upon Israeli evacuation of all the occupied Arab territories and reestablishment of full national rights for the Palestinian people. Furthermore, it recognized the PLO as the sole legitimate representative of the Palestinians.

This conference, which was particularly noteworthy as it came immediately after the Arabs' exercise of their military option and their wielding of the oil weapon, was attended by sixteen Arab heads of state and the Palestinian leaders. Though Jordan sent a delegation, King

Hussein absented himself due to the summit's decision to proclaim the PLO the sole legitimate representative of the Palestinian people. Libya refused to attend in protest at the allegedly limited concept of the strategy behind the war, and Iraq boycotted the conference in rage at not having been consulted on either the surprise October 1973 offensive or the ceasefire hastily accepted by Egypt on 22 October 1973 and later by Syria.

As part of his tour to explain the Arabs' use of the "oil weapon," Saudi Oil Minister Yamani conferred in Washington on 5 December 1973 with Secretary of State Kissinger and other U.S. officials. He explained that Saudi Arabia would be willing to remove its total ban and resume a schedule of increased production corresponding to a schedule of withdrawal by Israel from occupied Arab lands. But in a news conference held the next day, Kissinger, without making any commitments, responded that in light of active U.S. engagement in peace efforts in the Middle East "discriminatory measures against the United States and pressures are no longer appropriate."

In their fourth meeting, held in Kuwait in early December, OAPEC ministers began to express a greater measure of flexibility. Their communiqué issued on 8 December announced their readiness to lift the Arab oil embargo against the United States to coincide with the beginning of the implementation of a schedule for withdrawal of Israeli forces from the occupied Arab territories. Furthermore, they declared that once a withdrawal formula was approved, a schedule for the gradual return of oil production to its September 1973 level would be drawn up to go along with the implementation of the stages of withdrawal. Supplies of oil to "African countries and friendly Islamic states" were also to continue uninterrupted "to the extent that they have valid contracts, even if it means an increase in production." Many of those countries either had never established diplomatic relations with Israel or had severed such relations before or during the hostilities of October 1973 as an expression of support for the legitimacy of the Arab cause. A number of African countries had further called upon all countries, Arab and non-Arab, to impose a total economic embargo, and in particular an oil embargo, against Israel. This decision was made by the ministerial council of the Organization of African Unity, which was held in Addis Ababa on 21 November 1973 and attended by forty-two African countries.

On 21 December 1973 the Geneva Conference on the Middle East, convened under the cochairmanship of the United States and the Soviet Union, opened with general statements of policy by the participating countries' foreign ministers. U.S. Secretary of State Kissinger pledged a U.S. effort to seek a settlement according to a four-point approach: (1) scrupulous adherence to the truce; (2) first priority given to separation of Egyptian and Israeli forces; (3) the accord to include Israeli withdrawal, recognized borders, security arrangements and guarantees, and settlement of the Palestinian problem; and (4) recognition that Jerusalem "contains places considered holy by three great religions."

The opening of the Geneva conference had its impact on the fifth OAPEC meeting held in Kuwait on 24–25 December, which took further steps to relax oil-production cutbacks. Saudi Oil Minister Yamani said that such steps were taken as a result of favorable shifts in some countries' positions in the Arab-Israeli conflict. The 25 percent cutback was eased to 15 percent of the September 1973 level of production effective 1 January 1974, while the extra 5 percent reduction that had been originally scheduled for January was dispensed with altogether. Japan, which had already issued two statements endorsing UN Security Council resolutions on the Middle East conflict, was allowed "special treatment which would not subject it to the full extent of the across-the-board cutback measures." This was explicitly justified not only by "the change in Japan's policy towards the Arab cause," but also by "the deteriorating economic situation in Japan." It was also decided to resume oil exports to Belgium via Rotterdam (up to the level of September 1973 imports) and to supply "certain friendly countries," presumably Britain, France, and Spain, with their actual oil requirements even in excess of the 1973 level.[37] The embargo imposed against the Netherlands remained intact, despite the earlier declaration of the Dutch government's spokesman on 4 December to the effect that his government "considers that the Israeli presence in occupied territories is illegal."[38] As for the United States, the oil ministers' communiqué made a conciliatory gesture expressing the hope that the "desire of the United States government to participate in the search for a just and peaceful settlement of the problem will be fruitful and will lead to results beneficial to the peoples of the world and in particular to bilateral relations between the Arab and the American peoples."

Subsequent to President Sadat's public proposal to end the embargo against the United States, and in the wake of the Egyptian disengagement agreement with Israel and the Syrian objection to it, OAPEC's oil ministers met—for the sixth time since the embargo began—in Cairo on 2 January 1974 to deal with two issues: (1) the question of suspending the oil embargo against the United States, and (2) the type and dimensions of Arab aid to African states that were feeling the impact of the worldwide energy squeeze. Sadat suggested providing the United States with 85 percent of its imported oil needs after Israel and Syria signed a disengagement agreement, and reducing the cutback to other nations from 25 percent to 15 percent; but Sadat's proposal was turned down. Kuwait's authoritative newspaper al-Rai al-'Am opposed any removal of the embargo, saying that pressure on Washington should continue at least until Israel withdrew from all occupied Arab territories. Semiofficial newspapers in Libya and Iraq followed with no less adamant statements.

The OAPEC meeting concluded with no explicit mention of the Egyptian proposal in the joint communiqué, and both issues—the fate of the embargo and future decisions on output totals—were tabled until the next OAPEC meeting planned for 14 February 1974. Considerable emphasis, however, was placed on recommendations regarding aid to Africa, but there ensued no firm commitment, apparently because the Arabs feared that financial grants would draw negative responses from other oil-producing countries like Iran and Nigeria that were determined to maintain their own influence in Africa, or from big powers that were vying for more influence within these developing countries.

For his part, Sadat was anxious that the Arab oil-producing states moderate their stand on the oil embargo against the United States to prove to Washington that helping Egypt against Israel could pay off, and to show Kissinger the influential role Egypt played within the Arab world. The Syrian objection to the lifting of the embargo was due to the political stalemate on the Golan Heights issue and fear that lifting the oil embargo would weaken Syria's bargaining position. Further, the oil-producing countries clearly enjoyed their new-found power and importance too much to let Sadat dictate their policies to them, especially because the main objective of the oil embargo had not yet been realized, and an Israeli commitment to evacuate the occupied Arab territories did not seem imminent. Faisal in particular did not want to side with either Syria or Egypt, but rather hoped to make use of the differences between the two main combatants to enhance his own position as arbiter in Arab affairs. The growing Saudi influence on inter-Arab affairs had been one of the spectacular developments in the Arab world since the October war, and Faisal was determined to nurture it carefully.

Until late January 1974, King Faisal's role was mainly as a mentor to Arab oil policy, particularly in the Arab Gulf oil-producing countries. The visit of the Syrian president to Saudi Arabia on 2 February 1974 gave an impetus to Saudi influence in Arab politics, causing Faisal to express his own views on major political issues such as the desirability of a separation-of-forces agreement along the Golan Heights ceasefire line. It was oil that gave him the power to do so, and Saudi oil power began to assert itself not only internationally, but also in inter-Arab affairs. Syria wanted Faisal to keep up the oil boycott against the United States in order to lend force to its demand for an immediate Israeli commitment to withdraw from the Golan Heights. Sadat, however, wanted the boycott eased in recognition of the U.S. contribution to the Egyptian-Israeli agreement. In both instances, Faisal became the final arbiter. This development had strong domestic repercussions in Saudi Arabia.

Within the Saudi regime differences began to sharpen. Some influential Saudis objected to any measures that would further strain U.S.-Saudi relations. They felt alarmed at the prospect that a U.S. arms embargo might be sparked by a prolonged oil embargo, a move that could jeopardize Saudi security—internal as well as external. Others feared that to go along with Sadat might lead to an erosion of Saudi Arabia's role as a formulator of Arab political attitudes toward Israel, which had given Saudi Arabia a new preeminence in inter-Arab affairs. This preeminence had become the source of a new pride among educated young Saudis, a pride to which they had aspired for a long time.[39]

On 10 January 1974 Secretary of State Kissinger announced that the oil-consuming nations should not seek individual agreements with oil producers to protect their supplies because such "unrestricted bilateral competition will be ruinous for all concerned." Nearly two weeks later, on 22 January 1974, Kissinger expressed his expectation that the Arab oil embargo would be terminated after the implementation of the Egyptian-Israeli disengagement agreement. However, when this did not materialize, Kissinger warned on 6 February 1974 that continuance of the Arab oil embargo in light of U.S. peace efforts was a "form of blackmail" that would affect the course of future U.S. diplomacy. The U.S. secretary's remarks seemed directed largely at King Faisal to pressure him to modify his attitude. However, such statements only helped to enhance the image of the Saudi monarch in the Arab world and had little impact on Saudi oil policy.

At the Algiers Arab mini-summit conference held on 13 February 1974 and attended by Syrian President Hafez al-Assad, Faisal, and Algerian President Boumediene, Sadat made an effort to persuade King Faisal to lift the oil embargo. The Saudi monarch agreed in principle to do so, although he held out on the question of timing, wishing to let the Syrians use the embargo to strengthen their initial negotiating stand. The foreign ministers of Egypt and Saudi Arabia were dispatched to Washington on 16 February to present the Arab views and to indicate enough of a change in Syria's attitude to encourage Kissinger to resume diplomatic initiatives.

By early March Secretary Kissinger had surmounted the major obstacle to the commencement of disengagement talks between Israel and Syria. The Syrian-Israeli disengagement (eventually signed in Geneva on 31 May 1974), was modeled on the Egyptian-Israeli disengagement agreement. It involved high stakes for the United States for it presented a favorable opportunity to end the Arab oil embargo as well as to cool the Gulf states' rapprochement with the Soviet Union.[40]

After several postponements, the seventh OAPEC meeting convened in Tripoli on 13 March 1974. The delays were symptomatic of the various currents underlying the present stage of the oil offensive. Originally, the Tripoli meeting was scheduled earlier, but at the insistence of Egypt and Saudi Arabia, it was shifted to Cairo on 10 March, at which time the Egyptians hoped to receive the credit for announcing the suspension of the embargo. President Sadat and King Faisal had promised Kissinger during his latest Middle East tour that the embargo against the United States would be cancelled. In return, Kissinger assured them of continued efforts to advance a Golan Heights troop disengagement between Israel and Syria; but an agreement would not be worked out until after OAPEC lifted the embargo. Thus, the pressure was on the oil ministers to move first.

A number of Arab countries, namely Libya, Algeria, Iraq, and Syria, opposed and boycotted the Cairo session, threatening to meet separately if the resolution supported by Egypt, Saudi Arabia, Kuwait, Abu Dhabi, Qatar, and Bahrain was adopted. Fearing to lose the effectiveness of Arab unity of action, the Saudis and Egyptians gave in, and the OAPEC meeting was rescheduled for Tripoli. The ensuing six-hour session at Tripoli indicated a rift among oil producers on ending the oil embargo. The ministers adjourned the meeting and scheduled the next to be held on 17 March in Vienna. On the one hand, Algeria and Syria opposed ending the embargo because no progress had yet been made toward a separation-of-forces agreement on the Golan Heights; Iraq and Libya argued that U.S. policy in the Middle East was fundamentally hostile to Arab interests and that the embargo remained a just retribution. On the other hand, the Gulf states were in a more complicated position as their oil ministers had met with Sadat in Cairo and reached mutual understanding on the need to lift the embargo. However, they did not want to cause a rift in Arab relations, in which they would be accused of giving in to U.S. pressure without achieving any of the embargo's objectives. Further, they feared a return to the polarization of the Arab world into two camps. To placate Arab fears, Saudi Oil Minister Yamani gave an interview to Cairo's *al-Akhbar*, published 14 March 1974, in which he asserted: "If we agree to the resumption of oil supplies to the U.S., this would not mean that the use of the oil weapon is at an end. The oil weapon is still in our hands and the world will always be aware of it and will always be mindful of its interests in future."[41]

In Vienna on 18 March, the Egyptian-Saudi axis demonstrated its strength by succeeding in having OAPEC's eighth meeting decide to lift the oil embargo against the United States. Other decisions adopted by the meeting were:

(1) to treat both Italy and West Germany as friendly countries; their oil requirements to be provided within the limits of Arab oil production, but making sure that exported Arab oil does not replace non-Arab oil which was to be exported to these countries lest such oil be redirected to a country subject to the boycott or to the reduced production;

(2) to increase oil production in each Arab oil-producing country to the extent needed to enable it to carry out that decision.[42]

The embargo against the Netherlands, South Africa, Rhodesia, and Portugal continued. A communiqué issued at the end of the meeting reiterated the "basic objective" of the Arab oil measures. It stated that the aim was "to draw world attention to the Arab question in order to create an atmosphere conducive to the implementation of U.N. Security Council Resolution 242 calling for total withdrawal from the occupied Arab territories and the restoration of the legitimate rights of the Palestinian people." The communiqué made reference to a "new direction" in U.S. policy toward the Arab-Israeli conflict. It provided, however, that the decision would be subject to review on 1 June 1974. Algeria expressed the view that the lifting of the embargo was "provisional in nature and limited to the period expiring 1 June 1974." Iraq refused to attend the meeting; Libya and Syria, arguing that the time was not appropriate, refused to assent to the lifting of the embargo or to any increase in overall oil production.

As a result of the 18 March decision, countries importing Arab oil were classified as follows:

1. The "friendly states," which were allowed to import all their actual requirements of Arab oil;
2. The "neutral states," including the United States, which were allowed to import the equivalent of their average imports of Arab oil during the first nine months of 1973 or during the month of September 1973, whichever was greater; and
3. The "embargoed states," the Netherlands, South Africa, Portugal, and Rhodesia, whose supplies of Arab oil were cut off completely.

On 2 June 1974 Algeria unilaterally decided to resume oil shipments to the Netherlands. OAPEC's ninth meeting in Cairo decided not to reimpose the oil embargo against the United States. On 10 July nine Arab oil ministers meeting in Cairo announced the end of the oil embargo against the Netherlands, but its continuation against Portugal, South Africa, and Rhodesia. On 31 December 1974 Libya ended its oil embargo against the United States.

Thus, measures applied by the Arab oil-producing countries in their second major round included nationalization of foreign assets in Iraq, reduction of oil production, discrimination in oil exports, and embargoes of oil shipments to certain countries.

The 1973/1974 Oil Embargo: An Assessment

Objectives of the Embargo

The public announcement by the Arab oil ministers following their meeting in Kuwait on 17 October 1973 was made in two separate communiqués. The first included the resolution to impose the oil embargo; the second elaborated upon the political background and motivations behind that decision (see Appendixes C and D). An analysis of those two statements leads one to identify the objectives of the oil embargo as the following:

First, to express solidarity with the other Arab states engaged militarily with Israel and to play an active role in the achievement of the military and political objectives of the October war, namely, to compel Israel by military force to withdraw from all the territories it occupied during the 1967 June war.

Second, to put pressure on the international community to oblige Israel to (1) relinquish occupied Arab territories, and (2) restore "the legitimate rights of the Palestinian people in accordance with the United Nations resolutions."

Third, to reward "the countries that support the Arabs actively and effectively or that take important measures against Israel to compel its withdrawal." The political communiqué issued along with the resolutions of the conference asserted:

> The conferees are eager that this production cut should not affect any friendly state which has helped or will help the Arabs in a fruitful and effective manner. They will continue to be supplied with the same quantities of oil they used to obtain before the reduction.
>
> The same special treatment will be given to every state which adopts an important measure against Israel to persuade it to end its occupation of the usurped Arab territories.

These measures were aimed to convince "the great industrial states that consume Arab oil to adopt a measure or an action which indicates awareness of its general international commitment" and also to neutralize those states that "have acted in a manner which supports and strengthens aggression."

Fourth, to punish the various consuming countries that support and cooperate "with the Israeli enemy." Here the United States was singled out as "the principal and foremost source of the Israeli power which has resulted in the present Israeli arrogance and enabled the Israelis to continue to occupy our territories."

Fifth, to put pressure on the world community and prompt it to exercise its moral power to influence U.S. policies in the Middle East, which reflected unequivocal support for Israel. The aim was to make "the United States aware of the exorbitant price the great industrial states are paying as a result of its blind and unlimited support for Israel."

The concluding sentence of the communiqué, overlooked by many observers, put forth the bottom-line conditions that needed to be met for the embargo to be lifted. It specified that oil production would resume "when the world shows sympathy toward us and condemns the aggression against us." For the long term, the explicit objectives of the embargo were to force Israel to withdraw from Arab territories occupied in the 1967 war and restore the legitimate rights of the Palestinian people. However, the implicit short-term goal was to muster international support for the cause of the Palestinians, in itself believed to be a huge step toward achieving the longer-term goal of securing total Israeli withdrawal from the occupied Arab territories. This objective was made more explicit in the 8 December 1973 meeting of the Arab oil ministers during which it was made clear that the relaxation of the oil cutback measures was predicated on "an agreement on a timetable for a withdrawal." A statement issued at the time (see Appendix G) asserted that "if agreement is reached on withdrawal from all the territories occupied since 1967, foremost amongst them Jerusalem, in accordance with a timetable which Israel agrees to and whose implementation is guaranteed by the United States, the embargo on exports to the United States will be lifted as soon as the withdrawal program begins."

Here it is important to note a shift in the use of the embargo. At this stage, the Arab oil producers were enjoying the benefits of higher prices and lower production output,[43] and so their decision to continue the employment of the oil weapon was not deterred by economic considerations.

When the embargo ran its course and was finally lifted on 18 March 1974, the official statement issued was short, mild, and general, providing only a minimum description of the reasons behind the rescission and what specifically the cutbacks had achieved. A statement explaining the political reasons for ending the embargo said:

The ministers reevaluated the results of the Arab oil measures in light of its main objective, namely to draw the attention of the world to the Arab cause in order to create the suitable climate for the implementation of Security Council Resolution 242. The ministers took cognizance of . . . the signs which began to appear in various American circles calling (in various degrees) for the need of an evenhanded policy. American official policy assumed a new dimension vis-à-vis the Arab-Israeli conflict. Such a dimension will lead America to assume a position which is more compatible with the principle of what is right and just toward the Arab occupied territories and the legitimate rights of the Palestinian people.

In the background to the lifting of the embargo was the conclusion and partial implementation of agreements dealing with the disengagement of forces on the Egyptian and Syrian fronts. At a time of intense secret diplomacy conducted by Secretary of State Kissinger, one cannot but support the conjecture of many analysts that an agreement was being reached behind closed doors. The editors of the authoritative oil bulletin *Middle East Economic Survey* noted that "it is very possible that certain guarantees or 'best endeavour' promises were confidentially communicated by the U.S. to the Arab states concerned regarding the implementation of UN Resolution 242."[44] In support of this, it is significant to note that Sadat, who was establishing a close rapport with Kissinger, was one of those adamantly insisting that the oil embargo be terminated to give the United States an opportunity to prove the sincerity of its new evenhanded posture in the Middle East. With the exception of Libya and Syria, the Arab oil producers "felt that the United States had shown enough good will in influencing Israel to carry out military disengagement with Egypt" to warrant the lifting of the embargo.[45]

Most analysts of the Arab oil embargo have assessed the success of the oil weapon by evaluating its performance in terms of the ambitious political objectives of (1) compelling the Israelis to withdraw to the 1967 borders, and (2) restoring Palestinian rights. As those stated objectives were not achieved, the oil weapon has been discounted as ineffective.[46] Here it is important to note that these two objectives were the ultimate political goals of the Arab military initiative of 6 October 1973. The oil weapon was unsheathed to complement the Arab war effort, not to replace it. The Arab oil producers meeting in Kuwait were well aware of the real strength of the embargo, and no public statement was made to the effect that employing the oil weapon would by itself force Israel to withdraw from all the territories it occupied in 1967. On the contrary, official Saudi pronouncements throughout the embargo were vaguely worded to provide the Saudi government with flexibility to negotiate.

Embargo Impact on Target Nations

In assessing the impact of the 1973/1974 Arab oil embargo, it is important to note the difficulty of isolating the political dimension from the military and economic ones. It becomes hard to draw the line between what occurred as a direct result of the embargo and what occurred as a result of two major events that took place at the same time: (1) the October war, which preceded the embargo and provided the stimulus for initiating it,[47] and (2) the quadrupling of oil prices, which followed the war and the embargo declaration, and which was influenced by the environment created by both. Consequently, in considering the impact and achievements of the oil weapon, one needs to be aware that there is inevitable overlapping among the political, economic, and military dimensions.

The United States. The Arab oil embargo was one of the important elements influencing U.S. policy formulation and implementation. It brought pressure to bear on the United States to change its Mideast policies and adopt a more evenhanded approach.[48] It succeeded in changing U.S. priorities in foreign policy.[49] Prior to the embargo, U.S. policy in the Middle East focused on the maintenance of the status quo. It favored a cautious, slow approach to finding a comprehensive political settlement for the Arab-Israeli conflict. U.S. staunch support of Israel had caused a decline in U.S. credibility in the Arab world, particularly among Arab moderates. Following the embargo, the United States took the initiative to speed up the process of reaching a peace settlement[50] and made serious attempts to appear evenhanded.

Mixing Arab politics with oil economics caused the United States serious concern over access to oil, the stability of oil prices, and the security of oil sources. An agreement reached between the United States and Saudi Arabia in early April 1974 to strengthen economic, technological, and military cooperation underlined these concerns and the change in priorities. The threat of U.S. military intervention to secure the safety of the region or to seize oil installations in the case of oil-supply interruption was being considered seriously and discussed publicly for the first time.[51] The specter of another embargo stimulated U.S. efforts to keep the negotiation process going,[52] culminating in the 1979 Camp David agreement.[53]

Domestically, the Arab oil embargo evoked strong negative reaction in the United States. Its impact was blown out of proportion, mainly by the oil companies and the media. For years there had been widespread agitation in the United States by all industrial and manufacturing sectors to eliminate or drastically revise environmental control laws. The oil industry was persistent in its demands for the relaxation of laws and regulations governing oil and gas exploration and development, the building of pipelines, and the construction of refineries and deep-water terminals. In exaggerating the effect of the embargo, the oil companies took it as a pretext to raise oil prices, to force legislation removing environmental controls, to obtain greater tax benefits, and to create panic buying. They wanted to expand their shared monopoly to push the last remaining independent refiners and marketers out of the industry. Congressional lobbyists employed by the oil companies managed to persuade the Senate committee investigating the causes of the oil embargo in 1974 to drop its investigation into charges of oil-company profiteering. It was curious that at a time when there was supposedly an energy crisis, and when the United States lay under an Arab oil boycott, the profits of the U.S. oil companies reached unprecedented heights.

The companies hastily attempted to justify the huge profits.[54] In advertisements that filled entire pages of the country's largest-circulation newspapers, Texaco, for example, proclaimed in headline type, "Texaco earned $1.3 billion in 1973. Texaco invested $1.6 billion in 1973 to help fill your energy needs."[55] Mobil Oil advertised, "We just spent three months' profit in one morning," and "Are Profits Big? Right. Big Enough? Wrong."[56] The introduction to Standard Oil of Indiana's annual report stated: "In total, our 1974 capital and exploration budget will exceed $1.4 billion—more than $300 million above the 1973 level, and equivalent to nearly three times 1973 net earnings." At Exxon's annual stockholders' meeting, Chairman J. Kenneth Jamieson was reported to have reiterated the concept that "the industry and Exxon needed increasingly higher profits to finance the tremendous exploration and development needed to provide sufficient energy in the future."[57] Texaco and Gulf sent letters to all their stockholders claiming that increased taxes on the industry would impair their ability to provide future supplies. The Texaco letter stated:

> The tax reform proposals single out the petroleum industry for discriminatory and punitive taxes that would siphon off billions of dollars from the industry over the next five years. This is patently ill-considered legislation, since every dollar drained from this industry in the form of higher taxes is one less dollar that will be available to help achieve the goal of increased energy supplies.[58]

The Gulf letter warned:

> The ability of the oil and gas industry to generate capital and provide the nation with urgently needed energy supplies may soon be drastically impaired. The industry is, in fact, faced with the serious threat of restrictive

tax legislation. Congress is now considering tax legislation which, if enacted, would severely impair the industry's ability to develop energy resources and provide adequate supplies of fuel.[59]

Western Europe and Japan. The embargo led to dissension both among the Western European nations themselves and between them and the United States. Concern over long-term access to Arab oil and differences over what role to play in the search for a Middle Eastern political settlement resulted in mounting tensions between the traditional allies.[60] According to Leonard Silk of the *New York Times,* the embargo had "given the NATO alliance its most severe internal shock since France withdrew from military integration in 1966."[61] The Europeans blamed the United States "for trying to bully them into backing the American position on Israel, for not consulting with them, for giving them virtually no warning before putting American bombers and other forces on world-wide alert and for expecting them to risk a cut-off of their oil from the Middle East and North Africa on which Europe depends for more than 80 percent of its supply."[62] In turn the United States criticized the other members of NATO "for acting like a collection of small countries trying to hide in the woodwork, for not looking beyond this moment's or this winter's problems, for putting oil above principle, and for refusing to work with the United States to draw up a common policy toward the war—and the strategic threat of the Soviet bloc."[63] However, the Europeans were afraid throughout the embargo of the specter of recession, of unemployment, and of increasing hardships should the cuts continue.

Prior to the embargo Western Europe took the attitude of not interfering in U.S. Middle East peace initiatives. The embargo, however, led to a new sense of urgency in finding an acceptable resolution to the Palestine problem.

Throughout the period of the embargo, from 17 October 1973 to 18 March 1974, certain characteristics distinguished the relations among industrial nations, particularly Western Europe and Japan. Most pronounced among these were the self-centered approaches of the individual nations to ensure their supplies.[64] Long-term, bilateral agreements were signed between individual consumer and producer nations, such as those between Britain and Iran and between France and Saudi Arabia. However, such efforts did not negate Western attempts to unify their energy problem. Such policy was made through international initiatives such as the International Energy Agency and the Conference on International Economic Cooperation.

In their conferences and meetings, the individualistic concerns of the industrial nations frequently surfaced. The joint statement of the foreign ministers' meeting of the European Economic Community, held on 6

November 1973, called upon Israel and Egypt to return to the ceasefire lines of 22 October, i.e., before Israel had crossed the Suez Canal and encircled the Third Egyptian Corps. It declared that any peace settlement must take into account the legitimate rights of the Palestinians. However, this meeting failed to act on a Dutch request for the pooling of EEC oil resources should the Netherlands run out of oil as a result of the embargo. Fearing that such a policy might jeopardize their assured Arab oil supplies, Britian and France "vigorously opposed the joint oil pool."[65] On 22 November 1973, thirty-five days after the oil embargo was announced, Japan abandoned its neutral policy and adopted a policy closer to Arab views. The Japanese had only fifty-nine days of oil stockpiled, including the supplies aboard tankers en route. Caught by surprise, the country was not prepared psychologically and physically to face the crisis.[66] In recognition of these stands, the Arab producers exempted the EEC (with the exception of the Netherlands) and Japan from an additional 5 percent cut that was due on 1 December 1973.

In international conferences, the European community was often divided by French insistence that European countries negotiate individually with the oil-producing nations, and by the desire of the other eight EEC members to cooperate with the United States in talks between consumer and producer nations. On 9 January 1974, President Nixon called upon eight oil-consuming nations—Britain, Canada, France, Italy, Japan, the Netherlands, Norway, and West Germany—to meet in Washington on 11 February 1974 to discuss world energy problems. Nixon's move opposed an earlier French proposal, reported on 12 December 1973, for a summit meeting with broader scope between the European Economic Community and the Arab producer nations to discuss financial, technological, and energy relationships. Nevertheless, the U.S. position prevailed.

On 11 February 1974 the foreign ministers and finance ministers of Belgium, Britain, Canada, Denmark, France, West Germany, Ireland, Italy, Japan, Luxemburg, the Netherlands, and the United States conferred in Washington for two days. Following their deliberations, the participants issued a seventeen-point joint proposal. Key provisions included the following:

> 7. [The foreign ministers] affirmed that, in the pursuit of national policies, whether in trade, monetary or energy fields, efforts should be made to harmonize the interests of each country on the one hand and the maintenance of the world economic system on the other. Concerted international cooperation between all the countries concerned, including oil producing countries, could help to accelerate an improvement in the supply and demand situation, ameliorate the adverse economic conse-

quences of the existing situation and lay the groundwork for a more equitable and stable international energy relationship.

9. They concurred in the need for a comprehensive action program to deal with all facets of the world energy situation by cooperative measures. In so doing they will build on the work of the OECD. They recognized that they may wish to invite, as appropriate, other countries to join them in these efforts. Such an action program of international cooperation would include, as appropriate, the sharing of means and efforts, while concerting national policies, in such areas as:

The conservation of energy and restraint of demand.
A system of allocating oil supplies in times of emergency and severe shortages.
The acceleration of development of additional energy sources so as to diversify energy supplies.
The acceleration of energy research and development programs through international cooperative efforts.

11. Further, they have agreed to accelerate wherever practicable their own national programs of new energy sources and technology which will help the overall worldwide supply and demand situation.

12. They agreed to examine in detail the role of international oil companies.

17. They agreed that the preparations for such meetings of consumer countries should involve consultations with developing countries and other consumer and producer countries.

France opposed the proposals, calling for (1) "a comprehensive action program to deal with all facets of the world energy situation"; (2) establishment of a coordinating group to prepare for a consumer-producer conference; (3) formation of a coordinating group to integrate the actions of such a group; and (4) adoption of financial and monetary measures to avoid "competitive depreciation and the escalation of restrictions on trade and payments or disruptive actions in external borrowing."[67]

After the embargo was lifted the Europeans were left with the possibility of a future embargo. To avert the danger, they initiated an Arab-European dialogue, which aimed to create a cooperative relationship between Europe and the Arab world. Europe hoped to gain from this cooperation stable supplies of oil at reasonable prices, while the Arabs hoped to receive technological assistance as well as political support. (This dialogue later led to the European initiative that came close, in the Venice Declaration of 13 June 1980, to formal recognition of the Palestine Liberation Organization.)

The Washington energy conference established a twelve-nation Energy Coordination Group (ECG), which, during a meeting in Brussels on 8–9 July 1974, agreed in principle to pool member nations' oil resources in the event of a future energy crisis. According to the proposed plan, ECG members were to maintain large oil stocks and to reduce demand in times of emergency.

The two years following the embargo, 1974 and 1975, witnessed a decided tilt in Western Europe toward the Arab position. This shift in policy became most evident during the 1974 UN special debate on the Palestinian question. "Almost without exception, the Europeans agreed with the decision to hold the debate and to allow the PLO leader, Yassir Arafat, to address the General Assembly. Similarly, the majority went against Israel's wishes and spoke out for creation of a Palestinian state."[68]

For quite some time, relations between Israel and Western Europe deteriorated. In mid-March 1975 the *International Herald Tribune* observed:

Some European leaders began to show a genuine and growing concern for the plight of the Palestinian refugees. They began to question whether support for Israel was in accord with their own national interests. What all this meant became evident when the October war led to the Arab oil embargo and the world energy crisis.

Spurred by visions of a Europe without gasoline for automobiles and homes without heat, they hastily adopted what is known in Common Market circles as the "oil-in-our-time" resolution. Officials privately conceded that it was an unabashed attempt to appease Arab opinion by calling on Israel to meet almost every Arab demand short of giving up its own existence.

Since then relations between Israel and Western Europe have appeared to be plunging towards their lowest point. European governments, either individually or collectively through the Common Market, have scolded Israel for intransigence in dealing with the Arabs and they have paid increasing attention to calls for recognition of the Palestine Liberation Organization and creation of an independent Palestinian state on the Israeli-occupied West Bank of the Jordan.

Those who are members of the North Atlantic Treaty Organization have resisted efforts by the United States to encourage military support for Israel within NATO. In fact, some NATO members such as France and Britain are selling arms and material to the Arab countries.

Almost every week brings some sign of European-Israeli tensions. Within the last month, several countries, notably France and Britian, were accused of acquiescing in Arab efforts to discriminate against Jewish banks and businesses.[69]

Britain, essentially regarded as a close friend of Israel, felt after the embargo that it "must maintain a low profile because of its present need for Arab oil."[70] Even before the oil embargo French-Israeli relations were strained and difficult; afterward they became worse. West Germany, which before the embargo prided itself on having a "special relation" with Israel, moved further away from Israel than any other country. Germany's dependence on Middle Eastern oil "caused it to play down its sentiments and make certain obeisances to the Arabs,"[71] and to pursue a policy of Middle Eastern neutrality. Before the embargo the Dutch government was the staunchest friend of Israel within the European Common Market, and the Netherlands was punished for this when the OAPEC meeting singled it out as the chief target of the oil embargo. "Since then the Dutch have been more circumspect and have gone along with the various Common Market declarations and policies disliked by Israel."[72]

The Third World. Oil-importing Third World states, though not targets of the embargo, were hit hard by the increasing cost of oil. Arab diplomacy focused on generating support of Arab causes, particularly in Africa, where support of Israel had been traditionally strong.[73] The African mood was expressed by Senegal's President Léopold Sédar Senghor, who said, "The Arabs have numbers, space, and oil . . . they outweigh Israel."[74] Commenting on African attitudes, Merie Sirkin wrote: "The biggest immediate factor that [the Africans] would face is a complete cutoff of their petroleum if they did not take immediate action to isolate Israel and express their solidarity with the Arab cause. There was no subtlety in the Arab threat. It was clearly and openly expressed not only to the Africans but to everyone else."[75]

For their political support, Third World countries, and in particular the African governments, were hoping that the major Arab oil producers would give them preferential treatment in terms of oil supplies and prices and invest petrodollars in their economies. A. Akinsanya noted: "Thus, when OAPEC decided to use Arab oil as a weapon to alter some major powers' policies toward Israel, African states hoped they would be spared the adverse effects of the oil embargo."[76] However, as the Africans failed to receive their anticipated economic aid for the political support given to the Arabs,[77] there was some disenchantment within a number of African states. The threat of an oil embargo had caused the political shift in support from Israel to the Arab nations, but it was the petrodollars that, utilized properly, could have maintained the continuity and endurance of such policies.[78]

Embargo Performance in General

Seen in the light of the years that have elapsed since its employment, the Arab oil embargo achieved the following:

1. The 1973 Arab oil embargo reaffirmed the "special relationship" between Saudi Arabia and the United States. The Saudis still put their trust in the United States to achieve a peace settlement in the Middle East. For King Faisal, "American leverage on Israel is the best safeguard against another Middle East war and a potentially more bitter confrontation with the West. To be drawn into that vortex again would expose his regime to unpredictable hazards and permit a further advance of Soviet influence in the Middle East."[79] On its part, the United States still hoped that Saudi Arabia, the biggest oil exporter in the world with one of the largest financial reserves and with growing world influence, "will cooperate with the West to solve the related problems of security of oil supplies, the size of the bill, and how the consumers can pay."[80]

2. The Arab oil embargo brought the Palestinian issue persistently to the fore, causing world public opinion to favor finding a permanent solution to the Palestine problem. This shift, which depressed Israel's morale and weakened its bargaining power, was most notably exemplified in the United Nations in 1974 when the PLO was invited to participate in the deliberations of the General Assembly on the question of Palestine. A resolution to invite the PLO to address the General Assembly carried by 105 votes in favor, 4 opposed, and 20 abstaining. PLO Chairman Yasser Arafat subsequently addressed the assembly, and the PLO was later granted observer status by a vote of 95 nations in favor, 17 opposed, and 19 abstaining. In its Resolution No. 3236 adopted on 22 November 1974, the General Assembly fully recognized the inalienable rights of the Palestinian people to self-determination, national independence, and sovereignty.

3. The embargo and the hike in oil prices that followed led to the emergence of new power centers in international affairs. Oil-exporting countries, either individually or through OPEC, began to play a more prominent role in politics. Most affected was Saudi Arabia, whose role in Arab and Muslim affairs suddenly expanded as it became a major financier of development projects in the Third World and of military assistance to Syria and Egypt. The Saudis used this newly found power to restrain the radical tendencies in the Arab world and emphasize the moderate ones. It exerted great effort to seek a comprehensive settlement of the Arab-Israeli conflict based on a modified version of UN Resolution No. 242. This policy climaxed in Fahd's eight-point peace plan, known as the Saudi Initiative of November 1980, in which the Saudi government implied its willingness to recognize Israel in return for Israeli withdrawal from the 1967 occupied Arab territories, including the Arab section of Jerusalem.

4. The Arab oil embargo and the environment that followed the October war forced Israel into diplomatic isolation. Growing Arab

affluence resulted in impressive diplomatic gains, for example, the rupture of diplomatic relations between a number of African and Asian states and Israel, and the recognition of the PLO. It led many nations to improve political, economic, and diplomatic ties with the Arab world in order to assure continuous access to oil or to obtain preferential trade or investment agreements with the Arab oil producers. Many nations, among them Western Europe nations[81] and Japan,[82] began to express interest in the plight of the Palestinian refugees and concern for their well-being. Some of them began to question whether support for Israel's militarily aggressive policies was in their own national interests.

5. The embargo served to give the Arabs greater control over their own natural resources, increasing their political and economic strength.[83] It advanced Arab independence in pursuing oil policies and demonstrated the Arabs' ability to act as a unified entity in international affairs.[84] At the same time, it undermined Western oil interests in the Middle East because it encouraged nationalization of Western oil properties without fear of repercussions or boycotts for the oil produced in nationalized fields. It led to curtailment of the traditional domination of the oil trade by the integrated international oil companies known as the "seven sisters" by the new power of the oil-exporting countries who now controlled both the volume of production and the price of crude oil.

6. The embargo caused an increased awareness among industrial nations of the scarcity of natural resources. It brought home the fact that the world is on the threshold of a scarcity of low-cost oil at a time of growing world demand.

7. It fueled interest in production, leading to substantial growth in the search for secure sources of oil, spurring oil exploration efforts in high production cost areas, and decreasing the oil companies' interest in the low production cost of Third World oil. It increased the industry's perception of the risks involved in the production of oil in non-OPEC countries. It led to more coal, tar sand, and oil-shale–derived liquid fuels, along with more dependence on nuclear and solar energy to reduce energy vulnerability. The embargo also stimulated energy conservation, which helped reduce long-term world oil demand. It led to widespread efforts to educate the public in consuming nations on the need to conserve energy.

8. Arab production cutbacks increased U.S. and Soviet home oil production, accelerating the exhaustion of domestic resources and decreasing reserves. In a world of increasing scarcity, depleting domestic reserves could threaten the national security of the nations concerned. This possibility helped to alter the strategic panorama, making both superpowers attach greater strategic importance to the Middle East and increasing the likelihood of nuclear confrontation in the rivalry to increase

influence in the region. While the United States stepped up its military presence to meet what it considered to be a growing Soviet threat in the Gulf, the Soviet Union increased its arms shipments to Iraq, which flew MIG-23 fighter-bombers over Iran and the Gulf states.[85] The potential for confrontation was heavily underlined.

9. The oil embargo shattered the illusion that rich trading countries such as the major Western European states and Japan had unlimited economic power. As Klaus Knorr observed: "It was a number of militarily weak oil-producing states that displayed economic coercive power and demonstrated that the wealthy industrial countries are extremely vulnerable. There was nothing in their wealth that would have permitted them to mount an effective counter-threat against the Arab oil-exporting states."[86] Thus the embargo exposed the limitations of military or economic retaliation against the Arab producers because military intervention could be undermined by sabotage of the oilfields or the threat of invoking Soviet military power, with an attendant risk of nuclear confrontation. Sabotage would place the consuming nations in a much worse energy crisis than before, as production from destroyed wells could be restored only after two to three years. The impracticality of attempting to use a food embargo in response to the oil embargo was revealed in hearings before the House Foreign Affairs Committee on 21 November 1973.

10. In addition to its political repercussions, the oil embargo made itself strongly felt economically. The greatest impact was caused not so much by the oil cutback itself as by the environment it created, which made it possible for all oil producers to quadruple their prices. In less than one year's time oil prices rose from an average $2.50 a barrel (before October 1973) to over $10.00 a barrel by late April 1974, when the embargo was lifted. Among other things, the price hikes fueled inflation, created or exaggerated balance-of-payments deficits, and resulted in a flow of dollars from consuming to producing countries. This in itself had a great effect on the world monetary system and international trade in general, as well as on the financial and psychological status of the various international trading partners.[87] The embargo seriously disrupted Western economies, revealing their economic and political vulnerability. As the analyst Szyliowicz asserted:

The production cutbacks and the embargo of October dramatically highlighted the vulnerability of the industrialized nations of the West and commanded the most immediate attention, but, as the weeks passed and the flow of oil was resumed, the price dimension came increasingly into prominence as economists warned of the consequences of the transfer of wealth to the oil-producing states.[88]

The sharp increases in prices and the enormous windfall earnings made non-Arabs reluctant to undercut prices, and at the same time caused the Arabs no serious loss of income despite lower production.

A final assessment of the embargo leads one to become aware of its different effects on different countries. Some, like the United States, were inconvenienced; others, like Europe and Japan, were alarmed; non–oil-producing Third World nations were hurt;[89] and the Soviet Union benefited. The irony is that the embargo was most effective against Europe, Japan, and the Third World, which had no power and were in no position to solve the Mideast problem directly. In general, one cannot but observe the impressive economic and political impact of the oil weapon, which led Professor Harmut Brosche to describe it as "one of the most successful weapons introduced into world politics during the last years."[90]

Analyzing the impact of the Arab oil weapon, the Egyptian journalist Salah Muntasser pointed out in *al-Ahram* of 23 October 1974 ten fundamental changes that define new conditions affecting any future oil embargo. Muntasser's analysis is realistic and merits quotation *in extenso* as an appropriate way of concluding this discussion:

1. Gone forever are the long-standing fears of employing Arab petroleum for the cause of Arab rights. The basis of these fears was the impression that the world would turn against the Arab nation should it employ its petroleum to serve its cause. But what really happened is that the world (even America) had taken steps of cooperation to solve the Mideast problem more than it showed the feeling of enmity and hatred.

2. That "ownership" is one thing, but "domination" is another. The petroleum crisis had demonstrated that the world respects the "dominator" more than it does the "owner."

3. The Arab decisions to cut production and stop exports to the United States are what paved the way in front of all the producing nations to increase prices and in the sizeable form the increases took.

4. The oil decisions laid bare the true relationships and understandings among the big Western nations, between the United States and Europe, among the European states themselves within the Common Market, and among America, Europe, and Japan. Below the crust that covered these relationships appeared divisions and signs of deterioration and separation among these nations, in spite of all the alliances and interests that bind them together.

5. The first petroleum war caused changes that showed the absence of any relationship between producing and consuming nations.

6. As a consequence of the Arab oil war, the producing countries had taken actions that used to be thought of as cardinal sins which excited fear and terror.

To speak of "nationalization" was considered blasphemy, yet in Iraq, Algeria, and Libya nationalization decisions were issued against huge corporations which seemed like states and empires.

Before the October War under the principles of participation, the height of success for the Arab countries was to participate in the ownership of 25 percent of the operating companies on their territories. That percentage was to increase to 51 percent in 1983. Today the host countries own 60 percent of all the companies which are not totally nationalized. In Saudi Arabia, 100 percent ownership of Aramco is under consideration. Should this happen, the same situation will be transferred to the other host countries.

7. The petroleum war had convinced all the producing countries—and not only the Arabs—that the greatest income lies not in increasing production but in limiting it, and that the anticipated future value of oil is greater than its present value.

8. The increase in oil prices had raised the income of the Arab oil producers from 30 million dollars to 150 million dollars a day, resulting in what has become known as an "Arab surplus of funds."

9. The "prosperity" which found its way to the Arab countries has helped no doubt in ending many problems among those nations.

10. The power of oil—whether on the Arab or international levels— had its source in the unity of nations:

- on the Arab level, within OAPEC, which issued the curtailment and embargo decisions.
- on the international level, inside OPEC, which issued the price increase decisions.

It must be understood that within these two organizations, there will be efforts to dismantle and break these entities, and these are the most dangerous schemes being planned.

Factors Softening the Embargo's Impact

In addition to the mild winter in Europe during the embargo, a number of other factors helped to cushion its impact.

First, throughout the embargo crisis, oil-importing countries attempted to soften the impact by decreasing consumption. In Europe, curbs on private consumption were strictly observed: Gasoline use was reduced through restrictions on Sunday driving; rationing and speed limits were imposed; heating and lighting were forcibly reduced through rationing of fuel deliveries; early closings were required of business establishments and public offices; and reductions were made in street lighting and television transmission times. However, these measures were more a direct response to higher prices than to anticipated shortages. Oil kept flowing to Europe, and the threat of an oil crisis in the short run at least did not seem very serious. At a time when the Saudi oil minister was claiming that not a single drop of oil was being exported to the West, the *New York Times* wrote: "The energy crisis is a dramatic paradox: crude oil flows in huge quantities, but information about it has been cut to a murky trickle."[91] Romano Prodi and Alberto Clo asserted:

> It is difficult to ascertain to what extent governmental policies helped to limit the growth of demand. A certain slowing down in oil consumption had already been apparent in the latter part of 1973. The winter of 1973–74 was also unusually mild in Western Europe. The decrease in consumption may have stemmed partly from the exceptional increase in the price of petroleum products, a result of the increased costs of crude oil and the rise in the level of excise taxes. In any event, there was at no time a real shortage of petroleum on the European market. Consumption simply responded to the increase in prices, thus, incidentally, casting some doubt on the presumed "rigidity" of petroleum demand. Between October 1973 and April 1974 the reserves of oil products in the countries of the European Community never descended below the 80-day equivalent of consumption; and in Italy the reserves in fact increased by 23 percent.[92]

Second, production increases by non-Arab nations such as Iran, Nigeria, and Indonesia helped to some extent to offset the Arab oil cutbacks. Increased sales from Iraq and the Soviet Union also undermined the effectiveness of the oil embargo. Oil producers not participating in the embargo took advantage of rising prices by increasing sales to the West. The Soviet Union rerouted some of its Western European oil deliveries "in order to benefit from higher prices in particular markets," and "resold Arab oil to West European states, realizing a handsome profit."[93] Nevertheless, "the commanding position of Arab producers in the world market—60 percent, or 20 million barrels a day from Arab sources before the October War"[94]—made full substitution from non-Arab sources for the nearly 5 million barrels a day that were cut back nearly impossible.

Third, the distribution policies of the multinational oil companies helped to meet the oil demands of countries under the embargo, though at higher prices for consumers. For instance, the oil companies quietly diverted non-Arab oil to the Netherlands[95] and the United States, the main targets of the embargo. In addition, responsibility for the allocation of oil among consuming nations fell mainly upon the international oil companies, which allocated resources largely in accordance with the economic forces of the market. The policy of price discrimination that the oil companies followed allowed countries such as the Netherlands, West Germany, and the United States to receive oil, while other countries such as Italy and Belgium, which did not increase the prices of refined products, were left without deliveries.

Fourth, lack of a unified Arab embargo policy hindered implementation of the embargo and reduced its effectiveness. Three facts make this readily apparent:

1. Not all Arab producers implemented the production cutback agreed to in OAPEC meetings. From the start, Iraq, which was having problems marketing its oil, found this a golden opportunity to expand oil production and thus generate much-needed new income.[96] The Iraqis claimed that fighting beside Syria on the Golan Heights had caused their financial reserves to drop. To defend his country's position, Vice-President Saddam Hussein in December 1973 denounced the cutbacks as having been devised by "reactionary ruling circles well-known for their links with America." He argued that such a cutback "generally harmed other countries more than America" and "led to results which run counter to its stated purpose." It is a "serious political mistake," he warned, to implement policies that tend to hurt allies and potential allies (Europe and Japan) more than avowed enemies. The Algerian criticism that the effectiveness of the embargo depended on the tightness of oil supplies in general failed to convince the Iraqis to change their oil policy and join the other OAPEC members. But in view of its small production, compared to the overall cutback of Arab production, Iraq's refusal to join the embargo was of limited practical importance.

2. No serious attempt was made by Arab producers to control the destinations of the oil tankers carrying oil exports to Europe and the United States. As a result, the embargo could not be effectively applied. Haykal, wrote in his book *The Road to Ramadan* (1975):

> In fact the embargo had little effect, apart from a psychological one, on the countries it was aimed at. I remember asking Sheikh Yamani, the Saudi Oil Minister, how the embargo worked. He said that every tanker captain was required to give a pledge that he would not discharge his cargo in any of the embargoed countries—that was all. "But what else can we do?" he asked. Naturally some captains gave the pledge and broke it, while others discharged their oil at, say, London, whence it was transferred in another tanker to Rotterdam. They also adjusted supplies so that the embargoed countries got their oil from producing countries where the embargo was not being applied, like Nigeria. This may have been a little more expensive but did not worry the oil companies which, as usual, passed on the extra cost to the consumers.[97]

This attitude could be attributed to two factors: (1) reluctance to lead the oil crisis into a head-on collision with the industrial nations, and

(2) the high cost of the war effort resulted in a cash-flow shortage at a time when hard currency was badly needed to pay the Soviet Union for armaments and to provide aid and arms for Egypt, Syria, and Jordan.

3. As in the 1967 situation, the tendency of the conservative Arab oil producers was to use the oil weapon both as an instrument to apply pressure on Western nations, and as a safety valve to release domestic pressure in their own countries and the Arab world. The prevailing militant mood in the debate over implementation of the oil weapon was sparked by military initiatives by Egypt and Syria against Israeli occupation forces. However, as the fighting continued, more pressure was exerted by Arab public opinion on the oil producers to throw their oil weapon into the battle. Most of that pressure was exerted on Saudi Arabia's King Faisal, whose stand determined not only Saudi oil policies but also those of the oil-rich Gulf emirates. As a result, Faisal acted not so much to hurt the West as to maintain primacy among the Arabs.[98] In late October 1973 Saudi Oil Minister Yamani told a visiting delegation of U.S. congressmen that "King Faisal has done his best in the last two weeks to represent American interests. We did not want the embargo. We hope that we can do something, but there must be something that we can show as change."[99]

In retrospect, Arab oil continued to flow to all the nations placed under the embargo.[100] In fact, Saudi oil continued to arrive in the United States throughout the period of the embargo, albeit at a sharply reduced rate. The figures on crude-oil imports for the embargo period published by the U.S. Commerce Department on 9 April 1974 affirmed this fact.[101] This was the first official confirmation of the Arab oil leak since November 1973 when the U.S. Federal Energy Office declared a moratorium on announcing the statistics. (This was because the department did not wish to jeopardize the continuation of shipments by disclosing the origin of supplies.) These figures indicated that leading Arab oil producers "leaked" oil to the United States in spite of their embargo on deliveries. The figures showed that Saudi Arabia shipped 257,187 barrels of oil to the United States in January 1974, and a further 552,212 barrels in February. Tunisia continued to ship small amounts of oil to the United States throughout the embargo and shipments continued to arrive from Kuwait, the United Arab Emirates, and Algeria during November and December 1973. Subsequent denials by the oil companies and the producing nations, as well as by William Simon, the Federal Energy Office administrator, failed to undermine or cast doubts on these figures, which proved beyond doubt that the oil embargo was breached.

Though the figures are not specific, the *Wall Street Journal* thought it was fair to presume that most of the oil imported from Europe during the period of the embargo was Arab oil.[102] Moreover, Saudi Arabia increased its production during the few months before the embargo so that when curtailments occurred during the embargo their impact was softened. Christopher Rand, a Middle East business specialist, asserted: "King Faisal of Saudi Arabia had already upped Aramco's production by a million barrels a day during the hot months of July and August, thus allowing him to reduce production when the war began and still retain normal supply levels for the year."[103]

John Lichtblau, head of the U.S. Oil Institute's research department, said in published reports on 19 September that only 6.4 percent of U.S. oil consumption in the first months of 1973 was derived from Arab sources. Lichtblau said that rather than freezing exports to the United States, the Arab suppliers increased their volume 63 percent by September as compared with the same period in 1972.[104]

Soviet Reaction

During the 1956 Suez crisis and the 1967 and 1973/1974 Arab oil embargoes, the Soviet Union consistently encouraged the Arabs to use oil as a political weapon against Western nations.[105] The Soviets hoped to exploit the oil embargo for political purposes—to drive a wedge between the Arabs and the West and to isolate the United States from its allies; economically, the Soviets also hoped to benefit from the oil cutbacks. Rather than holding its exports to normal levels, "the Soviet Union has consistently taken advantage of Arab embargoes by furthering its oil export drive."[106] As early as 9 February 1973 Moscow's radio station Peace and Progress announced in English to Africa:

> The Arab countries are studying the possibility of joint steps to resort to economic sanctions against states that support the Israeli aggressive course. United States dependence on oil is growing on a colossal scale. More and more voices are being heard in Arab capitals demanding that Arab oil be used as an active weapon in the struggle against the forces of imperialism that have turned Israel into a country which is their agent in the Middle East.[107]

On 30 August 1973, more than a month before the embargo, Radio Moscow aired a program in Arabic called "Arab Oil in the Service of the Arab Peoples' Interests," in which it was said that "large sections of Arab public opinion are calling for the use of all economic resources of the Arab countries in the struggle for the removal of imperialist aggression."[108]

Prior to the 1973 oil embargo, an article in the pro-Soviet journal *New Times* claimed that the Arabs' use of the oil weapon could bring about "a more constructive approach" to the Mideast peace process (pressuring Israel to withdraw from occupied territories) on the part of Western European states.[109] In its news and commentaries during the October war, the Soviet Union tended to support the use of Arab oil as a political weapon against the United States. In its Arabic broadcasts to the Middle East, Radio Moscow on 17 October 1973 linked U.S. military aid to Israel to the oil question, saying that U.S. aid had angered the Arabs, who were forced to use "all means available" in their struggle. One day later this service said the United States had shrugged off Arab warnings of an oil boycott and if the Arabs used "all means" at their disposal, including oil, they would be successful more quickly in achieving their aims.[110] On 21 October commentator Boris Rachkov in *Moskovskaya Pravda* described the Arabs' use of the oil weapon as "justifiable."[111] On 28 November 1973 *Pravda*'s correspondent Viktor Kudryatsev reported from Cairo: "The Arab countries are using oil effectively as a political weapon."[112]

Throughout the embargo, the Soviet media endorsed the oil weapon and reported all Arab oil actions and decisions. When the embargo was finally lifted in March 1974, the Soviets favored its continuation. Soviet policy regarding the use of the Arab oil weapon reflected the paradox of the USSR's commitment to support national liberation movements in the Third World while at the same time pursuing a policy of détente and peaceful coexistence with the West.

Chinese Reaction

China plays a peripheral role in Middle East oil politics.[113] However, it supported the use of oil as a political weapon, which it maintained had dealt a "heavy political and economic blow" to imperialism.[114] In a communiqué published on 27 December 1974, the official Chinese news agency Xinhua claimed that between 1948 and 1972 over 10,000 million tons of oil were shipped off "by foreign monopolies," while they "squeezed" profits of $40,000 million. This amount, the Chinese agency reported, was four times as much as the United States' total oil investment in the Third World and Arab countries. The might of the oil weapon, Xinhua suggested, had shattered the oppressive gloom of the "no peace, no war" situation in the Middle East, which had been created by the imperialists. The Third World learned, as a result of Arab action, the real value of raw materials and how they could be used in the "struggle" with the imperialists, the communiqué suggested. China accused the Soviet Union of having given public and official support to the Arab oil embargo while at the same time supplying crude oil at gigantic profits to the United States and demanding cash for costly weapons from the Arab states. This communiqué reflected the Chinese position, which viewed the embargo as strengthening the resolve of Third World nations to use their natural resources as political weapons.

The Threat of Military Intervention

One radical reaction to the oil embargo was the U.S. threat to use force to ensure the continuous flow of oil. In an interview with *Business Week* in the first week of January 1975, Secretary of State Kissinger cryptically announced, "I am not saying that there's no circumstance where we would not use force."[115] He added that the White House would be prepared to go to war in the Middle East "only in the gravest emergency." One of his aides commented: "He could have brushed questions about military force aside, as he has done before. But he probably wants to let the possibility hang there in front of the oil producers as a kind of inducement for not pushing prices any higher, and maybe bringing them down."[116] Secretary Kissinger's hypothesis that force might have to be used to counter what he termed economic "strangulation" was based on four assumptions:

1. that another Arab oil embargo similar to the one imposed in 1973 would essentially "strangle," (i.e., destroy) the industrial economies of the world, including that of the U.S.;
2. that nation-states have the right to defend themselves against the threat of such strangulation;
3. that force against the embargo-supporting states will be needed to obtain oil; and
4. that open discussion of such actions is desirable.[117]

A few days later, Kissinger retracted his statement. "I was speaking hypothetically about an extreme situation. . . . We were not talking, as is so loosely said, about the seizure of oil fields. This is not our intention. That is not our policy."[118]

The threat of Western military action to control the supply of oil was also raised by President Gerald Ford in an interview with *Time* magazine on 20 January 1975.

Question. Moving to foreign policy, can you tell us more about the idea of using force in the Middle East and under what circumstances?

President Ford. I stand by the view that Henry Kissinger expressed in the *Business Week* interview. Now, the world "strangulation" is the key word. If you read his answer to a very hypothetical question, he didn't say that force would be used to bring a price change. His language said he wouldn't rule force out if the free world or the industrialized world would be strangled. I would reaffirm my support of that position as he answered that hypothetical question.

Question. What would your definition of "strangle" be?

President Ford. Strangulation, if you translate it into the terms of a human being, means that you are just about on your back.

The same theme was reiterated by President Ford at a news conference held on 21 January 1975.

Although a number of articles appeared in the U.S. press advocating the option of military action against the oil producers in the event of an oil embargo,[119] the idea was received negatively by the American people.[120] Military intervention, said a Washington policymaker, would be considered "only as absolutely a last resort to prevent the collapse of the industrialized world and not just to get the oil price down."[121] Another analyst argued that U.S. military action in the Gulf would be self-defeating, as it would have to be against those same conservative regimes that have been stemming the tide of radicalism in their region for the last two decades. The use of force or the threat of force in the Gulf area, no matter how hypothetical the possibility might be, would surely undermine moderation and promote radicalism—something the United States has been trying to avert for a generation.[122] Moreover, a clinical strike and takeover of the Gulf oil wells "would not guarantee the United States any more oil than it now imports, at lower prices than it now pays, or with faster delivery than it now receives."[123]

On the matter of military intervention, Ian Smart observed:

It is nevertheless a fact that a small number of countries whose military strength, separately or together, is relatively trivial were able to impose a politically motivated embargo on nations much stronger militarily without even having to consider seriously the possibility of a military reaction. The Western countries, against which Arab economic strength was primarily turned, did not seek to transform their own superior military strength into countervailing power.[124]

Smart gave the following reasons to explain this attitude:

There were many reasons for the industrialized oil-importing countries to refrain from using military force in 1973–74: constraints of a nuclear world, fears of creating serious tensions with the Soviet Union and within the West as well, thoughts of long-term damage to relations with all Arab governments, doubts about the effectiveness of military action, and, above all, the intuitive perception that certain new norms of international behaviour had come to prevail.[125]

In his book *Superpower Intervention in the Middle East*, Peter Mangold maintained that U.S. threats to take over the oilfields were taken "seriously" by the Gulf oil producers.[126] However, the former U.S. ambassador to Saudi Arabia (1973–1975) and former director of the U.S. Office of Fuel and Energy, James E. Akins, cast some doubt on this view. Akins wrote:

> We will have to await the release of the pertinent documents before judging whether the United States did intend to invade, but I know from the Arab leaders themselves that they assumed, possibly incorrectly, that the United States was governed by rational men who would never take a step which would surely have such disastrous consequences for the United States and its allies. The Arabs knew, better than those who threatened invasion, the ease with which oil fields could be sabotaged and kept out of production.[127]

There is no doubt that the threat to use force did cause alarm, but more among U.S. allies in the area than U.S. adversaries. Many perceived the imminence of such threats as merely a pretext to extend U.S. hegemony over the Gulf area, particularly in the aftermath of the Vietnam defeat. But in the final analysis, the threat to use force was a political blunder by Secretary of State Kissinger. It indicated serious U.S. concern for the effects of the oil embargo at a time when the U.S. government's policy was to underplay the embargo's impact, treating it as ineffective, impractical, and counterproductive. If that was the case, why should the U.S. secretary of state go so far as to threaten to use military force to end the situation, at the same time risking a major confrontation with the Soviet Union?

7
Conclusions:
Lessons of Oil Leverage

As the echo of the 1973 October war cannons fades into history, the impact of the chain reaction of events that the war set in motion becomes more evident. The military mood in the Arab world precipitated the oil embargo, and the embargo, combined with the unexpected military outcome, gave the Arabs a whole new sense of their power and capacity. A militant, united, and frustrated Arab world, unable to attract international attention or sympathy to its problems, was forced to resort to drastic measures that it otherwise might not have used.

It is obvious that at this point in history oil is the single most important commodity in world trade. As a universal commodity it is unique; it is the only commodity that cannot be forgone or replaced in the short run. Vigorous programs of energy conservation might lessen the oil needs of industrialized nations but would not cancel that need. Oil-energy alternatives are possible, but not probable in the very near future. Until other sources of supply can be found oil will remain, comparatively speaking, one of the least expensive, most practical, and most available sources of energy, and with two-thirds of the world's known reserves, the Arab Middle East will continue to be one of its main suppliers.

Furthermore, a significant feature that dominated the consuming and producing countries' relations will not last forever. In the past, few of the major oil consumers produced enough oil to meet their demands (with the exception of the United States, Britain, and the USSR), while no major producing country had sufficient domestic demand to absorb its output. This formula no longer holds true. Increased Soviet and U.S. oil demand and the increasing tendency of Arab and other producer countries, especially in North Africa, to move toward industrialization are leading to an increasing demand for oil. It is becoming more obvious that imported oil will not be able to make up the difference between domestic supplies and anticipated world industrial demand. In concluding our discussion of the main cases in which oil played a major role in international affairs, the question left to be answered is: What are the lessons to be learned from employing oil as a political weapon, for both the actors who exercised their oil leverage and the targets against whom the weapon was directed?

Lessons for Senders:
Making Oil Leverage Most Effective

New nationalistic governments with radically different economic and political approaches from their predecessors have emerged in a number of the oil-exporting countries. Their say in their national oil industries has increased tremendously, and their share in the profits has been greatly enlarged. Furthermore, they have been more inclined to give higher priority to politics than to economics. Some have exhibited an increased tendency to put their natural resources to political use. Whether these objectives were achieved or not is irrelevant; oil embargo policies are unlikely to be discarded in any future conflict.

The skill and sophistication with which the embargo was used in 1973 as compared to 1967 signify that in the future such a tactic should be considered seriously by potential target countries. Many factors could lead to its employment: some are regional, i.e., related to the Arab-Israeli conflict; others are international, i.e., related to North-South confrontations. The most serious prospect for the application of the oil weapon lies in the Arab-Israeli dispute. Should another war be fought, or should negotiations for a lasting settlement in the area end in a stalemate, the mood and environment created in the Arab world would lead Arab oil-producing states to resort to the oil weapon once again. If this happens, oil power will exert considerable economic leverage. Here the attitude of Saudi Arabia is of central importance: Its political and economic weight determines the flow of events. Saudi restraint will only hold to a certain point. Beyond this point Saudi Arabia cannot but assume the direction of the Arab tide. Internal political stability in Saudi Arabia and the Arab world will therefore play a decisive role.

To rely on Arab internal conflicts and differences to blunt the oil weapon shows political naiveté and a failure to understand both the Arab mentality and Arab norms of behavior. It is a fact that the Arabs are a patchwork of several racial and religious communities with varying stages of social and economic evolution, rigid geographical barriers, sharp political divisions, deep divergences of opinion, no permanent collective will, and scores of linguistic dialects. It is also true that only on a few occasions has recent Arab history recorded harmony and accord. But however much they may be divided among themselves, the

Arabs have an abnormally strong sense of solidarity against the outsider. This tradition, reflected in the Arab proverb "I and my brother against our cousin; I and my cousin against the outsider," appears in many of the political attitudes of the Arabs today. This was particularly true during the 1967 and 1973 Arab-Israeli wars. Those who view the 1967 and 1973 Arab solidarity as the exception rather than the rule, and so assume hopefully that internecine conflicts will diffuse the effect of future oil embargoes, fail to appreciate the extent of the tradition and culture of the people. As much as the Arabs are unstable, they are unpredictable; as much as they are determined, they are emotional. It takes only one issue to bring them closely together and no issue at all to sunder them apart.

Two examples that demonstrate the volatility of Arab attitudes are Saudi-Egyptian relations and Palestinian-Arab relations. Traditionally the Saudis and Egyptians were the nations most in discord in the Arab world—two regimes at opposite political poles. But during the 1967 and 1973 wars, they were the two best allies that a cause can bring together. From ignoring Egyptian calls to use its oil as a political weapon in 1956, to giving lip service in 1967 to the Arab oil embargo, to leading the political battle in 1973 by employing its oil leverage to pressure its Western allies, Saudi Arabia moved a long way. The Egyptians moved no less far: from describing the autocratic Saudi regime as a decadent tool of Western imperialism to embracing it as its loving, brotherly neighbor. The Palestinian-Arab love-hate relationship is somewhat similar. One day, Palestinians in the Arab countries are treated like unwelcome guests; the next, their leaders are given twenty-one gun salutes.

In their 1973 application of oil leverage, the Arab oil producers failed to learn all the lessons that the 1956 and 1967 episodes taught. Looking back at the three episodes together allows us to draw eight conclusions about how oil leverage can be applied most effectively.

1. The oil producers should not leave the planning and organization of an oil embargo until after the oil weapon has actually been deployed. Rather, there ought to be a "think tank" formed at the headquarters of the oil producers' associations (OPEC and OAPEC) that would work out the details of imposing and implementing an embargo once a decision is taken. Here, it is important to compile an energy profile of all possible targets that would include all relevant data, particularly the targets' energy needs and consumption patterns, as well as future energy trends and forecasts. Major foreign sources of supply should also be identified, particularly if they are nonmembers of the oil producers' associations.

2. The oil producers should assign priority to developing their industry and diversifying their economies. Meeting domestic economic and social

demands is essential for diffusing counterleverages. Great efforts should be directed at satisfying internal economic needs.

3. The oil producers should make serious attempts to decrease imports and weaken trade linkages, particularly with consumer nations that might become embargo targets. In this respect, diversification of import sources is essential. A major oil producer such as Saudi Arabia ought not to depend heavily on one major industrial nation such as the United States, which is a likely target of an embargo. If Saudi Arabia could turn to Japan for technology, to Australia and Argentina for foodstuffs, to Switzerland for medical supplies, to France for weapons, to Germany for manufactured goods, and to Europe for an area in which to invest its petrodollars, there would not be much left for the United States to use as a powerful counterleverage in the face of a future Saudi oil embargo, except perhaps the use of force, which in the long term might prove counterproductive. However, it is essential that this diversification of imports be initiated early, and not left until an embargo is imposed.

4. As the oil weapon is most effective when it is collectively rather than unilaterally deployed, cohesion and cooperation among the various oil-producing nations is essential. It needs to be understood that internal conflicts such as the Iranian-Iraqi war are not in the producers' best interest and can only weaken their oil leverage. Here, success depends on the extent to which economic and political linkages among the producers are stronger than those between the senders and the target nations. For example, the chances for success of the 1967 and 1973 embargoes were adversely affected by the close relations between Saudi Arabia and the United States, and the tense relations between Saudi Arabia and Egypt.

5. The coordination between OAPEC and OPEC needs to be intensified. The Arab oil producers need to enlist the support of non-Arab oil producers, so that even if the latter would not join them in using the oil weapon, they would not take advantage of the oil-supply situation during an embargo to increase their own production and move in on the markets of the Arab nations.

6. The oil producers need to assert control over the international allocation system, which is still dominated by the multinational oil companies. During past embargoes, the oil companies allocated the world's supply of crude on the basis of demand, regardless of whether or not the consumer nation was targeted for the embargo. Control of allocations by the senders would eliminate the possibility that oil could reach a country under the embargo by rerouting. At the same time it would not impose hardships on countries classified by the senders as "friendly." In the past, such "friendly" nations have suffered because the oil companies found it more profitable to give priority in allocations

to countries under the embargo who were willing to pay higher prices as part of the cost of defusing the embargo.

7. Protective measures should be taken so that efforts to pressure the target nations do not damage the senders' economies. Consequently, the oil producers need to create an emergency fund at the producers' associations' headquarters to alleviate the financial burdens that an oil embargo may impose on sender countries. The employment of the oil weapon is most effective if it is accompanied by production cuts. Because these production cutbacks may pose an economic and political threat to the senders, some more severe than others, the emergency fund could provide financial assistance during the embargo. The absence of such a fund could lead to fragmentation and leakage.

8. In planning embargo strategy, the producers need to exploit the seasonal factor. An oil embargo imposed at the beginning of winter, when there is a high, inelastic demand on oil for heating, is more effective than an embargo imposed in early summer, when an elastic demand on oil for traveling represents a large share of the market.

In sum, decisionmakers in sender countries need to appreciate that though an embargo is reversible, it is not as easily lifted as imposed. Consequently, before leaving themselves to the dictates of the moment when they may find themselves joining in such actions, it is crucial that the road be paved long before, by planning, outlining, and organizing the mechanisms as well as the philosophy behind the embargo.

Moreover, in their efforts to use oil leverage most effectively, the oil producers need to consider the counterleverage options open to the target nations. The target nations have at least six of these countermeasures available to use in response to the oil weapon.

1. *The Psychological Option.* Once an embargo is contemplated or imposed, senders need to guard against the possibility that targets may launch a media campaign directed at their own citizenry to underplay the impact and effectiveness of the embargo. The aim of such propaganda is to undermine the utility of the oil weapon and to describe such measures as double-edged or counterproductive. As official statements and government data of the target nation are carefully monitored and all relevant statistics indicating that the embargo is having substantial effects on any sector of the economy are usually censored, senders ought not to be discouraged and consider that the effect of their weapon has been blunted merely from lack of tangible evidence that indicates otherwise.

2. *The Political Option.* The target nation may withdraw its political support for the regime of the sender and may attempt to undermine

that regime by giving financial, political, or military support to the government's opposition. This may result in political instability in the sender nation and undermine the power of the regime, posing a serious challenge to its authority.

The sender can guard against this, first, by making the imposition of the oil embargo a national issue that enjoys the support of the masses, and, second, by sharing the decision to impose the embargo with all the major political parties and centers of power in the country.

3. *The Diplomatic Option.* The target nation may raise the ante and close the embassies and consulates of the sender nation, sever diplomatic relations, and expel the senders' diplomats and their families. Senders may retaliate in kind.

4. *The Economic Option.* The target nation may react by imposing its own economic sanctions against the producer, particularly in areas where the other country is most vulnerable. To increase the effectiveness of this leverage, the target nation may attempt to enlist the support of those allies who are convenient alternative sources of supply of relevant commodities. In this case, the senders' defense is to develop their own economies and decrease their dependencies on foreign imports of goods and technology.

5. *The Financial Option.* The target nation may attempt to hold the petrodollar investments of the oil sanctioner "hostage," in order to weaken the senders' economies and deprive them of the hard currency needed to offset the loss of oil revenues that result from a decrease in oil exports. The U.S. freeze of Iranian assets during the 1980 hostage crisis and the British freeze of Argentinian assets during the 1982 Falklands crisis have indicated that industrial nations are ready and willing to use the "freeze weapon" to counter coercive measures directed against them. The senders can guard against this possibility by shifting their investments and bank holdings from financial centers located in highly probable target nations, such as New York, London, Amsterdam, and Paris, to neutral capitals such as Geneva, Zurich, Luxemburg, and Athens.

6. *The Military Option.* The target nation may opt to use force to secure the flow of oil. Consequently, the oil producers ought to work out contingency plans to meet this possibility. It is very naive on the part of the oil sanctioners to assume rational behavior on the part of the target and so discount the possible use of force; in the target's perception this alternative may in fact seem "highly rational" and "most useful." As the objectives of the military option would be to secure the flow of oil by occupying and controlling the oilfields and oil installations without inflicting too much damage on these facilities, it would then be necessary for the oil sanctioners to circumvent this by planning to

inflict maximum damage on the oil facilities once any clear sign of military intervention appears.

Lessons for Potential Targets: Minimizing the Effects of Oil Leverage

The 1973 October war and the subsequent Arab oil embargo led the industrial nations to the formulation of joint positions on a number of major world issues. The developed countries rallied to one another's support. They felt that if the embargo succeeded it would mean the end of consumer prosperity and economic cooperation. The embargo power illustrated the old scenario where trouble brings together conflicting parties in the face of an outside threat. The target industrial nations feared that if one country weakened in the face of the embargo others would follow suit. However, this stand by no means meant that these nations had ultimately decided to end the state of disintegration, internal conflict, and political disarray that has traditionally characterized the Western scene.

As the oil embargo brought the European community closer together, it widened the gap between the United States and its European allies. The November 1973 declaration issued by the foreign ministers of the European Economic Community, supporting the demand for an Israeli withdrawal from occupied Arab territories, was widely interpreted in the United States as a capitulation to the oil leverage. Without doubt, the declaration's immediate context and stimulus was the threat to European oil supplies, but it did not represent any sudden or dramatic change of policy. It was, in fact, the first formal and independent expression of an attitude that has long been in evidence in Western Europe: dissatisfaction with the dangerous instability created by the indefinite Israeli occupation of Arab territories. It is of significance here that, while the Arab-Israeli issue is deeply involved in U.S. domestic policy, to the Europeans the creation of Israel was a symbol of absolution for the persecution of European Jews. Whereas the U.S. government's strong pro-Israeli stance conflicted with its national interests as far as its dealings with the Arab and Third World nations were concerned, it coincided with U.S. public opinion. The European attitude, though not domestically popular, was more balanced and coincided with vital financial and economic considerations.

It is in the national interest of major oil consumers who may eventually find themselves the targets of the oil weapon to guard themselves against such a possibility by seeking to minimize conflict with the producers and having multiple policy options available should those conflicts fail to be resolved. To defend themselves against the oil weapon, potential embargo targets need to heed the following observations:

1. Potential target nations must attend to major political and economic problems that may produce such serious conflicts that oil producers, individually or collectively, would find that using their oil leverage is their optimum policy option. On the political level, the tendency to use oil as a weapon would be greatly decreased if the Middle East were stabilized by completing the process of settlement of the Arab-Israeli conflict that was begun at Camp David in 1979. Strong U.S. support of Israeli policies and Egypt's withdrawal from the Arab "confrontation front" have enabled Israel to consolidate a permanent occupation of the Palestinian West Bank and Gaza, Arab Jerusalem, the Syrian Golan Heights, and the Lebanese south. Continued U.S. acceptance of such Israeli policies only exacerbates the present dilemma, feeding radicalism and making future oil embargoes highly probable. Persistent Israeli belligerence will only continue to create an explosive situation, particularly as the full capacity of the Palestine issue for political destabilization has yet to be experienced. On the economic level, the major issues that have been the focus of the North-South dialogue need to be resolved so as to decrease the possibility of an OPEC-led embargo against the industrial nations.

2. Potential target nations need to adopt energy policies that will make them less vulnerable to drastic supply restrictions. The policy options that have received extensive treatment by other scholars include: conservation, stockpiling, development of alternative energy resources, decreasing import dependency, and diversification of sources of imports.

3. Potential target nations need to resolve the economic and political differences among them on a number of issues and organize themselves in a manner that would make an embargo ineffective.

4. Industrial nations need to increase cooperation and coordination on energy matters within the EEC and the International Energy Agency (IEA) and continue the dialogue between those consumer organizations and both oil producers' organizations.

One main lesson that potential targets can derive from the 1967 and 1973 Arab oil embargoes is that although an oil producer's economy may depend on the commodity it uses as political leverage, in cases where the conflict is perceived as having assumed crisis proportions and where emotional traumas affect masses of people, the sender's need to score political points will outweigh economic considerations. The 1967 and 1973 oil embargoes demonstrate that regardless of the Arab economies' dependence on oil, in cases such as the war with Israel, Arab emotions outweigh all questions of economic gain or loss.

Appendix A
Baghdad Oil Conference, 5 June 1967

In accordance with the invitation of the Government of the Republic of Iraq, the representatives of all the Arab oil producing countries and of those Arab countries participating with them in their conference at Baghdad held on 24 and 25 Safar 1387, corresponding to 4 and 5 June 1967, met and considered the question of the treacherous Israeli aggression against the Arab nation, categorically denounced and condemned this aggression and any support for it in whatever form, and unanimously resolved the following:

First: To cut off the flow of Arab oil and prevent its delivery directly or indirectly to countries which commit or take part in aggression against the sovereignty or territory or territorial waters of any Arab state, with particular reference to the Gulf of Aqaba.

The conference means by aggression which would lead to cutting off the flow of oil the following:

1. Direct armed aggression on the part of any state in support of Israel.

2. Provision of military assistance to the enemy in any form whatsoever.

3. Attempts to secure the passage of commercial vessels through the Gulf of Aqaba under military protection of whatever form.

The Conference recommends the setting up of a permanent committee, composed of the Foreign Ministers of the Arab states, which would be convened within 48 hours of an invitation for it to do so by any Arab state with a view to determining what stands have been adopted such as might be deemed to constitute aggression.

Second:

1. The Conference resolved that the undertaking by any state of armed aggression, directly or indirectly, against the Arab states would subject the funds of companies and nationals belonging to such state in the Arab countries, including the funds invested by the oil companies, to the laws of war.

2. The Conference recommends all the Arab states to convene an emergency meeting to apply the same decision to all other funds invested by companies or nationals of the aggressor states, and warns all foreign oil companies operating in the Arab countries of the consequences of their conveying oil to the Zionist gangs in Occupied Palestine, irrespective of the source of point of origin of this oil, be it directly, indirectly, or through collaboration with other parties; it

also reaffirms the liability of these companies to the application of the provisions of the unified Boycott of Israel Law.

The Conference considers that the signing of any declaration infringing the sovereignty of the Arab states over the Gulf of Aqaba would constitute an act which would justify the prohibition of tankers of the signatory state from carrying Arab oil. A committee composed of the Ministers of Oil in the oil producing countries shall be formed to take the necessary measures (in this connection).

The Conference appeals to all the Islamic States and friendly oil producing states, and particularly Iran, to take all necessary measures to prevent the delivery of oil to the Zionist entity in Occupied Palestine in any form whatsoever.

Appendix B
Decision to Lift Oil Embargo, 1 September 1967

The Conference of Arab Ministers of Finance, Economy and Oil had recommended the possibility of employing the stoppage of the flow of oil as a weapon in the battle. However, after careful study of the matter, the Summit Conference concluded that the oil flow could itself be used as a positive weapon in that Arab oil represents an Arab asset which could be used to strengthen the economies of those Arab states which were directly affected by the aggression, thereby enabling them to stand firm in the battle. The Conference therefore decided to resume oil pumping operations on the grounds that this is an Arab asset which can be put to use in the service of Arab aims and in contributing towards enabling those Arab states which were subjected to aggression and a consequent loss of economic resources to stand firm in their resolve to eliminate the effects of the aggression.

The oil producing states have in fact already made a positive contribution towards enabling the countries affected by the aggression to stand their ground in the face of any economic pressure. The conferees approved the proposal presented by the Kuwait Government for establishing an Arab economic and social development fund, in line with the recommendation of the Conference of Ministers of Finance, Economy and Oil which was held in Baghdad.

Appendix C
OAPEC Ministerial Council Statement on Production Cutbacks, 17 October 1973

The Organization of Arab Petroleum Exporting Countries (OAPEC) Ministerial Council ended its meetings at 2130 today after holding a session at the Kuwait Sheraton Hotel under the chairmanship of Algerian Industry and Energy Minister Belaid Abdessalam. The Council meetings had begun this morning at the OAPEC premises in Kuwait in response to an invitation by the Kuwait Government to "discuss oil matters under the present circumstances." The Ministerial Council issued the following press statement on its meetings:

The Arab oil-exporting countries are contributing to the world's prosperity, welfare and economy by exporting quantities of this valuable natural wealth. Although the production of many of these states has exceeded the limits required by their local economies and the needs of their future generations for energy and sources of income, they have continued to increase their production, sacrificing their own interests for the sake of international cooperation and the interests of the consumers.

It is known that Israel occupied by force vast areas of three Arab states in the June 1967 war, and that it is continuing its occupation unmindful of the UN resolutions and the various appeals for peace from Arab and peace-loving states. Although the world community is committed to implement the UN resolutions and prevent the aggressor from reaping the fruits of his aggression and seizing the lands of others by force, most of the great industrial states that consume Arab oil have not adopted a measure or an action which indicates awareness of its general international commitment; some of them, rather, have acted in a manner which supports and strengthens aggression.

The United States became active before and during the current war, supplying Israel with all sources of strength which increase its arrogance and enable it to defy the legitimate rights and the principles of general international law which are not subject to argument.

Israel caused the closure of the Suez Canal in 1967, burdening the European economy with the consequences. In the war taking place now, it has hit the exporting ports in the eastern Mediterranean, burdening Europe with another cut in its supplies.

For the third time there is a war resulting from Israel's defiance of our legitimate rights with the backing and support of the United States. This prompts the Arabs to adopt a decision not to continue to make economic sacrifices by producing quantities of their valuable oil in excess of what is justified by the economic factors in their states unless the world community arises to put matters in order, compel Israel to withdraw from our occupied lands and make the United States aware of the exorbitant price the great industrial states are paying as a result of its blind and unlimited support for Israel.

Therefore, the Arab oil ministers meeting on 17 October in the city of Kuwait have decided to begin immediately the reduction of production in every Arab oil-producing country by no less than five percent of the production for the month of September. The same procedure will be applied every month and production will be reduced by the same percentage of the previous month's production until the Israeli forces are completely evacuated from all the Arab territories occupied in the June 1967 war, and the legitimate rights of the Palestinian people are restored.

The conferees are eager that this production should not affect any friendly state which has helped or will help the Arabs in a fruitful and effective manner. They will continue to be supplied with the same quantities of oil they used to obtain before the reduction. The same special treatment will be given to every state which adopts an important measure against Israel to persuade it to end its occupation of the usurped Arab territories.

The Arab ministers appeal to all peoples of the world, most of all the American people, to support the Arab nation in its struggle against Israeli colonialism and occupation. They emphasize the sincere desire of the Arab nation to cooperate fully with the peoples of the world, and the Arab nation's readiness to supply the world with oil despite all sacrifices when the world shows sympathy toward us and condemns the aggression against us.

Appendix D
Resolution to Impose Oil Embargo, 17 October 1973

The Oil Ministers of the member States of OAPEC held a meeting in the city of Kuwait on the 17th of October 1973 to consider employing oil in the battle currently raging between the Arabs and Israel. Following a thorough discussion of this question the Oil Ministers,

Considering that the direct goal of the current battle is the liberation of the Arab territories occupied in the June 1967 war and the recovery of the legitimate rights of the Palestinian people in accordance with the United Nations resolutions;

Considering that the United States is the principal and foremost source of the Israeli power which has resulted in the present Israeli arrogance and enabled the Israelis to continue to occupy our territories;

Recalling that the big industrial nations help, in one way or another, to perpetuate the status quo, though they bear a common responsibility for implementing the United Nations resolutions;

Considering that the economic situation of many Arab oil producing countries does not justify raising oil production, though they are ready to make such an increase in production to meet the requirements of major consumer industrial nations that commit themselves to cooperation with us for the purpose of liberating our territories;

Decided that each Arab oil exporting country immediately cut its oil production by a recurrent monthly rate of no less than five percent to be initially counted on the virtual production of September, and thenceforth on the last production figure until such a time as the international community compels Israel to relinquish our occupied territories or until the production of every individual country reaches the point where its economy does not permit of any further reduction without detriment to its national and Arab obligations.

Nevertheless, the countries that support the Arabs actively and effectively or that take important measures against Israel to compel its withdrawal shall not be prejudiced by this production cut and shall continue to receive the same oil supplies that they used to receive prior to the reduction. Though the cut rate will be uniform in respect of every individual oil exporting country, the decrease in the supplies provided to the various consuming countries may well be aggravated proportionately with their support to and cooperation with the Israeli enemy.

The Participants also recommend to the countries party to this resolution that the United States be subjected to the most severe cut proportionately with the quantities of crude oil, oil derivatives and hydrocarbons that it imports from every exporting country.

The Participants also recommend that this progressive reduction lead to the total halt of oil supplies to the United States from every individual country party to the resolution.[1]

[1]This resolution was not signed by the Oil Minister of Iraq.

Appendix E
Communiqué: Conference of Arab Oil Ministers, Kuwait, 4–5 November 1973

The Arab oil ministers met again in Kuwait on 4 November 1973 to discuss the question further and decided that the initial production cut be 25% of the September level, and a further 5% from the production of each of the following months. The 25% cut should also include the complete halt of all oil shipments to both the United States and the Netherlands.

The Arab Oil Halt to the United States and Holland

The Arab oil producing countries have decided to halt their oil supplies to the United States and Holland and to any other country supporting Israel.

This decision is by no means directed against the peoples of the United States or Holland. It is in fact directed against their governments' hostile policies towards the Arab people.

The Arab people fully realize the interests of other people and want to develop closer ties with the people of the United States and Holland, who must also realize where their interests lie.

The Arab Oil Exporting Countries would like the American and Dutch people to know that the halt in oil supplies to their countries will continue until such a time as Israeli forces are fully withdrawn from all occupied Arab territories and the Arab people of Palestine regain their lawful rights.

The Arab Oil Ministers would like to draw the attention of the American people to the fact that the United States Government itself adopted similar policies of banning shipments of arms, strategic materials such as oil, and even foodstuffs to countries considered hostile to the United States.

Appendix F
Resolution on Oil, Sixth Arab Summit Conference, Algiers, 28 November 1973[1]

The Conference resolves to continue using oil as an economic weapon in the battle until such time as the withdrawal from the occupied Arab territories is completed and the national rights of the Palestinian people are restored, in accordance with the following bases:

—Maintenance of the embargo on countries supporting Israel.

—Maintenance of the progressive cuts in oil production to the extent that the reduction in income accruing to any of the producing countries should not exceed one-quarter on the basis of the 1972 income level.

—Formation of a committee composed of the Ministers of Foreign Affairs and Oil of the Arab oil producing states with the following functions:

(1) To draw up a list classifying states in accordance with the following categories: friendly countries, neutral countries, and countries supporting the enemy.

(2) To follow up the implementation of the decision on the use of oil.

(3) To review the list of countries with a view to reclassifying a country from one category to another in the light of its commitment to implement the political line decided upon by the Arab Summit or if it adopts a political, economic or military stand in harmony with such political line.

(4) To give any neutral country which is reclassified into the friendly category the same quantities of oil as it used to import in 1972 on condition that it undertakes not to re-export such oil, either in the form of crude or refined products.

(5) The re-export of oil from any country to a hostile state is not permissible.

The above-mentioned committee will meet to draw up the classification of countries into the three categories, notification of which will be passed on to the Arab oil producing states and the states from which the oil is exported with a view to implementation.

---

[1]The conference was attended by the heads of state of sixteen Arab countries, not including Iraq and Libya; Jordan sent a lower-level delegation.

Appendix G
Resolution, Arab Oil Ministers, on Lifting Oil Embargo Against the U.S., Kuwait, 8 December 1973

The Arab Ministers of Oil and their representatives signatory to this resolution met in Kuwait on 8 December 1973, after reviewing their resolution issued on 18 November 1973 relating to the suspension of the five percent reduction for the European Common Market countries with the exception of Holland decided upon for December, subject to the proviso that the reduction of five percent of December production levels will continue thereafter for all non-exempted countries in January, have adopted the following resolution:

Firstly: If agreement is reached on withdrawal from all the territories occupied since 1967, foremost amongst them Jerusalem, in accordance with a timetable which Israel agrees to and whose implementation is guaranteed by the United States, the embargo on exports to the United States will be lifted as soon as the withdrawal program begins, and at that point the general reduction applicable to it will be determined on the basis that it should not exceed or be less than the prevailing percentage applicable to the oil consuming countries at the time the embargo is lifted. The percentage reduction will then be applied to the United States in the same way as to Europe and the rest of the world.

Secondly: When agreement on a timetable for a withdrawal is reached the Arab Oil Ministers implementing this resolution will meet to draw up a timetable for the gradual restoration of production to the level of September 1973 in a manner corresponding to the stages of the withdrawal.

Thirdly: The friendly African and Islamic countries will be given the full quantities contracted for in concluded contracts, even if this necessitates an increase in production by a percentage which will guarantee that their domestic requirements are met, provided it is ascertained that there is no possibility to re-export to countries to which oil exports are embargoed.

The Representatives of Abu Dhabi, Bahrain, Algeria,
Saudi Arabia, Syria, Qatar, Kuwait, Libya, Egypt

Appendix H
Text of Decision to Lift Oil Embargo, 18 March 1974

1. Italy and the Federal Republic of Germany shall be treated as friendly countries. Their oil requirements shall be provided within the limits of Arab oil production, but making sure that exported Arab oil does not replace non-Arab oil which was to be exported to these countries lest such oil be redirected to a country subject to the boycott or to the reduced production.

2. The embargo on oil shipments to the United States shall be lifted with the provision that this decision, like the other decisions, shall be reviewed at a meeting the Arab oil ministers will hold in Cairo on 1 June 1974.

3. The production of each Arab country shall be increased to the level that will enable it to implement this decision.

Notes

In addition to material in the notes, sources of information, including quoted material, communiqués, newspaper publications, conference resolutions, official government position papers, etc., used in this book are the *Middle East Monitor* (Washington) (hereafter referred to as *MEM*), the *Middle East Economic Survey* (Nicosia) (hereafter referred to as *MEES*), *Facts on File* (New York), Keesing's *Contemporary Archives* (New York), and *Arab Report and Record* (London).

Introduction

1. For a history and analysis of this conflict culminating in the 1951 nationalization, see Lawrence Paul Elwell-Sutton, *Persian Oil: A Study in Power Politics;* N. S. Fatemi, *Oil Diplomacy;* Marvin Zonis, *The Political Elite of Iran;* Robert Graham, *Iran: The Illusion of Power,* pp. 64–67; and Jahangir Amuzegar, "Nationalism Versus Economic Growth," *Foreign Affairs* 44, no. 4 (July 1966): 651–661. For an account of British involvement during this period, see Leonard Mosley, *Power Play: Oil in the Middle East,* Chapters 15 and 16. A review of the legal dispute of the nationalization decree in the World Court and the UN Security Council is found in Alan W. Ford, *The Anglo-Iranian Oil Dispute of 1951–52.*

2. Richard W. Cottam, a former State Department officer and an Iranian specialist, asserted that the shah was put back into power "as a result of a CIA-backed and in large part CIA-directed coup" (*Nationalism in Iran,* p. 332). Michael Karl Sheehan, in *Iran: The Impact of United States Interests and Policies, 1941–1954,* considers U.S. involvement in the overthrow of Mossadeq and the pre-Mossadeq period during which the United States pressured the shah to introduce land and political reforms. See also David Wise and Thomas B. Ross, *The Invisible Government,* and Kermit Roosevelt, *Countercoup: The Struggle for Control of Iran.*

3. Among the books that give a general treatment of the 1956 Suez crisis are: Kenneth Love, *Suez: The Twice-Fought War;* Michael Adams, *Suez and After: Year of Crisis;* P. Johnson, *The Suez War;* Hugh Thomas, *Suez;* Robert R. Bowie, *Suez 1956;* Moshe Dayan, *Diary of the Sinai Campaign;* Anthony Eden, *The Memoirs of Anthony Eden: Full Circle;* Harold Macmillan, *Riding the Storm: 1956–1959;* Anthony Nutting, *No End of a Lesson;* A. S. Protopopov, *The Soviet Union*

and the Suez Crisis of 1956; Andre Beaufre, *The Suez Expedition: 1956;* A. J. Barker, *Suez: The Seven Day War.*

4. The literature on the 1967 Arab oil embargo is very scant. While almost all other episodes of economic leverage have been discussed and analyzed thoroughly, to our knowledge there exists no study that deals with this event in depth. Of some 635 entries on economic leverage listed in the bibliography of our book *Economic Sanctions: Ideals and Experience,* not a single one deals exclusively with the 1967 Arab oil embargo. One reason for this neglect lies in the fact that the accepted wisdom in the field is to view the episode as an unsuccessful effort that served no purpose and had no significance. (See our article, "The 1967 Oil Embargo Revisited," *Journal of Palestine Studies* 13, no. 2 (Winter 1984):65–90.

5. OPEC's successful efforts in 1973/1974 to assume unilateral control over oil prices gave it so much publicity in Western media that the public as well as a good number of scholars have tended to erroneously identify OPEC rather than OAPEC as the organization instituting the embargo. See, for instance, Robert D. Cantor, *Introduction to International Politics* (pp. 6, 48); Lawrence Solomon, *Energy Shock, After the Oil Runs Out* (p. 9); Robin C. Landis and Michael W. Klass, *OPEC: Policy Implications for the United States* (pp. 1, 32–33); Michael W. Klass, et al., *International Minerals: Cartels and Embargoes* (p. 3); Robert L. Wendzel, *International Politics, Policymakers and Policymaking* (p. 185); John Charles Daly, moderator, *Energy Security: Can We Cope with a Crisis* (p. 1); Paul W. MacAvoy, *Energy Policy: An Economic Analysis* (p. 17); Duane Chapman, *Energy Resources and Energy Corporations* (pp. 30–31).

Chapter 1: The Leverage of Oil, 1956

1. For a political portrait of the man in the context of the Egyptian milieu of his time, see P. J. Vatikiotis, *Nasser and His Generation.* A comprehensive introduction to modern Egyptian history is Derek Hopwood's *Egypt: Politics and Society, 1945–1981.*

2. Ann Williams, *Britain and France in the Middle East and North Africa,* p. 117.

3. For a Western perspective, see J. Dougherty, "The Aswan Decision in Perspective," *Political Science Quarterly* 74 (March 1959):21–45.

4. Williams, *Britain and France,* p. 121.

5. For a book that documents the British presence in Egypt and traces the major events in Egypt's struggle for independence, see Peter Mansfield, *The British in Egypt.*

6. Mansfield, *The British in Egypt,* p. 312.

7. It was the Chinese leader Chou En-Lai who either originally suggested or helped to persuade Soviet Premier Nikita Khrushchev to supply arms to Egypt in 1955, thus decisively changing the course of events in that region. For a careful and well-researched history of Chinese policy in the Middle East, see Yitzhak Shichor, *The Middle East in China's Foreign Policy, 1949–1977.*

8. Townsend Hoopes, *The Devil and John Foster Dulles,* p. 337.

9. On the 1955 Czechoslovakian arms agreement, see Wilton Wynn, *Nasser of Egypt: The Search for Dignity*, and Uri Ra'anan, *The USSR Arms the Third World: Case Studies in Soviet Foreign Policy*.

10. Charles L. Robertson, *The Emergency Oil Lift to Europe in the Suez Crisis*, p. 12.

11. Noble Frankland and V. King, eds., *Documents on International Affairs, 1956*, pp. 69–70.

12. *Times* (London), 27 July 1956, p. 10.

13. Robert R. Bowie, *Suez 1956*, p. 18.

14. Anthony Nutting, *No End of a Lesson: The Story of Suez*, pp. 32–33.

15. Mark Arnold-Forster, "An Act of Folly Without Justification," *Guardian* (London), 30 July 1976, p. 9. This is an excellent article tracing "diplomatic and military moves which led to U.N. sanctions against Britain, France, and Israel and ended Britain's imperialist buccaneering."

16. "Europe's Achilles Heel," *Economist*, 4 August 1956, p. 382.

17. Robert Murphy, *Diplomat Among Warriors*, p. 461.

18. The London *Economist* wrote on 17 November 1956:

Never since the war have the Russians sounded such an alarm or spoken with such a threatening voice as they now have over the Suez crisis. Broadcasts were interrupted on Moscow radio and additional news bulletins introduced. After the beginning of hostilities the headlines of Soviet newspapers proclaimed: Aggression Against the Egyptian People Must Be Stopped Immediately. The campaign reached its peak with the threatening Notes to Britain and France broadcast on November 5th. [p. 578]

Eugene Rabinowitch (in "The First Year of Deterrence," *Bulletin of the Atomic Scientists*, Chicago, 13, January 1957:2–8) argued that it was the Soviet (Nikolai Bulganin's) threat of missile warfare rather than UN resolutions and U.S. diplomatic pressures that forced the withdrawal of British and French troops. In contrast, J. M. Mackintosh maintained that the Soviet Union avoided participation in the 1956 conflict and that its threats against Britain, France, and Israel were not issued until after the crisis had abated and seemed primarily directed toward a propaganda advantage with respect to the position of the United States. See J. M. Mackintosh, *Strategy and Tactics of Soviet Foreign Policy*, pp. 185–187. Also John Erickson, specialist in Soviet military affairs, stated that the Soviets "to all intents and purposes crippled the strike capacity of Egypt" by withdrawing their forty-five Ilyushin-28 strike bombers to Upper Egypt and Syria before the Anglo-French attack.

19. Nutting, *No End of a Lesson*, p. 31. The intricate diplomacy preceding the Anglo-French-Israeli attack is extensively treated in Michael A. Guhin's book *John Foster Dulles: A Statesman and His Times*.

20. This appraisal of the situation was generally shared in Britain. See, for example, an editorial in the *Times* (London), 1 August 1956; also James G. Eayrs, ed., *The Commonwealth and Suez: A Documentary Survey*, pp. 33–37.

21. Moshe Dayan, *Diary of the Sinai Campaign*, p. 59. Many British officials as well as French applied to Nasser such analogies as the "Mussolini of the

Nile": See R. A. Butler, *The Art of the Possible: The Memoirs of Lord Butler*, pp. 188–189.

22. Anthony Eden, *The Memoirs of Anthony Eden: Full Circle*, p. 478.

23. Bowie, *Suez 1956*, p. 26. See also Peter Calvocoressi et al., *Suez Ten Years Later: Broadcasts from the B.B.C. Third Programme*. In these broadcasts, the participants highlight the importance of the invasion to France's Algerian policy.

24. Ernest Stock, *Israel on the Road of Sinai, 1949–1956*, p. 5.

25. See Michal Bar-Zohar, *Ben Gurion: The Armed Prophet*, p. 197. The collusion with Israel was disclosed a month later, when the London *Guardian's* correspondent in Tel Aviv was able on 19 November to confirm that the French had known of the Israeli plans in advance. The same day the *New York Times* had been informed of a Franco-Israeli scheme to attack Egypt "on or about October 16."

26. Stock, *Israel on the Road of Sinai*, p. 215.

27. N. Safran, *From War to War: The Arab-Israeli Confrontation 1948–1967*, p. 53.

28. Bowie, *Suez 1956*, p. 66.

29. Quoted in Dwight D. Eisenhower, *The White House Years: Waging Peace, 1956–1961*.

30. This assumption is based on the "rational actor" model, which assumes that decisionmakers will: (1) select the objectives and values that a given policy is supposed to achieve and maximize; (2) consider the various alternative means to achieve these purposes; (3) calculate the likely consequences of each alternative course; and (4) choose the course most likely to attain the objectives originally selected. In the case of Egypt, British policymakers anticipated a move on the part of the Egyptian Revolutionary Council or the Egyptian masses to sacrifice Nasser "to save Egypt" and the Egyptian revolution. An insightful analysis of the complex processes of decisionmaking during foreign-policy crises is Graham T. Allison, *Essence of Decision: Explaining the Cuban Missile Crisis*. Allison defined rationality as "consistent, value-maximizing choice within specified constraints" (p. 30). It is highly instructive to compare the rationale and expectations of the Eden government in its planning to invade Egypt with that of the Kennedy government in the 1961 Bay of Pigs fiasco. See Irving L. Janis, *Victims of Groupthink*.

31. Peter Lyon, *Eisenhower: Portrait of the Hero*, p. 715. See also Donald Neff, *Warriors at Suez: Eisenhower Takes America into the Middle East*.

32. James A. Nathan and James K. Oliver, *United States Foreign Policy and World Order*, p. 244.

33. M. S. Venkataramani, "Oil and U.S. Foreign Policy During the Suez Crisis 1956–7," *International Studies* (New Delhi) 2, no. 2 (October 1960):106.

34. Europe's military power and NATO forces in Europe and the Mediterranean were highly dependent on Middle Eastern oil. See John C. Campbell, *Defense of the Middle East: Problems of American Policy*, p. 229. See also the testimony of John Foster Dulles: U.S., Congress, Senate, *The President's Proposal on the Middle East, Hearings Before the Committee on Foreign Relations and the Committee on Armed Services*, 85th Cong., 1st sess., 1957.

35. Arnold-Forster, "An Act of Folly," p. 9.

36. Tom Little, *Modern Egypt*, p. 175.

37. Ibid.

38. Nathan and Oliver, *United States Foreign Policy*, p. 274.

39. John Spanier, *American Foreign Policy Since World War II*, 7th ed., p. 86.

40. Ibid.

41. "The Cost for France," *Economist*, 10 November 1956, pp. 498–499.

42. *Scotsman* (London), 19 November 1956.

43. *Economist*, 17 November 1956, p. 600. See also *New York Times*, 23 November 1956.

44. "Gunboat Diplomacy," *Economist*, 10 November 1956, p. 505.

45. *Economist*, 17 November 1956, p. 600.

46. Ibid.

47. Nathan and Oliver in *United States Foreign Policy and World Order* stated: "The Suez crisis had its origins in Dulles's and Eisenhower's obsession with international communism and their inability to grasp fully non-Western nationalism" (p. 243).

48. The pledge of U.S. financial assistance was disclosed by the French premier, Guy Mollet, in a press conference reported in the *New York Times*, 13 September 1956, p. 1.

49. See U.S., Congress, Senate, *Emergency Oil Lift Program and Related Oil Problems, Joint Hearings Pursuant to Senate Resolution 57*, 85th Cong., 1957.

50. Robert Engler, *The Politics of Oil*, p. 261.

51. *Times* (London), 17 November 1956. See also the *Daily Mail* (London), 20 November 1956.

52. Comments by some of the French, Italian, and German press are found in Robertson, *Emergency Oil Lift*, p. 22.

53. Ibid., p. 21.

54. U.S., Congress, Senate, *Emergency Oil Lift Program*, p. 1818.

55. Anthony Nutting, *Nasser*, p. 413.

56. Ibid.

57. *Economist*, 23 February 1957, p. 649.

58. At the same time, a resolution introduced in the UN General Assembly demanded an end to all aid to Israel until its withdrawal.

59. Eisenhower sent a letter in which he warned that the Israeli position endangered the peace efforts and risked grave consequences for Israel. See Brian Urquhart, *Hammarskjold; The Years of Decision*, p. 182. Bulganin also sent a strong warning. See David Ben-Gurion, *Israel: A Personal History*, pp. 508–512. See also Stephen D. Isaacs, *Jews and American Politics*, pp. 250–251.

60. For an informative analysis of the Israeli forces' withdrawal, see Walid Abi-Mershed, *Israeli Withdrawal From Sinai*.

61. S. Karpov, "The Closure of the Suez Canal: Economic Consequences," *International Affairs* (Moscow) (April 1974):83.

62. *Times* (London), 28 July 1956. See also "Oil Is Critical," *Economist*, 10 November 1956, pp. 523–526.

63. *New York Times*, 19 August 1956. See also "The Distribution of Middle East Oil Supplies," *Economist*, 10 August 1956, p. 525.

64. See "TAPLine," *Economist*, 11 August 1956, p. 471.

65. *New York Times*, 19 August 1956.

66. *Manchester Guardian*, 2 November 1956.

67. Nutting, *Nasser*, p. 172.

68. *New York Herald Tribune*, 5 November 1956. For an account of the IPC construction in the years 1932 to 1934 from its oilfield in the vicinity of Kirkuk, Iraq, to the Mediterranean ports of Haifa (Palestine) and Tripoli (Lebanon), see Iraq Petroleum Company, Limited, *The Construction of the Iraq Mediterranean Pipe-line; A Tribute to the Men Who Built It.*

69. *Daily Mail* (London), 24 September 1956.

70. *Manchester Guardian*, 14 November 1956.

71. "The West Through Arab Eyes," *Economist*, 10 November 1956, p. 493.

72. Ibid., p. 492. See also Fred J. Khoury, *The Arab-Israeli Dilemma*, p. 539.

73. *Economist*, 1 December 1956, p. 794.

74. *New York Herald Tribune*, 13 December 1956.

75. *Economist*, 10 November 1956, p. 493.

76. Little, *Modern Egypt*, p. 175.

77. Robertson, *Emergency Oil Lift*, p. 20.

78. Ibid., p. 21.

79. *New York Times*, 28 July 1956.

80. *Financial Times* (London), 11 August 1956.

81. Under the Marshall Plan stimulus, Western Europe shifted to oil, thus becoming the major market for imports. See Engler, *Politics of Oil*, pp. 202, 217–220.

82. *Scotsman* (Edinburgh), 19 November 1956. For a well-informed discussion of Europe's demand for oil in 1956 see Organization of European Economic Co-operation (OEEC), *Europe's Growing Needs of Energy: How Can They Be Met?* OEEC, *Europe's Need for Oil: Implications and Lessons of the Suez Crisis*, and George Lenczowski, *Oil and State in the Middle East.*

83. *Scotsman* (Edinburgh), 19 November 1956.

84. *Financial Times* (London), 21 November 1956.

85. *Manchester Guardian*, 19 November 1956.

86. *Daily Telegraph* (London), 19 November 1956.

87. *Times* (London), 21 November 1956.

88. *Manchester Guardian*, 21 November 1956.

89. *Times* (London), 27 November 1956.

90. *Financial Times* (London), 20 November 1956.

91. *Financial Times* (London), 19 November 1956.

92. *Times* (London), 27 November 1956.

93. Karpov, "Closure of the Suez Canal," p. 84.

94. *New York Times*, 21 November 1956.

95. John M. Blair, *The Control of Oil*, p. 3.

96. P. H. Frankel, "Oil Supplies During the Suez Crisis—On Meeting a Political Emergency," *The Journal of Industrial Economics* 6 (February 1958):86.

This article focuses on the measures taken by the European countries to (1) increase the flow of supplies, and (2) avoid extremes of profits being made or losses being sustained by individual operations.
97. Ibid., p. 100.

Chapter 2: The Leverage of Oil, 1967

1. James A. Bill and Carl Leiden, *Politics in the Middle East*, pp. 265–266. This excellent introductory book is topically organized, focusing on problems and patterns of the Middle Eastern power structure.

2. Bourguiba's advocacy in the early 1960s of a negotiated settlement to the Arab-Israeli conflict did not endear him to the Arab masses and led to his alienation in inter-Arab politics. For a detailed account of Bourguiba's mediation efforts in 1965, see Samuel Merlin, *The Search for Peace in the Middle East: The Story of President Bourguiba's Campaign for a Negotiated Settlement Between Israel and the Arab States.*

3. George Lenczowski, *U.S. Interests in the Middle East*, p. 23. Though this book reflected the most widespread view of the interplay of ideology and politics in Arab affairs, not all Middle East experts shared it. Malcolm Kerr, for example, dissents from this school and makes commendable efforts to dispel the claim, often made in Arab cold war studies, that Arab interpolitics can be understood simply in terms of "revolutionary" and "conservative" ideologies. See Malcolm Kerr, *The Arab Cold War: Gamal Abd Al-Nasir and His Rivals, 1958–1970*, 3rd ed., and *Regional Arab Politics and Conflict With Israel.*

4. On Saudi history and politics, see Emile Nakhleh, *The United States and Saudi Arabia, A Policy Analysis;* David E. Long, *Saudi Arabia;* Helen Lackner, *A House Built on Sand: The Political Economy of Saudi Arabia;* and William B. Quandt, *Saudi Arabia in the 1980s: Foreign Policy, Security, and Oil.*

5. The modern kingdom of Saudi Arabia dates from 1932 when Abdul Aziz Ibn Saud unified the dual kingdoms of Hijaz and Najd and proclaimed himself king. Ibn Saud's death in 1953 placed his eldest son, Saud Ibn Abdul Aziz, on the throne, and his second son, Faisal, was named heir apparent. In March 1958 Faisal was granted executive powers, and on 2 November 1964 he became king after Saud was deposed by a family decision. Faisal ruled Saudi Arabia until 25 March 1975 when he was assassinated by a nephew. He was succeeded by Crown Prince Khalid, who died of a heart attack in 1982 and was succeeded by the present king, Fahd. Valuable scholarly accounts of the founder king of Saudi Arabia are: Harold C. Armstrong, *Lord of Arabia, Ibn Saud: An Intimate Study of a King;* David Howarth, *The Desert King: Ibn Saud and His Arabia;* Ameen Rihani, *Maker of Modern Arabia;* Mohammed Almana, *Arabia Unified: A Portrait of Ibn Saud.*

6. The *New York Times* of 3 August 1956 wrote:

The Beirut newspaper *Al Rawad* voiced the sentiment of many Arabs in an editorial today protesting that "a handful of sheikhs" were squandering huge oil revenues that could be used to finance the Aswan High Dam in Egypt and other projects and to arm the Arab countries. It suggested that Egypt join with Syria and Lebanon, which have no oil, and Saudi Arabia, to agree on a joint development plan based on the oil revenues of all Arab countries.

7. In 1963 Mohamed Hassanein Haykal, editor of the Cairo daily *al-Ahram*, disclosed that Aramco was allowing King Saud to draw as much as three years' royalities in advance so that he could strengthen the anti-Nasser tendencies of the Syrian secessionist regime. "The Saudi king had already spent 7,000,000 pounds on financing the secessionist coup itself. But when his expenditures began to exceed all limits without anything to show for them, Aramco, tired of the whole thing, was among the powers that counselled Saud's replacement by Faisal, who was expected to be more provident than his brother" (*al-Ahram*, 22 February 1963).

8. See Gamal Abd El-Nasser, *The Philosophy of the Revolution*. This is a vivid account of the spirit in which the coup of 23 July 1952 was realized.

9. *Economist*, 3 October 1970, p. 13. For a scholarly sympathetic view of Nasser and his presidency see Nejla M. Abu Izzeddin, *Nasser of the Arabs*.

10. Under the monarchy, 95 percent of the wealth of Egypt was in the hands of a thin stratum of pashas, landlords, bankers, and merchants who with their families formed less than 1 percent of the population. Most of the Egyptian nobility were of Turkish descent—King Farouk himself was a descendant of Albanian adventurers who came to Egypt with the Turks—living in the luxury described in Oriental fairy tales while millions of peasants, workers, men, women, and children of all ages were living in unimaginable misery. More than half of Egypt's population suffered from bilharziasis—the terrible eye disease that causes blindness—and more than two-thirds of the children died before reaching the age of six. Thirty years was the average life expectancy in Egypt. "Allah has rightly made mortality so high; we would all starve if it were not so," was the social philosophy of the aristocracy. See Carolus, "The Ten Plagues of Egypt," *Nation*, 23 August 1952, pp. 145–147.

11. See Hisham Sharabi, *Government and Politics of the Middle East in the Twentieth Century*, p. 216. For a critical analysis of Nasser, see Robert St. John, *The Boss: The Story of Gamal Abdel Nasser*, and Keith Wheelock, *Nasser's Egypt*.

12. Miles Copeland, *The Game of Nations*, pp. 172–177. While Copeland described how the CIA attempted to buy Nasser, Wilbur Crane Eveland in *Ropes of Sand: America's Failure in the Middle East* exposed the deployment of assassination teams by the CIA to eliminate the Egyptian president.

13. The dominant political ideology in Egypt at this time, i.e., Nasserism, a product of a number of historical events, forces, and trends, produced a climate in Egypt and the Arab world that facilitated the acceptance of the leadership role that Cairo played in inter-Arab politics.

14. Stephen Duguid, "A Biographical Approach to the Study of Social Change in the Middle East: Abdullah Tariki as a New Man," *International Journal of Middle East Studies* 1, no. 3 (July 1970):202.

15. A. I. Dawisha saw the foreign-policy objectives of the Nasser years as shifting back and forth among (1) a maximum objective of "comprehensive unity," (2) a minimum objective of "Arab solidarity," and (3) an intermediate objective of "revolutionary change." See A. I. Dawisha, *Egypt in the Arab World*.

16. *President Gamal Abdel Nasser's Speeches and Press-Interviews*, p. 351.

17. A. I. Dawisha, "Intervention in the Yemen: An Analysis of Egyptian Perceptions and Policies," *Middle East Journal* (Winter 1975):48.

18. For background on Yemen's history, see Manfred Wenner, *Modern Yemen: 1918–1966*. An outstanding study devoted to the events antedating the 1962 revolution is Robert W. Stookey's *Yemen: The Politics of the Yemen Arab Republic*. On the Yemeni civil war, see Edgar O'Ballance, *The War in Yemen*; Dana Adams Schmidt, *The Yemen: Unknown War*; John S. Badeau, *The American Approach to the Arab World*.

19. For a comprehensive, well-documented account that covers both political and military aspects of Nasser's intervention and war in Yemen, see Ali Abdel Rahman Rahmy, *The Egyptian Policy in the Arab World: Intervention in Yemen 1962–1967 Case Study*. The author, an Egyptian scholar who served as a major in the Regular Army of Egypt during the Yemeni war, placed the episode in the context of the inter-Arab politics of the time.

20. Anthony Nutting, *Nasser*, p. 349.

21. Interview with *Look* magazine, 4 March 1968; also reported in the *Times* (London), 5 March 1968.

22. Dawisha, "Intervention in Yemen," p. 55.

23. Ibid., p. 58.

24. *Egyptian Gazette*, 8 February 1966.

25. *Guardian* (London), 28 April 1966.

26. Dawisha, "Intervention in Yemen," p. 60. An incisive inquiry that attempted to explain how and why the 1967 June war came about is that of Theodore Draper, *Israel and World Politics*. Draper argued that the penetration of the eastern Mediterranean by the Soviet Union, which sought the elimination of Western interests and influences in the area, upset the unstable equilibrium that had existed since 1956 and started the chain of events that eventually culminated in the June war. The authors of the present book disagree; they view the chain of causes as extending further back—to 1948 and the unresolved Palestinian problem.

27. David Hirst, "Arab Oil Reprisals," *Guardian* (London), 29 May 1967. This insightful article shows a good deal of understanding of Arab psychology and politics.

28. A collection of original, well-documented essays on the 1967 June war by recognized scholars is Ibrahim Abu-Lughod, ed., *The Arab-Israeli Confrontation of June, 1967: An Arab Perspective*; see also "The Arab-Israeli War," *Foreign Affairs* 46 (January 1968):304–346, and Elias Samo, ed., *The June 1967 Arab-Israeli War: Miscalculation or Conspiracy?* Other works are Michael Howard and Robert Hunter, *Israel and the Arab World: The Crisis of 1967*; Hal Kosut, ed., *Israel and the Arabs: The June 1967 War*; Charles Douglas-Home, *The Arabs and Israel*.

29. As British protectorates, the three Gulf sheikhdoms presumably would have had to obtain British approval to attend the conference. Inviting the two transit countries, Lebanon and Syria, was primarily designed to bring Syria— which had blown up the pipeline from Iraq to the Mediterranean without prior consultation during the 1956 Suez crisis—into coordinated planning right from the start.

30. An excerpt from the "Arab Oil Ministers' Communiqué," Baghdad, 5 June 1967.

31. Robert W. Stookey, *America and the Arab States: An Uneasy Encounter,* pp. 208–209.

32. In a press conference held in May 1967, President Nasser declared that he did not agree to the destruction of oil installations unless "the Arab governments failed to do their duty." Syrian and Egyptian calls for sabotage intensified in tone during and immediately after the war. For example, on 12 June 1967 the Syrian newspaper *al-Thawra* called on the Arab people to "destroy all that is American and British in the Arab homeland. They should wreck military bases and strike at petroleum companies in the first place." (Quoted also in the *Egyptian Gazette,* 13 June 1967.)

33. An excellent analysis of political, social, and psychological conditions in the Arab states in the aftermath of the June war is Michael Adams, *Chaos or Rebirth: The Arab Outlook.*

34. A valuable book that discusses the Arab states' relations after the 1967 war is Fouad Ajami's *The Arab Predicament: Arab Political Thought and Practice Since 1967.* Ajami maintained that three rival groups emerged after 1967 with proposals for the future of Arab society: (1) the radicals, who called for a wholesale rejection of tradition along the lines of Cuba and China; (2) the Muslim fundamentalists, who called for a return to traditions; and (3) the conservatives, who regained their strength as a result of the 1967 humiliation of the secular pan-Arabists.

35. "Saudi Minister Urges Arabs To Reconsider Oil Boycott," *Financial Times* (London), 1 July 1967. Yamani substantiated his statement with figures putting Saudi losses since the beginning of the embargo at approximately $25 million, adding that his country's losses from then on would not be less than $250,000 a day (also quoted by Nicholas Herbert, "More Moderation on Arab Oil: Boycott Value Questioned," *Times* [London], 1 July 1967). See also *New York Times,* 1 July 1967. On 2 July the *New York Times* wrote: "The Arabs, as usual, had a proverb to fit the situation. *Rahet el sakra; wa ijit el fakra:* "Gone the wine fumes; thinking resumes."

36. During a visit to the United States, King Hussein was quoted by the Associated Press as saying on 30 June 1967 that he was perfectly satisfied that neither British nor American aircraft helped Israel, though he did have at a certain point a feeling that they could have been involved.

37. Quoted in "Saudi Call To Resume Oil Supplies," *Times* (London), 8 July 1967.

38. *New York Times,* 9 July 1967.

39. "Arab Rift Appears on Oil Flow to West," *New York Times,* 10 July 1967.

40. "U.A.R. Ends Truce With King Faisal," *International Herald Tribune,* 10 July 1967.

41. "Iraqi Ministers Denounce Saudi Oil Move," *Egyptian Gazette,* 11 July 1967.

42. "Iraqis Say Lackeys Must Be Destroyed," *Egyptian Gazette,* 10 July 1967.

43. Ibid.

44. Ibid.

45. Reported by *Egyptian Gazette,* 13 July 1967.

46. *International Herald Tribune,* 10 July 1967.

47. *Egyptian Gazette,* 4 July 1967.

48. *International Herald Tribune,* 13 July 1967.

49. This was the first time oil was pumped through the pipelines since they were closed down by order of the Lebanese government on 7 June, two days after the eruption of the Arab-Israeli war. Some forty-five miles of the pipeline passed through the southern part of Syria, now occupied by the Israeli army, which showed no interest in interfering with it.

50. "Oil Boycott Confirmed in Kuwait Talks," *Times* (London), 15 July 1967.

51. Since 1962, Egypt had backed the Yemeni Republican regime of President Abdullah Sallal, while Saudi Arabia backed Royalists loyal to the deposed Imam Badr of Yemen. Various other Yemeni factions had oscillated between the two sides. The Jedda Accords, which provided for the formation of a transitional government of Republicans and Royalists, was never put into effect.

52. "Attack on Embargo," *Daily Telegraph* (London), 17 August 1967.

53. David Hirst, "Arabs Now Plan To Put Pressure on Oil Companies," *Guardian* (London), 22 August 1967.

54. These recommendations, though officially secret, were revealed by Cairo's authoritative daily *al-Ahram* and quoted by the official Egyptian news agency Middle East News. See the *Financial Times* (London), 31 August 1967.

55. "Oil Parley Vows Arab 'Solidarity,'" *New York Times,* 21 August 1967.

56. The other three Arab summit conferences were held in Cairo in January 1964, Alexandria (Egypt) in September 1964, and in Casablanca (Morocco) in September 1965. Absent from the Fourth Arab Summit Conference were Syria's President Nureddin al-Attasi, Algeria's President Houari Boumediene, Morocco's King Hassan II, Tunisia's President Habib Bourguiba, and Libya's King Idris I.

57. See D. C. Watt, "The Arab Summit Conference and After," *World Today* (October 1967):447.

58. Colin Jones, "Arabs Agree to a Resumption of Oil Supplies to West," *Financial Times* (London), 2 September 1967. Despite disapproval of the Arab summit's resolution lifting the oil embargo, Iraq decided to resume oil shipments, while Syria made no attempt to close the pipeline that carries Iraqi crude across Syrian territory.

59. Thomas F. Brady, "Khartoum Aftermath," *New York Times,* 7 September 1967.

60. Nutting, *Nasser,* p. 434.

61. Mohamed Hassanein Haykal, "In Frankness," *al-Ahram* (Cairo), 8 September 1967.

62. T. T. Connors, *An Examination of the International Flow of Crude Oil, With Special Reference to the Middle East,* p. 29.

63. Christopher Tugendhat, *Oil: The Biggest Business,* p. 284.

64. Dmitriyev, "Arab Oil Resources," *International Affairs* (Moscow) (August 1967):102.

65. L. Sedin, "The Arab Peoples' Just Cause," *International Affairs* (Moscow) (August 1967):28.

66. I. Belyayev and E. Primakov, "The Situation in the Arab World," *New Times* (Moscow), 27 September 1967, p. 10.

67. Before the war, Britain's stockpile was sufficient for four months' normal consumption. In addition, there were routine stocks that were said to equal forty-five days' consumption. See Sam H. Schurr and Paul T. Homan, *Middle Eastern Oil and the Western World: Prospects and Problems*, pp. 80, 82.

68. *Petroleum Economist* (January 1974):17.

69. Leonard Mosley, *Power Play: Oil in the Middle East*, p. 345.

70. *Economist*, 22 July 1967, p. 344.

71. Fawwaz Trabulsi, "The Palestine Problem: Zionism and Imperialism in the Middle East," *New Left Review* 57 (September-October 1969):85.

72. Thomas F. Brady, "Oil Stoppage Perilous," *New York Times*, 13 June 1967.

73. Daniel Crecelius, "Sa'udi-Egyptian Relations," *International Studies* (New Delhi) 14 (October-December 1975):578.

74. *New York Times*, 11 June 1967.

75. Thomas Barger, *Arab States of the Persian Gulf*, p. 40.

76. Christopher Tugendhat, "Oil Lessons That Must Be Learnt," *Financial Times* (London), 10 June 1967.

77. Later, the flow of oil from Nigeria was interrupted by the outbreak of fighting and a full blockade between Biafra and the federal government.

78. A statement by a U.S. Department of Defense spokesman as reported in the *New York Times*, 11 June 1967.

79. Brady, "Oil Stoppage Perilous."

80. Michael Fulda, *Oil and International Relations: Energy Trade, Technology and Politics*, p. 274.

81. In contrast to Eisenhower in 1956, President Lyndon Johnson, who before the war had failed to dissuade Israel from launching its preemptive strike, made no attempt once the war was over to pressure Israel to withdraw from occupied Arab territories. This policy created the dilemma that eventually led to the 1973 October war and the Arab oil embargo. See William B. Quandt, *Decade of Decisions: American Policy Toward the Arab-Israeli Conflict, 1967–1976*.

82. Thomas G. Paterson, J. Garry Clifford, and Kenneth J. Hagan, *American Foreign Policy: A History*, p. 586.

83. The dominant view of Western policymakers and scholars is to consider the 1967 Arab oil embargo ineffective, impractical, costly, and thus unsuccessful. See, for instance, J. E. Hartshorn, "Oil and the Middle East War," *World Today* 24, no. 4 (April 1968):157; Walter Laqueur, *The Struggle for the Middle East*, p. 127; George W. Stocking, *Middle East Oil, A Study in Political and Economic Controversy*, p. 459; Hanns Maull, *Oil and Influence: The Oil Weapon Examined*, p. 2.

Chapter 3: The Growing Momentum of Arab Oil Leverage, 1959–1973

1. U.S. Federal Trade Commission, *The International Petroleum Cartel*, p. 45.

2. Concern over access to oil resources, thrust upon the Western powers as a result of World War II, ignited serious U.S. official concern for Middle Eastern

oil, especially Saudi Arabian oil. This was the case in spite of the fact that in 1943 the United States produced nearly 67 percent of the world's petroleum. For judicious and detailed analysis of the origins of U.S. strategic interests in the Middle East with particular focus on the special U.S.-Saudi relationship, see Aaron David Miller, *Search for Security: Saudi Arabian Oil and American Foreign Policy, 1939–1949.* Miller pointed out that midway through World War II a number of U.S. experts on economic and petroleum issues clearly foresaw future U.S. dependence on Saudi oil. Marian Kent in *Oil and Empire: British Policy and Mesopotamian Oil, 1900–1920* provided a well-documented account of the diplomatic maneuvers of the British government in its attempt to obtain control of Mesopotamian oil; by contrast, John Darwin in *Britain, Egypt, and the Middle East: Imperial Policy in the Aftermath of War, 1918–1922* examined Britain's role in certain areas of the Middle East during the Lloyd George coalition government. He argued that strategic considerations and the safety of India in particular were the most important policy items and dismissed oil resources policy as a low-priority item. However, during World War II Anglo-U.S. rivalry in the Middle East was intense. Efforts to reach an Anglo-U.S. oil agreement remained unsuccessful. See Barry M. Rubin, *The Great Powers in the Middle East, 1941–1947.* For background on the competition for control of oil resources among major powers, see Ludwell Denny, *We Fight for Oil,* and Louis Fischer, *Oil Imperialism: The International Struggle for Petroleum.*

3. D. P. O'Connell, *The Law of State Succession,* p. 106.

4. For more details on Middle Eastern oil concessions, see Zuhayr Mikdashi, *A Financial Analysis of Middle Eastern Oil Concessions: 1901–1965;* Muhamad A. Mughraby, *Permanent Sovereignty Over Oil Resources: A Study of Middle East Oil Concessions and Legal Change;* Shavarsh Toriguian, *Legal Aspects of Oil Concessions in the Middle East;* Simons G. Siksek, *The Legal Framework of Oil Concessions in the Arab World;* Henry Cattan, *The Evolution of Oil Concessions in the Middle East and North Africa.*

5. It is important in considering these concession agreements to be aware that they were granted by three types of governments: (1) governments subject to foreign domination—as was the case in Algeria; (2) immature governments— as was the case in the Gulf; and (3) governments that did not represent the will of the people—as was true in the majority of cases.

6. *The Middle East and North Africa, 1973–74,* p. 65. A UN commission established in 1958 suggested that nationalism, expropriation, and requisition of foreign concessions may be justified on grounds of public utility, security, and national interest, provided an appropriate compensation is paid.

7. In this context it is important to note that at times strategic considerations were taken into account in granting these concessions. For example, it is not true, as Michael B. Stoff claimed in *Oil, War, and American Security: The Search for a National Policy on Foreign Oil, 1941–1947,* that money was the *only* consideration in the Saudi grant of an oil concession to a U.S. company. Aaron David Miller in *Search for Security: Saudi Arabian Oil and American Foreign Policy, 1939–1949* (pp. 20–21) was more correct in suggesting that the major factor was to counterbalance the then-dominant British influence in the area.

8. *Economist,* 31 July 1971, p. 51.

9. *Economist,* 18 January 1958, p. 231.

10. For a detailed discussion of the relationship between the oil companies and the producer states (especially Saudi Arabia and Kuwait), see Derek Hopwood, ed., *The Arabian Peninsula: Society and Politics*.

11. Fuad Rouhani, *A History of OPEC*, p. 45.

12. *Petroleum Week*, 20 June 1958, p. 40.

13. Tariqi expressed similar views in another interview with *al-Khalij al-Arabi* (Saudi weekly), 20 April 1961.

14. Explanatory memorandum issued on 12 December 1961 by the Iraqi government in conjunction with legislation expropriating 99.5 percent of IPC's concession area.

15. For the impact of the newcomers on the oil industry, see Michael Tanzer, *The Political Economy of International Oil and the Underdeveloped Countries*, pp. 21–22 and 36–37.

16. For the history and performance of OPEC during this period, see Zuhayr Mikdashi, *The Community of Oil Exporting Countries: A Study in Governmental Cooperation*; Rouhani, *A History of OPEC*; and Ghadar, *The Evolution of OPEC Strategy*.

17. These "new men" fall under the same category defined by William R. Polk, who described them as "those who possess the skill, the discipline, the orientation and the motivation to modernize society." See William R. Polk, "The Middle East: Analyzing Social Change," *Bulletin of the Atomic Scientists* (January 1967):13.

18. For more details, see Kemal S. Sayegh, *Oil and Arab Regional Development*.

19. For an informative analysis of the personal impact of Tariqi, see Stephen Duguid, "A Biographical Approach to the Study of Social Change in the Middle East: Abdullah Tariki as a New Man," *International Journal of Middle East Studies* 1, no. 3 (July 1970):195–220.

20. J. E. Hartshorn, *Oil Companies and Governments*, p. 301.

21. David Hirst, *Oil and Public Opinion in the Middle East*, p. 105.

22. *Egyptian Economic and Political Review* (Cairo) 5 (July 1959):23.

23. Ibid.

24. "The First Arab Petroleum Congress," *World Today* 15 (June 1959):253.

25. Ibid., p. 247.

26. *Egyptian Economic and Political Review*, p. 23.

27. *Study on the Fifth Arab Petroleum Congress, 1965*, pp. 4–5.

28. Ibid., pp. 5–6.

29. Ibid., p. 6.

30. Ibid.

31. Ibid., pp. 12–13.

32. Rouhani, *History of OPEC*, p. 161.

33. *MEES*, 17 November 1967.

34. *Selected Documents—1968* (Vienna: Organization of Petroleum Exporting Countries, June 1969), p. 371.

35. *Egyptian Gazette*, 16 January 1968.

36. *Egyptian Gazette*, 10 September 1968. The literature on OAPEC is scant. A major work on its development and growth is Mary Ann Tetreault, *The*

Organization of Arab Petroleum Exporting Countries: History, Policies and Prospects. Other informative studies on the organization are: Karen A. Mingst, "Regional Sectorial Economic Integration: The Case of OAPEC," *Journal of Common Market Studies* 16, no. 2 (December 1977):95–113; Organization of Arab Petroleum Exporting Countries, *A Brief Report of the Activities and Achievements of the Organization, 1968–1973.*

37. J. E. Hartshorn, "Oil and the Middle East War," *World Today* (April 1968):157.

38. *Egyptian Gazette,* 11 September 1968.

39. As reported by *MEES,* 13 September 1968, pp. 6–7.

40. Iraq's role in OAPEC and OPEC is discussed in Edith Penrose and E. F. Penrose, *Iraq: International Relations and National Development.*

41. *Egyptian Gazette,* 12 January 1968.

42. Ibid.

43. *Egyptian Mail,* 11 January 1969.

44. *Egyptian Gazette,* 11 March 1969.

45. *Daily Telegraph* (London), 16 January 1970.

46. *Baghdad Observer,* 8 January 1970.

47. *Baghdad Observer,* 9 January 1970.

48. *Egyptian Gazette,* 13 April 1970.

49. *Times* (London), 13 April 1970.

50. *Egyptian Gazette,* 27 April 1970.

51. *Egyptian Gazette,* 25 May 1970.

52. Ibid.

53. *Egyptian Gazette,* 29 June 1970.

54. *Egyptian Gazette,* 30 June 1970.

55. *Financial Times* (London), 30 June 1970.

56. *Egyptian Gazette,* 19 October 1970.

57. *Le Commerce du Levant* (Beirut), 30 December 1970.

58. *Guardian* (London), 11 June 1971.

59. *Al-Kifah* (Baghdad), 9 June 1971.

60. *Egyptian Gazette,* 14 October 1971.

61. *Times* (London), 8 June 1971.

62. *New York Times,* 13 June 1971.

63. *Al-Nahar* (Beirut), 19 October 1971.

64. *Financial Times* (London), 20 October 1971.

65. *Guardian* (London), 10 December 1971.

66. *Egyptian Mail,* 4 March 1972.

67. *Egyptian Gazette,* 10 March 1972.

68. *Egyptian Gazette,* 21 June 1972.

69. *Financial Times* (London), 21 June 1972. The loan, which came mainly from Kuwait, Abu Dhabi, and Libya, was nearly $169 million. Iraq received $151 million and Syria $18 million.

70. *Egyptian Gazette,* 21 June 1972.

71. *New York Times,* 21 June 1972.

72. *Middle East Economic Digest* (London), 21 July 1972.

73. *Middle East Economic Digest* (London), 29 December 1972, p. 1492.

74. *Middle East Economic Digest* (London), 17 November 1972.

75. *Times* (London), 5 September 1973.

76. *Egyptian Gazette*, 5 September 1973.

77. *Times* (London), 5 September 1973.

78. *International Herald Tribune*, 5 September 1973.

Chapter 4: The Control of Oil, 1967–1973: Participation and Nationalization

1. For a survey of oil company/producer country relations with a focus upon the post-World War II period, see George Ward Stocking, *Middle East Oil: A Study in Political and Economic Controversy*. Also, an extensive review of oil-producing countries in the Middle East is Benjamin Shwadran, *The Middle East, Oil, and the Great Powers*.

2. Sheikh Abdullah Tariqi, interview with *al-Sha'b* (Cairo), 30 April 1959.

3. David Hirst in *Oil and Public Opinion in the Middle East* (p. 22) maintained that "It is no accident that the slow decline in Iraqi oil production which had set in towards the end of the Kassem era suddenly gave way to substantial increase."

4. Muhammad Ahmad Salim, *al-Akhbar* (Cairo), 13 January 1958.

5. *Al-Siyassah* (Beirut), 15 April 1958.

6. For historical background on Aramco's operations in Saudi Arabia, see *Handbook: Oil and the Middle East*. For a discussion of the Aramco concession, see Raymond F. Mikesell et al., *Foreign Investment in the Petroleum and Mineral Industries: Case Studies of Investor–Host Country Relations*. An astute analytical interpretation of the complicated linkages between the U.S. government, U.S. oil companies, and Saudi Arabia is found in Irvine H. Anderson's book, *Aramco, the United States, and Saudi Arabia: A Study of the Dynamics of Foreign Oil Policy, 1933–1950*.

7. Ali Jamal, *Bina al-Watani* (Cairo monthly), 6 October 1960.

8. Speech at Ouargla, Algeria, 28 September 1964.

9. *Al-Bilad* (Riyadh; Saudi daily), 2 November 1959.

10. Two schools of thought with regard to nationalization of natural resources emerged. The first, led by Palestinian economist Dr. Yusef Sayigh, dismissed nationalization as "inflexible" and a "one-shot affair." See Yusif Sayigh, "Arab Oil in the Strategy of Arab-Israeli Confrontation," *Shu'un Filastiniya* [Palestine Affairs] (Beirut) no. 16 (December 1972); "Arab Oil and the Palestine Question: A Dialectical Relationship," *Shu'un Filastiniya*, no. 41/42 (January-February 1975); "Arab Oil Policies: Self-Interest versus International Responsibility," *Journal of Palestine Studies* 3 (Spring 1975):59–73. The other school of thought maintained that oil as a weapon is ineffective unless owned and that nationalization should therefore be the cornerstone of Arab oil policies. Once the oil industry was nationalized, it would become more feasible to impose restrictions on production and export. See Hasan Salman, *Toward Nationalization of Iraqi Petroleum*; Abdullah al-Tariki, "Nationalization of Arab Petroleum Industry Is a National Necessity,"

paper presented to the Fifth Arab Petroleum Congress, Cairo, 16–23 March 1965. See also *Study on the Fifth Arab Petroleum Congress, 1965,* pp. 104–118, and Tariki's "Nationalization of the Arab Petroleum Industry" [in Arabic], paper presented to the Eighth Arab Petroleum Congress, Algiers, 28 May–3 June 1972.

11. Stated in two papers submitted to the first two Arab petroleum congresses: "A Sovereign Nation's Legal Ability To Make and Abide by a Petroleum Concession," Cairo, April 1959, and "The Same World," Beirut, October 1960; see also Frank Hendryx, in the *New York Herald Tribune Monthly Economic Review* (June 1961), and "Congenial Arab Oil Congress," *Times Review of Industry* (December 1961):75.

12. Quoted by Harley C. Stevens in "Some Reflections on the First Arab Petroleum Congress," *Middle East Journal* (Washington) (Summer 1959):276.

13. Ibid., p. 277.

14. G. and H. S., "The First Arab Petroleum Congress," *World Today* 15 (June 1959):249.

15. Ibid.

16. Julian M. Snyder, "The Biggest Problem of the Arabs Getting Into the Club," *Vital Speeches of the Day* (New York), 15 March 1975, p. 327.

17. *Economist,* 14 October 1972.

18. For the U.S. reaction to the agreement, see M. A. Adelman, "Is the Oil Shortage Real?" *Foreign Policy* 9 (Winter 1972):81–82.

19. The London *Financial Times* disclosed that the amounts the host countries had to pay for their initial stakes were: Saudi Arabia, $500 million; Abu Dhabi, $162 million; Kuwait, $150 million; and Qatar, $71 million.

20. See Jamal Abdel Nasser, *Egypt's Liberation—The Philosophy of the Revolution,* pp. 106–109.

21. *News Chronicle* (London), 20 September 1956.

22. *Times* (London), 13 July 1959; see also *Economist,* 27 December 1958, p. 1180.

23. *Arab World* (Beirut), 6 April 1967.

24. *Daily Telegraph* (London), 24 June 1967.

25. For an informative analysis of the creation and development of ENI, see P. H. Frankel, *Mattei, Oil and Power.*

26. Only four of the sixteen Arab countries meeting at Baghdad to discuss the Iraqi proposal voted in favor of the ban: Iraq, Syria, Sudan, and the Yemen.

27. *Economist,* 1 May 1971, p. 70.

28. *Economist,* 19 June 1971, p. 82.

29. *Economist,* 3 July 1971, p. 73.

30. For an informative book dealing with this period, see Abdul Amir Kubbah, *The Libyan Kingdom: Its Oil Industry and Economic System.*

31. The Libyan Petroleum Law of 1955 was enacted in this manner to encourage oil companies to search for petroleum on a grand scale. See Petroleum Commission of Libya, *Petroleum Development in Libya, 1954 Through Mid-1961;* also Ibrahim Hangari, *The Libyan Petroleum Law, 1955, as Amended up to 1965.*

32. For a perceptive analysis of the major characteristics of the contemporary Libyan political scene, see Lisa Anderson, "Libya and American Foreign Policy," *Middle East Journal* 36, no. 4 (Autumn 1982):516–534.

33. A critical appraisal of both pre- and post-revolutionary Libya is J. A. Allen, *Libya: The Experience of Oil*. In analyzing the success and failure of both administrations, Allen capably distinguished between rhetoric and reality. See also Ruth First, *Libya: The Elusive Revolution*, and Frank C. Waddams, *The Libyan Oil Industry*.

34. *Economist*, 11 July 1970.

35. *MEM*, 15 April 1971.

36. *Financial Times* (London), 10 December 1971.

37. Ibid.

38. *MEES*, 11 May 1973.

39. *Le Monde* (Paris), 16 May 1973.

40. *MEES*, 16 May 1973.

41. *MEES*, 17 August 1973.

42. *Middle East Economic Digest* (London), 17 August 1973.

43. *International Herald Tribune*, 5 September 1973.

44. See *Economist*, 8 September 1973, pp. 69–70.

45. For the historical background, see Elie Kedourie, "Continuity and Change in Modern Iraqi History," *Asian Affairs* 61, no. 2 (June 1974):140–146; Abbas Kelidar, "Iraq: The Search for Stability," *Conflict Studies* 59 (July 1975); Majid Khadduri, *Independent Iraq: A Study in Iraqi Politics from 1932 to 1958*, and, by the same author, *Republican Iraq: A Study of Iraqi Politics Since the Revolution of 1958*.

46. *Financial Times* (London), 5 May 1961.

47. Statement to the Iraqi News Agency, 21 July 1960. For more details on the issue, see Benjamin Shwadran, "Middle East Oil 1961—II: Iraq-IPC Negotiations," *Middle Eastern Affairs* (November 1962):258–267.

48. In mid-August 1967 Iraq, in a demonstration of its firmness of purpose, introduced the new Law no. 97, giving its state-owned oil company INOC the exclusive right to explore and develop new territories.

49. See *Revolutionary Iraq 1968–1973*.

50. While Iraq's relations with the United States remained poor, its friendship with the Soviet Union was becoming a major factor in Iraqi foreign policy, particularly since the Soviet Union supplied the bulk of Iraq's military equipment. In May 1969, Iraq became the first non-Communist country to recognize the German Democratic Republic (East Germany) at ambassador level.

51. *MEM*, 1 July 1971.

52. Ibid.

53. On the party's history and ideology, see Kamel S. Abu Jaber, *The Arab Ba'th Socialist Party: History, Ideology, and Organization*; John F. Devlin, *The Ba'th Party: A History from Its Origins to 1966*; Gordon H. Torrey, "The Ba'th—Ideology and Practice," *Middle East Journal* 23 (Autumn 1969):445–470.

54. Iraqi News Agency (Baghdad), 19 May 1971.

55. *MEM*, 1 July 1971.

56. On the post-World War II Kurdish nationalist movement, see Lettie M. Wenner, "Arab-Kurdish Rivalries in Iraq," *Middle East Journal* 17 (Winter-Spring 1963). For an account of the Kurdish-Iraqi war, see David Adamson, *The Kurdish*

War, and Dana Adams Schmidt, *Journey Among Brave Men*. For a scholarly study of the Kurdish question in Iraq that focuses upon the approach of the Ba'th governments to the Kurdish rebellion from 1968 to 1975, see Edmund Ghareeb, *The Kurdish Question in Iraq*. Ghareeb examined the origins, evolution, and dynamics of Iraq's Kurdish question, concluding that the Kurds were unlikely to engage in another serious attempt to achieve independence by violence.

57. On 15 January 1969 the Iraqi Foreign Minister, Abd-al-Karim Shaikhli, speaking over Baghdad Radio, announced Iraq's rejection of the UN Security Council Resolution 242. Shaikhli explained the key to the Iraqi objection was that the resolution imposed on the victim (the Palestinians) "terms more cruel than those imposed on the aggressor" and that it apparently aimed "to liquidate the Palestine cause in return for withdrawal from territory occupied in June 1967." This statement—the first giving the official position of Iraq on the UN resolution—aligned Iraq with Syria (which has also rejected the Resolution) in opposition to the policies of Egypt and Jordan (who have accepted the resolution).

58. *MEM*, 1 June 1972.

59. The production cutback presented a serious threat to the national security of the Iraqi regime and many statements to this effect were made openly by Iraqi officials.

60. *MEM*, 15 June 1972.

61. *Economist*, 3 June 1972, p. 88.

62. A useful source of information on the events that led to the negotiations with the oil companies and to the eventual nationalization of IPC on 1 June 1972 is Adil Hussein, *Iraq: The Eternal Fire, 1972 Iraqi Oil Nationalizations in Perspective*. For an examination of the admixture of ideology and politics behind the 1972 Iraqi nationalization of IPC, see Abdul H. Raoof, "Ideology and Politics in Iraqi Oil Policy: The Nationalization of 1972," in Russel A. Stone, ed., *OPEC and the Middle East*, pp. 211–224.

63. *MEM*, 15 June 1972.

64. *Guardian* (London), 5 June 1972. The Arab Petroleum Congresses were organized by the Arab League. Their influence, however, waned due to the emergence of OAPEC. The Eighth Arab Petroleum Congress, held in Algiers in June 1972, "was notable in recommending that Arab oil-producing states take direct control of their oil industries and that they establish, through their national oil companies, direct links with countries importing Arab oil." (Frank C. Waddams, *The Libyan Oil Industry*, p. 300.)

65. *Egyptian Gazette*, 11 June 1972.

66. *Times* (London), 21 June 1972.

67. *MEES*, 2 March 1973.

68. Saddam Hussein, *On Current Issues* (Baghdad: Al-Thawra Publications, 1974), p. 80.

69. *Economist*, 13 October 1973, p. 16 (Iraqi Law No. 70, 7 October 1973).

70. *MEES*, 26 October 1973, pp. 3–7 (Iraqi Law No. 90, 21 October 1973). The reasons stated by the Iraqi News Agency for this action included the use of Dutch territory as "a bridgehead for assistance sent to the enemy," i.e., the supply by the Netherlands to Israel of crude oil from its imported stock, the

continuous flights of KLM to "transport mercenaries and assistance to the enemy," the initial opposition of the Netherlands to the issue of an unbiased communiqué by EEC members, the declaration of the Dutch foreign minister to Arab ambassadors of his country's support for Israel, the personal participation of the Dutch minister of defense in a demonstration staged in the Dutch capital to express support for Israel during the war, and the participation of various Dutch establishments and companies in collecting contributions for the Israeli war effort.

Chapter 5: The Shift from the Nasser Era to the Faisal Era, 1967–1973

1. For a detailed personal portrayal of the Saudi monarch, see Gerald de Gaury, *Faisal, King of Saudi Arabia*. Also see Willard A. Beling, ed., *King Faisal and the Modernization of Saudi Arabia*.

2. Sheikh Rustum Ali, *Saudi Arabia and Oil Diplomacy*, p. viii.

3. *Sada al-Usbu* (Bahrain), 1 April 1975: an off-the-record press interview given in the summer of 1972 but withheld from publication for almost three years at the request of King Faisal.

4. George Lenczowski, *Oil and State in the Middle East*, p. 188.

5. Emile Nakhleh, *The United States and Saudi Arabia: A Policy Analysis*, p. 13.

6. Among the oil-producing states, Saudi Arabia falls into a special category. Its oil reserves are by far the largest: in 1971 it had 23 percent of all known reserves in the world, compared to 10.5 percent in Kuwait, 9 percent in Iran, 5.5 percent in Iraq, and 4 percent in Libya. While in 1971 it produced less than 10 percent of total world production, Saudi Arabia was expected to produce over 20 percent by 1980. As the demands of the U.S. market multiplied, the country ready to satisfy these demands was Saudi Arabia.

7. Fouad Ajami, *The Arab Predicament: Arab Political Thought and Practice Since 1967*, p. 24.

8. The *Times* (London), 9 May 1967.

9. See Malcolm Kerr's article in *The Middle East: Quest for an American Policy*, edited by Willard A. Beling.

10. Shortly after Nasser's death, Mohamed Haykal, the still-influential editor of Cairo's leading daily *al-Ahram*, solemnly stated that he had abandoned his former belief in a strict dividing line between "reactionary" and "revolutionary" states. There were circumstances, he wrote in his weekly editorial, when "patience is revolutionary."

11. It has been a lifelong wish of Faisal to pray before his death in Jerusalem's Dome of the Rock, from which, according to Muslim traditions and teachings, Prophet Mohammed ascended into heaven astride the holy white steed Buraq. On the place of Jerusalem in Islamic and Arab history, see Ibrahim Abu-Lughod, ed., *The Arab-Israeli Confrontation of June, 1967: An Arab Perspective*. For a collection of articles that provide some idea of the complexity of the question of Jerusalem, see Joel L. Kraemer, ed., *Jerusalem: Problems and Prospects*. See

also E. M. Wilson, *Jerusalem: Key to Peace,* and O. Kelly Ingram, ed., *Jerusalem: Key to Peace in the Middle East.* For Israeli policies with regard to Jerusalem, see Michael Brecher, "Jerusalem: Israel's Political Decisions, 1947–1977," *Middle East Journal* 32, no. 1 (Winter 1978):13–34. An informative survey of the UN role in the Jerusalem issue is found in R. H. Pfaff, *Jerusalem: Keystone of an Arab-Israeli Settlement.*

12. Bernard Reich, *Quest for Peace: United States-Israel Relations and the Arab-Israeli Conflict,* p. 207.

13. Maurice Samuelson, "Sadat the Stayer," *New Statesman* (London), 10 October 1975, p. 432.

14. For Sadat's involvement with the Muslim Brotherhood see Anwar el Sadat, *In Search of Identity: An Autobiography,* pp. 22–24.

15. *Arab World* (Beirut), 28 June 1971.

16. *MEM,* 15 May 1972.

17. From 1969 to 1972, Henry Kissinger's strategy in the Middle East reflected a preference of freezing diplomacy while insuring Israeli military superiority. This approach was promoted to meet mounting Soviet military involvement in Egypt. However, once Sadat expelled the Soviets from Egypt, the United States failed to react by pressuring Israel for concessions, weakening Sadat's and Faisal's positions in the Arab world. (For Kissinger's Middle East policies see his memoirs, *White House Years.*)

18. *Le Monde* (Paris), 28 March 1973.

19. *Washington Post,* 18 April 1973. In 1964 the U.S. consumed about 588 million tons of oil and imported 100 million tons. By 1974 its consumption had increased to 785 million tons and its imports to 315 million tons.

20. *Financial Times* (London), 1 May 1973.

21. Sadat and Faisal agreed on the oil weapon strategy but disagreed on the tactics. While Faisal wanted to wait until Western dependence on Arab oil increased, making oil leverage highly effective, Sadat was pressed for time and advocated immediate action. See Walter Laqueur, *Confrontation: The Middle East and World Politics.*

22. "Kuwaiti Is Quoted on Oil as Weapon," *New York Times,* 14 March 1973.

23. In an earlier interview with the Tripoli daily *al-Fajr al-Jadid* (15 April 1973), Qaddafi expressed doubts "that the Arab oil-producing states would adopt an earnest attitude with respect to the use of oil as a weapon in the Middle East crisis." The Libyan leader accused Arab states at the time of "deceiving each other" and claimed that "if any one of them were to stop the flow of oil, its neighbors would hurry to raise their output." He maintained that "when we reduced our output after the revolution, Saudi Arabia raised its output. After we nationalized the oil, some of the Arab states hurriedly beat us to the markets to sell their oil." He stressed that he was "not referring to Kuwait and Saudi Arabia alone, but to all the Arabs who possess oil, even those with alleged progressive regimes."

24. *MEES,* 16 May 1973.

25. Anthony Sampson, "The Oil War," *Observer,* 17 November 1974.

26. *Al-Nahar* (Beirut), 22 April 1973.

27. For an informative background on Omani history and politics, see Robert G. Landen, *Oman Since 1856: Disruptive Modernization in a Traditional Arab Society.*

28. For additional reading on this issue, see "Details of the Iranian Invasion," *al-Talia* (Kuwaiti weekly), 12 January 1974, pp. 15–18; also *The Arabian Peninsula, Iran and the Gulf States: New Wealth, New Power, A Summary Record.*

29. The Saudis were also worried about the possibility that a radical group might manage to sink a supertanker in the Strait of Hormuz, which links the Gulf with the outside world. Such a move would have blocked oil shipments for months. For "fanciful scenarios" of oil-supply disruption through this bottleneck, see R. K. Ramazani, *The Persian Gulf and the Strait of Hormuz*, pp. 89–94.

30. *World Energy Demands and the Middle East*, p. 99, part I.

31. For a full text of Yamani's speech, see *World Energy Demands and the Middle East*, pp. 95–100.

32. Tareq Y. Ismael, "Oil: The New Diplomacy," in Tareq Y. Ismael, ed., *The Middle East in World Politics*, p. 236.

33. Sampson, "The Oil War."

34. "The King Speaks Out," *Middle East Perspective* (New York) 6, no. 5 (September 1973), 1.

35. Quoted by Sampson, "The Oil War."

36. Guy de Jonquieres, writing from Washington, D.C., in the *Financial Times* (London), 14 September 1973.

37. A spokesman for the Department of State said that "the idea of using force which was mentioned in the speech does not reflect in any way any thought within this administration."

Chapter 6: The Leverage of Oil, 1973/1974

1. Morris A. Adelman, "Is the Oil Shortage Real?" *Foreign Policy* (Winter 1972):73. Adelman, a widely known expert on world oil, had in the past been "spectacularly wrong about what he said would happen to oil prices in the 1960s. He said they would fall, and, as everyone knows by now, they have risen steadily and look like continuing to rise for the foreseeable future" (see the *Economist*, 7 July 1973, special survey, p. 12). Other works contributing to the debate were: David Hess, "Is Energy Crisis a Myth to Enrich Oil and Auto Tycoons?" *Philadelphia Inquirer*, 18 April 1973; "The Energy Crisis: Reality or Myth," *Annals of the American Academy of Political and Social Science* (November 1973); James Ring Adams, "The Great Debate," *Wall Street Journal*, 10 April 1973; Robert Hunter, *The Energy Crisis and U.S. Foreign Policy*; Edward Luttwak, "A New Look at the Energy Crisis," *Near East Report*, 18 April 1973.

2. Adelman, "Is the Oil Shortage Real?" p. 73.

3. Ibid., pp. 76–77.

4. Ibid., p. 90.

5. Ibid., p. 105.

6. From the transcript of the "Firing Line" program, "The Energy Crisis and Energy Policy," William F. Buckley, Jr., host, and Morris A. Adelman and Jock Ritchie, guests, p. 1. The program was taped in New York City on 13 September 1973 and originally telecast on PBS on 23 September 1973.

7. Anthony Sampson, "The Oil War," *Observer* (London), 17 November 1974.

8. Compare those views with the kind of thinking that abounded in the postembargo period stating that the Arab oil embargo, as led by Saudi Arabia, was caused by hidden "compelling economic considerations," i.e., absorptive capacity constraints in Saudi Arabia and conservation of a depleting asset. One such example is Uzi Arad, who argued that the marketing of oil "is a process in which economics is paramount and politics subsidiary. . . . In short, if Israel did not exist, the Saudis would have had to invent it" (see John Duke Anthony, ed., *The Middle East: Oil, Politics, and Development*, p. 22). Time has shown the error of the claim that Saudi Arabia wanted to cut production and used the October war as an excuse.

It is also very instructive to compare such a line of argument with that which prevailed during the 1967 oil embargo. Then, the argument was, "The Arab states will have to recognize that denying oil to the West is merely a form of economic suicide" ("Beyond the Oil Boycott," *New York Times*, 11 June 1967).

9. Joseph S. Szyliowicz, ed., *The Energy Crisis and U.S. Foreign Policy*, p. 229.

10. *Middle East Intelligence Survey* (Tel Aviv), 1, no. 3 (1 May 1973):24.

11. John W. Amos, "The Middle East: The Problem of Quarantine," in William W. Whitson, ed., *Foreign Policy and U.S. National Security*, p. 91, fn. 10.

12. James F. Akins, "The Oil Crisis: This Time the Wolf Is Here," *Foreign Affairs* (April 1973):468–469.

13. Ibid., p. 490.

14. Sampson, "The Oil War."

15. *MEES*, 12 October 1973.

16. Iraqi media gave this story top billing, even ahead of battlefield news. From the beginning, Iraqi media urged other Arab countries to follow Iraq's example to "hit and liquidate the U.S. interests completely and to nationalize the U.S. oil interests in particular as a punishment for those who support the Zionist enemy's aggression. . . . We also call on all the Arab countries to stop exporting oil to the United States" (Baghdad Radio, 7 October 1973).

17. Charles F. Doran, *Myth, Oil, and Politics*, p. 32.

18. *MEM*, 15 October 1973, p. 4.

19. See *MEES*, 26 October 1973, p. 2.

20. See "Middle East Oil Emergency," *Petroleum Press Service*, no. 11 (November 1973):407.

21. The mass media of those countries remained silent on the oil question, an attitude severely criticized by the Iraqi media. Baghdad's daily *al-Thawra*, in its editorial of 11 October 1973, protested: "It is very strange that conspicuous silence is maintained [by some Arab governments] in respect to oil. Arab oil-producing countries should nationalize America's share and stop the flow of oil to America as Iraq has already done."

22. An excerpt from the official Kuwait "Communiqué of OAPEC," 14 October 1973.

23. Iraq did not sign the communiqué. Radio Baghdad commented on 21 October 1973: "It was evident that the agent governments' representatives, particularly those of Saudi Arabia who are known for their close relations with U.S. imperialism, intended the adoption of such a weak decision to absorb the wrath of the Arab masses and to erase the slogan of using the oil weapon."

24. MEES, no. 52, 19 October 1973, pp. iii–iv. The communiqué was signed by all participants—Saudi Arabia, Kuwait, Libya, Algeria, Egypt, Syria, Abu Dhabi, Bahrain, and Qatar—except Iraq.

25. MEM, 15 October 1973.

26. R.H.C. Steed, "Oil, the Koran and King Faisal," Daily Telegraph (London), 15 March 1975.

27. For a study that explores the reasons why Aramco acquiesced to the order of the Saudi government to institute an oil embargo against the United States, see Louis Morano, "Multinationals and Nation-States: The Case of Aramco," Orbis 23, no. 2 (Summer 1979):447–468.

28. Anthony Sampson, "Oil War: The Arabs' Grand Slam," Observer, 24 November 1974.

29. See Dana Adams Schmidt, Armageddon in the Middle East, p. 212.

30. MEES, 26 October 1973, p. 5.

31. MEES, 19 October 1973, p. 4.

32. MEES, 2 November 1973, p. 1.

33. MEES, Supplement, 6 November 1973, pp. 2, 5.

34. MEES, 23 November 1973, p. 5.

35. Kissinger's diplomatic efforts to mediate during and after the 1973 war are discussed extensively in Jeffrey Z. Rubin, ed., Dynamics of Third Party Intervention: Kissinger in the Middle East.

36. MEES, 30 November 1973, p. 1.

37. For the full text, see the Financial Times (London), 27 December 1973.

38. The Dutch government "turned down Arab requests that the Netherlands make a new unilateral declaration on the Middle East backing the Arab cause." See Reginald Dale, "Arabs May Alter Attitude on Use of Rotterdam," Financial Times (London), 3 December 1973.

39. This was a time of more positive attitudes among young Saudis than when Peter Mansfield's report in the Sunday Times of London (6 August 1967) indicated that there were "serious mutterings of discontent in Saudi Arabia" as a result of Saudi failure to participate effectively in the 1967 Arab-Israeli war. "Many of the young Saudi elite feel bitterly ashamed. As one remarked: 'Despite our government's boasts that we were sending 20,000 troops to help Jordan, our only casualties in the war were two officers killed in an accident on holiday in Italy,'" reported Mansfield.

40. The continued U.S. policy of ignoring Arab overtures led to reports that Saudi Arabia would renew diplomatic relations with Moscow, helping to produce this chain of events: (1) In January, Kuwait dispatched a military mission to examine a possible arms deal in Moscow; (2) Abu Dhabi followed suit with a

similar mission to Yugoslavia, and in February a trade delegation from Hungary arrived to discuss commercial agreements; (3) Oman decided to establish diplomatic relations with Rumania.

41. On a number of other occasions Yamani left open the possibility of resorting to the oil weapon if peace should not be achieved in the Middle East. See, for example, his speech to the American Society of Newspaper Editors in Washington on 18 April 1975, quoted in the *Washington Post*, 19 April 1975.

42. Statement issued after the meeting. See the *New York Times*, 19 March 1974.

43. Stephen D. Krasner asserted that "without the enormous revenues generated by collusive pricing, oil would be a far less potent political weapon." See Krasner, "The Great Oil Sheikhdown," *Foreign Policy* (Winter 1973-74):123.

44. Quoted by Fuad M. Itayim, "Strengths and Weaknesses of the Oil Weapon," paper submitted to the Sixteenth Annual Conference of the International Institute of Strategic Studies, University of Sussex, 12–15 September 1974, p. 5.

45. Juan de Onis, "Two Countries Balk," *New York Times*, 19 March 1974. This medium-range objective of pressuring the U.S. to become more sensitive to Arab demands coincides with statements made by a number of Arab officials. The Algerian minister of energy, Belaid Abdessalam, maintained that the oil weapon was used in order "to call the world's attention to the injustices of the situation" (*U.S. News and World Report*, 31 December 1973, p. 21); the Saudi minister of foreign affairs Omar al-Saqqaf asserted that the oil weapon was used to put the case to the American people (*New York Times*, 31 December 1973, p. 5); Egyptian Ambassador Ashraf Ghorbal stated that "the oil weapon was used to gain attention to 25 years of suffering" (*New York Times*, 7 January 1974, p. 1). President Sadat declared that the oil weapon "was only a message to show the whole world that the Arabs after the 6th of October deserve to take their place under the sun" (*New York Times*, 25 February 1974, p. 1).

46. For instance, the Arab writer Kamal Hani concluded that while the oil weapon was indeed successful, it was a "catastrophe" as far as the stated objectives were concerned. See Kamal Hani, "The Disengagement Between Oil and the Interest of the Arab People" *al-Tariq* (Beirut) no. 4 (April 1974):16–17.

47. The Arab oil expert Fuad Itayim maintained that the 1973 October war was a watershed in Middle Eastern history, not because it heralded a shift in the military balance of power, but because it "ushered in the employment of the Arab oil on a massive scale as a bargaining counter." See Fuad Itayim, "Arab Oil: The Political Dimensions," *Journal of Palestine Studies* (Winter 1974):84. For two diametrically opposed points of view of the 1973 war, see Hassan al Badri, Taha el Magdoub, and Mohammed Dia el Din Zohdy, *The Ramadan War, 1973*, and Chaim Herzog, *The War of Atonement: October 1973*.

48. In his book *A Changing Image: American Perceptions of the Arab-Israeli Dispute*, Richard Curtiss traced the evolution of U.S. public opinion on the Arab-Israeli conflict and concluded that it is becoming more balanced and that this trend will continue.

49. Marwan Iskander in *The Arab Oil Question* contended that Arab oil provided Kissinger with a convincing and effective argument for exerting pressure

on Israel (see pp. 114–115). Similarly, Mohammad Hasan in his book *Harb al-Bitrol* [The Oil War] viewed the oil weapon as the *deus ex machina* for Kissinger's successful negotiations of the Sinai disengagement agreements (p. 173).

50. In "Uniqueness and Generality" (of the oil crisis), *Daedalus* 104, no. 4 (Fall 1975), Ian Smart maintained that the disengagement agreements between Egypt and Israel "were negotiated by an American secretary of state moved to a new urgency by the use of the Arab oil weapon" (p. 262). The well-known Lebanese journalist Ghassan Tueni argued that in the postembargo era, the oil weapon would continue to provide the impetus for U.S. pressure on Israel. See Tueni, "After October," *Journal of Palestine Studies* (Summer 1974):128.

51. It was Kissinger in his January 1975 interview with *Business Week* who initiated those threats. The same theme was later reiterated by President Ford in his interview with *Time* magazine, 20 January 1975, and by Secretary of Defense James Schlesinger in the *Washington Post*, 19 May 1975.

52. For a study analyzing the success of the Arab oil embargo in bringing an end to the Middle Eastern stalemate and starting a fresh round of negotiations for the political settlement of the Mideast conflict, see Mohammed Ahrari, "OAPEC and 'Authoritative' Allocation of Oil: An Analysis of the Arab Oil Embargo," *Studies in Comparative International Development* 14, no. 1 (Spring 1979):9–21.

53. Ironically, neither Saudi Arabia, the country that took the lead in the oil embargo, nor the Palestinians, for whose cause the embargo was imposed, were happy about this major development. For a critical view of the Camp David agreement, see Fayez A. Sayegh, "The Camp David Agreement and the Palestine Problem," *Journal of Palestine Studies* 8, no. 2 (Winter 1979):3–40.

54. The net income of the seven major oil companies in 1974 was $11,321 million as compared with $8,807 million in 1973. For criticisms of oil profits, see the *Wall Street Journal*, 21 January and 4 April 1974 and the *New York Times*, 8 and 27 April 1974.

55. *Wall Street Journal* and *New York Times*, 28 January 1974.

56. Reprinted in the *New York Times*, 25 January 1974.

57. *New York Times*, 17 May 1974, p. 53. Letter to stockholders from Maurice F. Granville, chairman of the board, 5 June 1974.

58. *Congressional Record*, 15 July 1974, p. E4703.

59. Ibid.

60. See Richard B. Mancke, *Squeaking By: U.S. Energy Policy Since the Embargo*. Mancke pointed out that "the near total inability of the United States and its European and Japanese allies to cope with the oil embargo reduced sharply the cohesion of the Western alliance" (p. 3).

61. Leonard Silk, "The Oil Weapon," *New York Times*, 6 November 1973.

62. Ibid.

63. Ibid.

64. West European imports in 1974 were 733 million tons (68 percent from the Middle East, 12 percent from North Africa (i.e., Libya and Algeria), and 8 percent from West Africa (Nigeria). For a discussion and comparison of the policies pursued by France and Germany in their search for adequate oil supplies

in the post-1973 period, see Horst Mendershausen, *Coping with the Oil Crisis: French and German Experiences.*

65. *Facts on File* 33, no. 1723, 4–10 November 1973, pp. 919–920.

66. Makoto Momoi, "Japan and the Persian Gulf and the Indian Ocean," in Abbas Amirie, ed., *The Persian Gulf and Indian Ocean in International Politics,* p. 167.

67. *Facts on File,* 34, no. 1736, 16 February 1974, pp. 97–98.

68. John M. Goshko, "Israel Assesses Its Support in West as Strains Continue," *International Herald Tribune,* 17 March 1975.

69. Ibid.

70. Ibid.

71. Ibid.

72. Ibid.

73. For an important study of Afro-Arab relations, see Anthony Sylvester, *Arabs and Africans: Cooperation for Development.* The author attributed the African switch to the Arab cause to the perception that Israel was intransigent in dealing with the West Bank and Jerusalem. Other factors included: Israel's association with what is labeled U.S. imperialism; Israel's flirtation with South Africa; greater Third World solidarity and sympathy for the Palestinian cause; and the rejection of the old image of Israel as an underdog fighting the dominant Arabs.

74. B. Rivlin and J. Fomerand, "Changing Third World Perspectives and Policies Toward Israel," in Michel Curtis and Susan A. Gitelson, eds., *Israel in the Third World,* p. 347.

75. Merie Sirkin, "Israeli-American Relations: The Fall From Grace," unpublished paper (Waltham, Mass.: African Studies Association, Brandeis University, 1975), p. 23, cited by Victor T. LeVine and Timothy W. Luke in *The Arab-African Connection: Political and Economic Realities,* p. 16. See also A. Gitelson, "Why Do Small States Break Diplomatic Relations With Outside Powers? Lessons From the African Experience," *International Studies Quarterly* 18 (December 1974):451–484.

76. A. Akinsanya, "The Afro-Arab Alliance: Dream or Reality?" *African Affairs* 75 (October 1976):525.

77. A. Bamisaye, "The Politics of Oil," unpublished paper (Waltham, Mass.: African Studies Association, Brandeis University, 1974), p. 15, cited in LeVine and Luke, *The Arab-African Connection,* p. 17. See also E. Chibwe, *Arab Dollars for Africa,* pp. 42–50.

78. On Arab petrodollars and Africa, see K. A. Hameed, "The Oil Revolution and African Development," *African Affairs* 75, no. 300 (July 1976):349–358; A. A. Mazrui, "Black Africa and the Arabs," *Foreign Affairs* 53, no. 4 (July 1975):725–742; A. Oded, "Slaves and Oil: The Arab Image in Black Africa," *Weiner Library Bulletin* 27 (1974):34–47; A. Raphael, "Arab Oil Wealth Starts To Flow in Africa," *African Development* 9, no. 25 (May 1975):24–27.

79. David Housego, "Saudi Arabia Keeps a Tight Hold on its Purse Strings," *Financial Times* (London), 3 December 1974.

80. Ibid.

81. For an essay reviewing the energy situation in Western Europe in light of the dramatic rise in oil prices, see George F. Ray, *Western Europe and the*

Energy Crisis. See also Albert H. Hourani, *Europe and the Middle East* (London: Macmillan, 1980).

82. For a descriptive analysis of Japan's feeling of vulnerability in oil matters, see Yuan-Li Wu, *Japan's Search for Oil: A Case Study on Economic Nationalism and International Security*. Other articles dealing with the topic are: V. Yorke, "Oil, the Middle East and Japan's Search for Security," *International Affairs* 57, no. 3 (Summer 1981):428–448; Masao Sakisaka, "Japan's Long-Term Vulnerabilities," in J. C. Hurewitz, ed., *Oil, the Arab-Israeli Dispute, and the International World*, pp. 52–64; Koji Taira, "Japan After the 'Oil Shock': An International Resource Pauper," *Current History* 68, no. 404 (April 1975):145–148.

83. See Frank Church, "The Impotence of the Oil Companies," *Foreign Policy* 27 (Summer 1977); see also the testimony of Morris Adelman: U.S., Congress, Senate, Committee on Foreign Relations, *Multinational Corporations and United States Foreign Policy, Hearings Before the Subcommittee on Multinational Corporations*, 94th Cong., 1st sess., 1975, pp. 11–12.

84. In his book *Le Petrole à l'Heure Arabe*, Nicholas Sarkis argued that the net success of the OAPEC oil policy was that it allowed the Arab world "to appear on the international scene as a coherent and powerful bloc" (p. 45).

85. See Drew Middleton, "Persian Gulf Emerging as Military Focus," *New York Times*, 22 January 1975.

86. Klaus Knorr, "International Economic Leverage and Its Uses," in Klaus Knorr and Frank N. Trager, eds., *Economic Issues and National Security*, p. 110.

87. For an analysis of the macroeconomic impacts of the oil price increases and the monetary and fiscal policies that were pursued in reaction to those increases by the United States, Western Europe, and Japan, see Edward R. Fried and Charles L. Schultze, eds., *Higher Oil Prices and the World Economy: The Adjustment Problem*. See also Thierry de Montbrial, "The Economic Effects of a Massive Increase in the Price of Oil," in Thierry de Montbrial, *Energy: The Countdown*, pp. 186–197.

88. Szyliowicz, *The Energy Crisis*, p. 185.

89. To alleviate the damage done by higher oil prices, Peter R. Odell and Luis Vallenilla in their book *The Pressures of Oil: A Strategy for Economic Revival* called for the creation of a joint OPEC-OECD fund to recompense the non–oil-producing Third World.

90. Harmut Brosche, "The Arab Oil Embargo and United States Pressure Against Chile: Economic and Political Coercion and the Charter of the United Nations," *Case Western Reserve Journal of International Law* 7, no. 3 (1974):6.

91. *New York Times*, 7 January 1974; *Wall Street Journal*, 7 January 1974.

92. Romano Prodi and Alberto Clo, "Europe," in Raymond Vernon, ed., *The Oil Crisis*, p. 101.

93. Arthur Jay Klinghoffer, "The Soviet Union and the Arab Oil Embargo of 1973–74," *International Relations*, no. 3 (May 1976):1018. See also Frank Gardner, "Not a Bad Profit for the Soviets—300 Percent," *Oil and Gas Journal* 72, no. 14 (April 1974):51.

94. Juan de Onis, "The Arab World, Use of 'Oil Weapon' Is Designed To Pay Political Dividends," *New York Times*, 28 November 1973.

95. See John M. Goshko and Jonathan Randal, "EEC Leaders Make Show of Unity on Oil," *Washington Post*, 16 December 1973; C. H. Farnsworth, "Common Market for Energy Sharing," *New York Times*, 15 December 1973.

96. For a discussion of how the Iraqi media manipulated the oil issue to put pressure on other Arab oil-producing states to take action against the United States, see William A. Rugh, "Arab Media and Politics During the October War," *Middle East Journal* 29 (Summer 1975):310–328.

97. Mohamed H. Heikal, *The Road to Ramadan*, p. 271.

98. See Joseph S. Szyliowicz, "The Embargo and U.S. Foreign Policy," in Szyliowicz, ed., *The Energy Crisis*, p. 206.

99. U.S. Congress, *The United States Oil Shortage and the Arab-Israeli Conflict*, p. 51.

100. The embargo reduced world oil flows only from 33 mbd in September 1973 to 28.8 mbd in November 1973. In 1973, OPEC exports increased to peak at 29 mbd.

101. See Joe Stork, "The Oil Weapon," in Naseer Aruri, ed., *Middle East Crucible*, pp. 353–357.

102. *Wall Street Journal*, 9 April 1974. See also *Times* (London), 10 April 1974, p. 21.

103. Christopher T. Rand, "The Arabian Fantasy: A Dissenting View of the Oil Crisis," *Harper's* (January 1974):43.

104. See *Brief* (Tel Aviv), no. 66, 16–30 September 1973, p. 1.

105. On Soviet relations with oil-producing states, see Lincoln Landis, *Politics and Oil: Moscow in the Middle East*. A historical analysis of Soviet relations with the Middle Eastern oil producers is found in A. Yodfat and M. Abir, *In the Direction of the Gulf: The Soviet Union and the Persian Gulf*. In this book the authors contended that the USSR was the first foreign power to recognize the Kingdom of Saudi Arabia. For a wide-ranging study of Soviet oil politics, particularly with regard to Middle Eastern oil, see Arthur J. Klinghoffer, *The Soviet Union and International Oil Politics*; B. Rachkov, "The Future of Arab Oil," *International Affairs* (Moscow) 8 (1970):32–37; Robert E. Hunter, *The Soviet Dilemma in the Middle East, Part II: Oil and the Persian Gulf*; A. S. Becker and A. L. Horelick, *Soviet Policy in the Middle East*; John A. Berry, "Oil and Soviet Policy in the Middle East," *Middle East Journal* 26, no. 2 (Spring 1972):149–160.

106. Klinghoffer, "The Soviet Union and the Arab Oil Embargo," p. 1011.

107. Paul Wohl, "Soviets Deny U.S.S.R. Is Behind Oil Embargo," *Christian Science Monitor* (London edition), 17 December 1973.

108. Ibid.

109. D. Volsky and A. Ustvatov, "Israeli Expansionists Miscalculate," *New Times*, no. 42 (October 1973):10. See also C. L. Sulzberger, "Having and Eating Oilcake," *New York Times*, 29 December 1973, p. 25.

110. William A. Rugh, "Arab Media and Politics During the October War," *Middle East Journal* 29 (Summer 1975):328.

111. Ibid.

112. Wohl, "Soviets Deny U.S.S.R." See also Victor Zorza, "Arab Oil Weapon in a Moscow Refinery," *Times* (London), 20 November 1973; also by the same

author, "Moscow May Find the Oil Weapon Double-Edged," *Times* (London), 11 December 1973.

113. China had always shown little interest in Middle Eastern oil. Between 1950 and 1973, China's policy toward the Middle East was limited to efforts to modify Soviet influence in the area. After 1973, however, China began to exhibit considerable interest in Middle Eastern trade. The Chinese intended to use trade with the Middle East as a means of improving their world balance of trade.

114. Clare Hollingsworth, "China Backs Arab 'Oil Weapon,'" *Daily Telegraph* (London), 28 December 1974.

115. *Business Week*, 13 January 1975, p. 69.

116. *New York Times*, 13 January 1975.

117. *Business Week*, 13 January 1975, pp. 66–76.

118. An interview given by Kissinger on "Bill Moyers' Journal: International Report," reproduced by the Department of State's Bureau of Public Affairs as "The Secretary-of-State Interview," 16 January 1975, p. 6.

119. The main advocate of U.S. military intervention was Professor Robert W. Tucker, whose article "Oil: The Issue of American Intervention," *Commentary* (January 1975), argued that a situation could well arise that would necessitate a resort to force to insure the security of oil supplies from the Gulf to the Western world and Japan. I. F. Stone in "War for Oil?" *New York Review of Books*, 6 February 1975, characterized Tucker's essay as "criminal nonsense" and termed the act of publishing it "irresponsible." Other articles by Tucker, reflecting a similar position, are "Further Reflections on Oil and Force," *Commentary* (March 1975); "Oil and American Power—Three Years Later," *Commentary* (January 1977). For more diverse views on the issue, see Tom Wicker, "Stating the Obvious," *New York Times*, 12 January 1975; Anthony Lewis, "Thinking the Unthinkable," *New York Times*, 12 December 1974; Charles L. Schultze, "Oil War: Fantasy No One Needs," *Washington Post*, 26 January 1975; Terence McCarthy, "The Middle East: Will We Go to War?" *Ramparts* (March 1975); Miles Ignotus [pseud.], "Seizing Arab Oil," *Harper's* (March 1975):45–62; Earl C. Ravenal, "Fear of Force in the Middle East: The Oil Grab Scenario," *New Republic* (January 1975); Dennis H. Wrong, "Oil, the Marines, and Professor Tucker," *Dissent* (Spring 1975); U.S. Library of Congress, Congressional Research Service, *Oil Fields as Military Objectives* (Washington, D.C.: Government Printing Office, 1975).

120. Only 10 percent of those interviewed by the Gallup Poll supported military action: "Mideast Invasion by U.S. Opposed," *Washington Post*, 23 January 1975; see also Leslie Gelb, "Why Did Mr. Kissinger Say That?" *New York Times*, 19 January 1975.

121. *Time*, 6 January 1975, p. 31.

122. Emile Nakhleh, *The United States and Saudi Arabia*, p. 58.

123. Ibid., pp. 58–59.

124. Smart, "Uniqueness and Generality," p. 278.

125. Ibid., p. 279.

126. Peter Mangold, *Superpower Intervention in the Middle East*, p. 76.

127. James E. Akins, "Book Review: *Superpower Intervention in the Middle East* by Peter Mangold," *Middle East Journal* 33, no. 2 (Spring 1979):221.

Glossary

ARAMCO. The Arabian-American Oil Company. Originally established in 1933 by Standard Oil Company of California (Socal) and later joined by three other U.S. multinational oil companies: Texaco (1936), Exxon (1948), and Mobil (1948).

Bandung Conference. The conference of Asian and African nations, held in Bandung, Indonesia, on April 18–24, 1955. It condemned "colonialism in all of its manifestations" and unanimously adopted a ten-point "declaration on the promotion of world peace and cooperation," incorporating mainly the principles of the U.N. charter. In the aftermath of the conference, Gamal Abdel Nasser of Egypt, Jawaharlal Nehru of India, and Josip Broz Tito of Yugoslavia emerged as the uncontested leaders of the newly born nonalignment movement. The Bandung conference had no successor.

Compagnie Française des Pétroles (CFP). French national oil company, the biggest European national oil company. Controlled by the French state. As an instrument of French oil policy, the company combines the interests of the state and private investors.

Concession. Cooperative access to supplies; has the character of a contract; generally given for a term of years but may be granted in perpetuity.

Iraq Petroleum Company (IPC). A consortium of British, Dutch, U.S., and French companies. British Petroleum, Compagnie Française des Pétroles, and Shell each owned 23.75 percent, while Esso and Mobil each owned 11.875 percent and the Gulbenkian Foundation, 5 percent.

Istanbul Convention. A conference held in Istanbul in 1888 and attended by Austria, France, Germany, Britain, Italy, the Netherlands, Russia, Spain, and Turkey. Conferees agreed that the Suez Canal should "always be free and open, in the time of war as in the time of peace, to every vessel of commerce or of war, without distinction of flag."

Jedda Accords. A ceasefire agreement between Nasser and Faisal reached in August 1965, which provided for the formation of a transitional government of Republicans and Royalists in Yemen to hold a plebiscite that would allow the Yemenis to decide for themselves which type of government they wanted. It stipulated the withdrawal of Egyptian forces within ten months from the date of the agreement and the suspension of all Saudi assistance to the Royalists.

Kuwait Oil Company (KOC). Owned in equal shares by Gulf Oil and British Petroleum.

Muslim Brotherhood. Muslim revitalization movement founded in 1928. Its leader, Hasan al-Banna, called for a purified Islam and denounced the growing secularism and Westernization of the Muslim world. Had a paramilitary organization and engaged in political assassinations.

OAPEC. Organization of Arab Petroleum Exporting Countries. Established 1968 to determine ways and means for cooperation among Arab oil producers in oil matters. Its members are Algeria, Bahrain, Egypt (membership suspended as of 17 April 1979), Iraq, Kuwait, Libya, Qatar, Saudi Arabia, Syria, and the United Arab Emirates.

Oasis Oil. A company that produced about one-third of Libya's oil; was owned jointly by Continental Oil and Marathon (one-third each), and by Amerada and Royal Dutch/Shell (one-sixth each).

OPEC. Organization of Petroleum-Exporting Countries. Established 1960 to unify and coordinate the oil policies of the producing countries. Its members are Algeria, Ecuador, Gabon, Indonesia, Iran, Iraq, Kuwait, Libya, Nigeria, Qatar, Saudi Arabia, United Arab Emirates, and Venezuela.

TAPLINE. Trans-Arabian Pipeline Company. Pipeline built across Saudi Arabia, Syria, and Jordan to the Zahrani refinery in South Lebanon in 1951 at a cost of more than $200 million. Of its 1,068 miles, 25.8 miles were in Lebanon, the Mediterranean terminus; 79.1 miles were in Syria; 110 miles were in Jordan; and the balance were in Saudi Arabia, where the pipeline originated. The pipeline moved about 325,000 barrels of oil a day for transshipment, mostly to Europe.

U.N. Security Council Resolution 242. A resolution approved unanimously on November 22, 1967, which aimed at bringing peace to the Middle East. It called for withdrawal of Israeli forces from Arab territories occupied in the 1967 war; an end to the state of belligerency between the Arab nations and Israel; acknowledgement of and respect for the sovereignty, territorial integrity, and political independence of every nation in the area; the establishment of "secure and recognized boundaries"; a guarantee of freedom of navigation through international waterways in the area; and a just settlement of the refugee problem.

Identifications of Officials

'Arif, Abdul Rahman. Became president of Iraq when younger brother, President Abdul Salam 'Arif, was killed in helicopter crash April 13, 1966. He was overthrown in a bloodless coup on July 17, 1968; living in exile.

'Arif, Abdul Salam. Headed an army coup that overthrew Abdul Karim Kassim in February 1963. Killed in helicopter crash near Basrah on April 13, 1966.

al-Assad, Hafez, Lt. Gen. Syrian president since March 1971 following a successful coup in November 1970 that overthrew another faction of the Ba'ath Party. Elected for second seven-year term as president in February 1978.

al-Atiki, Abdel Rahman. Kuwaiti Minister of Finance and Petroleum 1967–1975; Minister of Finance since 1975.

el-Barzani, Mulla Mustafa. Leader of Kurdish revolt against Iraq that was crushed by Iraqi army in March 1975. Died in exile in 1979.

Ben Bella, Ahmed. After Algerian independence in 1962, he was elected president September 15, 1963. Overthrown in bloodless coup June 1965 and was under house arrest until July 1979 when President Chadli Bendjedid released him.

Boumediene, Houari. Became second president of Algeria when he led a coup against Ben Bella in June 1965. Died in 1978 of cancer.

Bourguiba, Habib Ben Ali. Became first president of Tunisia after France granted Tunisia independence in 1957; re-elected in 1959, 1964, 1969; elected president for life by National Assembly in March 1975.

Farouk I. King of Egypt from 1936 until he was deposed and forced to abdicate by a group of officers led by Nasser in 1952. Died in exile in Rome in 1965.

Gulbenkian, Calouste. Armenian entrepreneur who became known as "Mr. Five Percent" because of his share in IPC.

Hassan II. King of Morocco since 1961. Survived coup attempts in 1971, 1972.

Ibn Abdul Aziz, Fahd. Became Saudi Arabia's king after his half-brother, King Khalid, died of a heart attack in 1982.

Ibn Abdul Aziz, Khalid. King of Saudi Arabia between 1975 and 1982.

Ibn Abdul Aziz al-Saud, Faisal. Became crown prince when brother, King Saud, ascended throne in 1953. Became king in March 1964 when Saud was deposed. Assassinated by a nephew March 25, 1975, at palace in Riyadh.

Ibn Saud. First king of Saudi Arabia (1932–1953).

Ibn Talal, Hussein. King of Jordan since 1953.

Idris I. Became king of Libya in 1951 when Libya achieved independence. Deposed in coup led by Col. Qaddafi September 1, 1969.

Kassim, Abdul Karim. Became Iraqi prime minister following a bloody military revolution on July 14, 1958; was executed by a coup led by the officers belonging to the Ba'ath Party in February 1963.

Mossadeq, Mohammed. Iran's prime minister who nationalized Anglo-Iranian Oil Company in 1951. Died in 1967 while under house arrest.

Naguib, Mohammed, Maj. Gen. Became Egypt's first president after the military coup that ousted King Farouk and ended the monarchy in July 1952. He was removed from office in November 1954 and placed under house arrest by Nasser who accused him of having links with Muslim Brotherhood militants who tried to assassinate Nasser in October 1954. Sadat freed him in 1971 but Naguib never reappeared in public. He died in August 1984.

Nasser, Gamal Abdel. Led a military coup which deposed King Farouk in July 1952; became president of Egypt in 1954. Died of heart attack in September 1970.

Pahlavi, Mohammed Reza. Became Shah of Iran in 1941 upon abdication of father, Reza Shah Pahlavi. His rule ended on January 16, 1979, when he was forced to leave Iran. Died in Cairo of cancer on July 27, 1980.

Qaddafi, Muammar. Chairman of Revolutionary Command Council of Libya. Led the army coup in September 1969 that deposed King Idris I.

Sadat, Anwar. Became president of Egypt when Nasser died in 1970. Assassinated October 6, 1981, by Moslem extremists.

Saladin. Legendary Muslim hero, a leader of chivalry, mercy, and compassion. He defeated the Crusaders and liberated Jerusalem in 1187 after it had lain for 88 years in the hands of the Franks, making it again a center of religious toleration and sparing the lives of its Crusader defenders.

Saud. King of Saudi Arabia (1953–64), succeeding his father, King Ibn Saud. Abdicated in 1965 after royal family transferred powers to his brother Faisal. Died in exile in 1969.

Tariqi, Abdullah Ibn Hamad. Saudi Director-General of Oil and Mineral Affairs (1955–1960); the first ever Saudi minister of oil (1960–1962); a founding father of OPEC, he was dismissed when Faisal returned to power in 1962 because of his radical views. He lives in exile.

Yamani, Sheikh Ahmed Zaki. Saudi Minister of Petroleum and Mineral Resources since 1962 when Tariqi was dismissed.

Bibliography

Books

Abi-Mershed, Walid. *Israeli Withdrawal From Sinai.* Beirut: Institute for Palestine Studies, 1965.

Abir, Mordechai. *Oil, Power and Politics.* London: Frank Cass, 1974.

Abu Izzeddin, Nejla M. *Nasser of the Arabs.* Beirut: Imprimerie Catholique, 1975.

Abu Jaber, Kamel S. *The Arab Ba'th Socialist Party: History, Ideology, and Organization.* Syracuse, N.Y.: Syracuse University Press, 1966.

Abu-Lughod, Ibrahim, ed. *The Arab-Israeli Confrontation of June, 1967: An Arab Perspective.* Evanston, Ill.: Northwestern University Press, 1970.

Adams, Michael. *Suez and After: Year of Crisis.* Boston: Beacon Press, 1958.

_____. *Chaos or Rebirth: The Arab Outlook.* London: BBC Publications, 1968.

Adamson, David. *The Kurdish War.* London: Allen and Unwin, 1964.

Adelman, M. A. *The World Petroleum Market.* Baltimore: Johns Hopkins University Press, 1972.

Adie, W.A.C. *Oil, Politics, and Seapower: The Indian Ocean Vortex.* Strategy Papers, 4. New York: Crane, Russack, for the National Strategy Information Center, 1975.

Ajami, Fouad. *The Arab Predicament: Arab Political Thought and Practice Since 1967.* Cambridge: Cambridge University Press, 1981.

Albrecht-Carrie, Rene. *Britain and France.* New York: Doubleday, 1970.

Ali, Sheikh Rustum. *Saudi Arabia and Oil Diplomacy.* New York: Praeger, 1976.

Allaun, F. *The Cost of Suez.* London: Union of Democratic Control, 1957.

Allen, J. A. *Libya: The Experience of Oil.* Boulder: Westview Press, 1981.

Allison, Graham T. *Essence of Decision: Explaining the Cuban Missile Crisis.* Boston: Little, Brown and Co., 1971.

Almana, Mohammed. *Arabia Unified: A Portrait of Ibn Saud.* London: Huchinson Benham, 1980.

Alnasrawi, Abbas. *Financing Economic Development in Iraq: The Role of Oil in a Middle Eastern Economy.* New York: Praeger, 1967.

Amirie, Abbas, ed. *The Persian Gulf and Indian Ocean in International Politics.* Tehran: Institute for International Political and Economic Studies, 1975.

Anderson, Irvine H. *Aramco, the United States, and Saudi Arabia: A Study of the Dynamics of Foreign Oil Policy, 1933–1950.* Princeton, N.J.: Princeton University Press, 1981.

Anthony, John Duke, ed. *The Middle East: Oil, Politics and Development.* Washington, D.C.: American Enterprise Institute for Public Policy Research, 1975.

Appleton, Sheldon. *United States Foreign Policy.* Boston: Little, Brown and Co., 1968.

The Arabian Peninsula, Iran and the Gulf States: New Wealth, New Power, A Summary Record. Washington, D.C.: Middle East Institute, 1973.

Armstrong, Harold C. *Lord of Arabia, Ibn Saud: An Intimate Study of a King.* London: Berker, 1934.

Aruri, Naseer, ed. *Middle East Crucible.* Wilmette, Ill.: Medina University Press International, 1975.

Askari, Hossein, and John Thomas Cummings. *Middle East Economics in the 1970s: A Comparative Approach.* New York: Praeger, 1976.

––––––. *Oil, OECD and Third World: A Vicious Triangle?* Austin: University of Texas Center for Middle Eastern Studies, 1978.

Background to the Middle East Situation 1958. New York and Washington, D.C.: British Information Services, April 1958.

Badeau, John S. *The American Approach to the Arab World.* New York: Harper and Row for the Council on Foreign Relations, 1968.

Badri, Hassan el, Taha el Magdoub, and Mohammed Dia el Din Zohdy. *The Ramadan War, 1973.* Dunn Loring, Virginia: T. N. Dupuy Associates, 1978.

Barger, Thomas. *Arab States of the Persian Gulf.* Newark, Dela.: Center for the Study of Marine Policy, 1975.

Barker, A. J. *Suez: The Seven Day War.* London: Faber and Faber, 1964.

Barrows, Gordon H. *The International Petroleum Industry.* New York: International Petroleum Institute, 1965.

Bar-Zohar, Michel. *Suez: Ultra-Secret.* Paris: Fayard, 1964.

––––––. *Ben Gurion: The Armed Prophet.* New York: Prentice-Hall, 1968.

Beaufre, Andre. *The Suez Expedition: 1956.* New York: Praeger, 1969.

Becker, A. S., and A. L. Horelick. *Soviet Policy in the Middle East.* Santa Monica, Calif.: RAND Corporation, September 1970.

Becker, Abraham, Bent Hansen, and Malcolm Kerr. *The Economics and Politics of the Middle East.* New York: American Elsevier Publishing Co., Inc., 1975.

Beling, Willard A. *The Middle East: Quest for an American Policy.* Albany: State University of New York Press, 1973.

Beling, Willard A., ed. *King Faisal and the Modernisation of Saudi Arabia.* Boulder, Colo.: Westview Press, 1980.

Ben-Gurion, David. *Israel: A Personal History.* New York: Funk and Wagnalls, 1971.

Bhattacharya, Anindya K. *The Myth of Petropower.* Lexington, Mass.: Lexington Books, 1977.

Bill, James A., and Carl Leiden. *The Middle East, Politics and Power.* Boston: Allyn and Bacon, 1974.

––––––. *Politics in the Middle East.* Boston and Toronto: Little, Brown and Co., 1979.

Bill, James A., and Robert W. Stookey. *Politics and Petroleum, The Middle East and the United States.* Brunswick, Ohio: King's Court Communications, Inc., 1975.

Blair, John M. *The Control of Oil.* New York: Pantheon, 1976.

Bowie, Robert R. *Suez 1956.* New York and London: Oxford University Press, 1974.

Bradley, Paul. *The Economics of Crude Petroleum Production.* Amsterdam: North Holland Publishing Co., 1967.

Bromberger, Merry and Serge. *Secrets of Suez.* London: Pan Books, 1957.

Bullard, Sir Reader. *Britain and the Middle East.* 3rd ed. London: Hutchinson University Library, 1964.

Burdett, Winston. *Encounter With the Middle East.* London: Andre Deutsch Ltd., 1970.

Burell, R. M. *Politics, Oil and the Western Mediterranean.* Beverly Hills, Calif.: Sage Publications, 1973.

Butler, R. A. *The Art of the Possible: The Memoirs of Lord Butler.* London: Hamish Hamilton, 1971.

Calvocoressi, Peter, et al. *Suez Ten Years Later: Broadcasts From the B.B.C. Third Programme.* London: British Broadcasting Corporation, 1967.

Campbell, John C. *Defense of the Middle East: Problems of American Policy.* New York: Harper, 1958.

Cantor, Robert D. *Introduction to International Politics.* Itasca, Illinois: F. E. Peacock Publishers, Inc., 1976.

Cattan, Henry. *The Evolution of Oil Concessions in the Middle East and North Africa.* New York: Oceana Publications, 1967.

_____. *Oil and Gas Leases.* New York: Oceana Publications, 1967.

Chapman, Duane. *Energy Resources and Energy Corporations.* Ithaca and London: Cornell University Press, 1983.

Chibwe, E. *Arab Dollars for Africa.* London: Croom Helm, 1976.

Childers, Erskine. *The Road to Suez.* London: MacGibbon and Kee, 1962.

Connors, T. T. *An Examination of the International Flow of Crude Oil, With Special Reference to the Middle East.* Santa Monica, Calif.: RAND Corporation, October 1969.

Copeland, Miles. *The Game of Nations.* London: Weidenfeld and Nicholson, 1969.

Cottam, Richard W. *Nationalism in Iran.* Pittsburgh, Pa.: University of Pittsburgh Press, 1964.

Crosbie, Sylvia K. *A Tacit Alliance: France and Israel From Suez to the Six Day War.* Princeton, N.J.: Princeton University Press, 1974.

Curtis, Michel, and Susan A. Gitelson, eds. *Israel in the Third World.* New Brunswick, N.J.: Transaction Books, 1976.

Curtiss, Richard. *A Changing Image: American Perceptions of the Arab-Israeli Dispute.* Washington, D.C.: American Educational Trust, 1982.

Daly, John Charles (moderator). *Energy Security: Can We Cope with a Crisis?* Washington, D.C.: The American Enterprise Institute for Public Policy Research, 1981.

Daoudi, M. S., and M. S. Dajani. *Economic Sanctions: Ideals and Experience.* London, Boston, Melbourne, and Henley: Routledge and Kegan Paul, 1983.

Darwin, John. *Britain, Egypt and the Middle East: Imperial Policy in the Aftermath of War, 1918–1922.* New York: St. Martin's Press, 1981.

Dawisha, A. I. *Egypt in the Arab World.* New York: John Wiley and Sons, 1976.

Dayan, Moshe. *Diary of the Sinai Campaign.* London: Weidenfeld and Nicholson, 1966.

De Chazeau, Melvin G., and Alfred E. Kahn. *Integration and Competition in the Petroleum Industry.* New Haven, Conn.: Yale University Press, 1959.

De Gaury, Gerald. *Faisal, King of Saudi Arabia.* London: Barber, 1966; New York: Praeger, 1967.

De Montbrial, Thierry. *Energy: The Countdown. A Report to the Club of Rome.* New York: Pergamon Press, 1979.

Denny, Ludwell. *We Fight for Oil.* 1928. Reprint. Westport, Conn.: Hyperion, 1975.

Devlin, Jim F. *The Ba'th Party: A History From Its Origins to 1966.* Stanford, California: Hoover Institution, 1976.

Diamond, Robert, ed. *Middle East: U.S. Policy, Israel, Oil and the Arabs.* Washington, D.C.: Congressional Quarterly, 1974.

Doran, Charles F. *Myth, Oil, and Politics: Introduction to the Political Economy of Petroleum.* New York: Free Press, 1977.

Douglas-Home, Charles. *The Arabs and Israel.* Rev. ed. London and Sydney: Bodley Head, 1970.

Draper, Theodore. *Israel and World Politics.* New York: Viking Press, 1968.

Eayrs, James G., ed. *The Commonwealth and Suez: A Documentary Survey.* London: Oxford University Press, 1964.

Eden, Anthony. *The Memoirs of Anthony Eden: Full Circle.* Boston: Houghton Mifflin, 1960.

———. *The Eden Memoirs: Facing the Dictators.* London: Cassell, 1962.

———. *The Suez Crisis of 1956.* Boston: Beacon Press, 1968.

Eisenhower, Dwight D. *The White House Years: Waging Peace, 1956–1961.* New York: Doubleday, 1965.

Elwell-Sutton, L. P. *Persian Oil: A Study in Power Politics.* London: Lawrence and Wishart, 1955.

Engler, Robert. *The Politics of Oil: A Study of Private Power and Democratic Directions.* New York: Macmillan, 1961; Chicago: University of Chicago Press, 1967.

Eveland, Wilbur Crane. *Ropes of Sand: America's Failure in the Middle East.* New York: Norton, 1980.

Fanning, Leonard M. *Foreign Oil and the Free World.* New York: McGraw-Hill, 1954.

Fatemi, Nasrollah Saifpour. *Oil Diplomacy: Powderkeg in Iran.* New York: Whittier Books, 1954.

Finer, Herman. *Dulles Over Suez: The Theory and Practice of His Diplomacy.* Chicago: Quadrangle Books, 1964.

Finnie, David H. *Desert Enterprises: The Middle East Oil Industry in Its Local Environment.* Cambridge, Mass.: Harvard University Press, 1958.

First, Ruth. *Libya: The Elusive Revolution.* Harmondsworth, England: Penguin, 1974.

Fischer, Louis. *Oil Imperialism: The International Struggle for Petroleum.* 1926. Reprint. Westport, Conn.: Hyperion, 1975.

Ford, Alan W. *The Anglo-Iranian Oil Dispute of 1951–1952: A Study of the Role of Law in the Relations of States.* Berkeley: University of California Press, 1954.

Frankel, P. H. *Mattei, Oil and Power.* London: Faber and Faber, 1966.

Frankland, Noble, and V. King, eds. *Documents on International Affairs 1956.* London: Oxford University Press, 1959.

Fried, Edward R., and Charles L. Schultze, eds. *Higher Oil Prices and the World Economy: The Adjustment Problem.* Washington, D.C.: Brookings Institution, 1975.

Fulda, Michael. *Oil and International Relations: Energy Trade, Technology and Politics.* New York: Arno Press, 1979.

Gallman, W. J. *Iraq Under General Nuri.* Baltimore: Johns Hopkins Press, 1964.

Ghadar, F. *The Evolution of OPEC Strategy.* Lexington, Mass.: Lexington Books, 1977.

Ghareeb, Edmund. *The Kurdish Question in Iraq.* Syracuse, N.Y.: Syracuse University Press, 1981.

Gold, Fern Racine, and Melvin A. Conant. *Access to Oil: The United States' Relationships with Saudi Arabia and Iran.* Washington, D.C.: Government Printing Office, 1977.

Graham, Robert. *Iran: The Illusion of Power.* New York: St. Martin's Press, 1979.

Grayson, Leslie E. *National Oil Companies.* New York: John Wiley and Sons, 1981.

Griffin, James M., and Henry B. Steele. *Energy Economics and Policy.* New York: Academic Press, 1980.

Guhin, Michael A. *John Foster Dulles: A Statesman and His Times.* New York and London: Columbia University Press, 1972.

Hamilton, Charles W. *Americans and Oil in the Middle East.* Houston, Tx.: Gulf Publishing Co., 1962.

Handbook: Oil and the Middle East. Rev. ed. Dhahran, Saudi Arabia: Arabian-American Oil Company, 1968.

Hangari, Ibrahim. *The Libyan Petroleum Law, 1955, as Amended up to 1965.* Tripoli, 1966.

Hartshorn, J. E. *Oil Companies and Governments.* London: Faber and Faber, 1962.

_____ . *Politics and World Oil Economics: An Account of the International Oil Industry in Its Political Environment.* New York: Praeger, 1962.

Hasan, Mohammad. *Harb al-Bitrol* [The oil war]. Cairo: Dar al-Kitab, 1974.

Hayter, W. *Hungary and Suez: The Kremlin and the Embassy.* London: Hodder, 1966.

Heikel, Mohamed H. *The Cairo Documents.* New York: Doubleday, 1972.

_____ . *The Road to Ramadan.* Glasgow: Collins, Sons and Co., 1976.

Hemsley, Stephan. *Oil in the Middle East.* London: Oxford University Press, 1968.

Herzog, Cham. *The War of Atonement: October, 1973.* Boston: Little, Brown and Co., 1975.

Hirst, David. *Oil and Public Opinion in the Middle East.* London: Faber and Faber, 1965; New York: Praeger, 1966.

Hoopes, Townsend. *The Devil and John Foster Dulles*. Boston: Little, Brown and Co., 1973.

Hopwood, Derek. *Egypt: Politics and Society, 1945–1981*. Winchester, Mass.: Allen and Unwin, Inc., 1982.

Hopwood, Derek, ed. *The Arabian Peninsula: Society and Politics*. Totowa, N.J.: Rowman and Littlefield, 1972.

Hourani, Albert H. *The Middle East and the Crisis of 1956*. London: St. Antony's Papers No. 4, Middle Eastern Affairs No. 1, 1958.

––––––. *Europe and the Middle East*. London: Macmillan, 1980.

Howard, Michael, and Robert Hunter. *Israel and the Arab World: The Crisis of 1967*. London: Institute for Strategic Studies, 1967.

Howarth, David. *The Desert King: Ibn Saud and His Arabia*. New York: McGraw-Hill, 1964.

Hudson, Michael. *Arab Politics*. New Haven, Conn.: Yale University Press, 1979.

Hunter, Robert E. *The Soviet Dilemma in the Middle East*. London: London Institute for Strategic Studies, October 1969.

––––––. *The Energy Crisis and U.S. Foreign Policy*. Washington, D.C.: Overseas Development Council, 1973.

Hurewitz, J. C., ed. *Oil, the Arab-Israeli Dispute, and the International World*. Boulder, Colorado: Westview Press, 1976.

Hussein, Adil. *Iraq: The Eternal Fire, 1972 Iraqi Oil Nationalization in Perspective*. Translated by A. W. Lulua. London: Third World Centre for Research and Publishing, 1981.

Ingram, O. K., ed. *Jerusalem: Key to Peace in the Middle East*. Durham, N.C.: Triangle Friends of the Middle East, 1978.

Iraq Petroleum Company, Limited. *The Construction of the Iraq Mediterranean Pipeline: A Tribute to the Men Who Built It*. London: St. Clements Press, 1934.

Isaacs, Stephen D. *Jews and American Politics*. New York: Doubleday, 1974.

Iskandar, Marwan. *The Arab Oil Question*. Beirut: Arab Monograph, Middle East Economic Consultants, 1974.

Ismael, Tareq, ed. *The Middle East in World Politics*. Syracuse, N.Y.: Syracuse University Press, 1974.

Issawi, Charles. *Oil, the Middle East and the World*. New York: Library Press, 1972.

Jacoby, Neil H. *Multinational Oil*. New York: Macmillan, 1974.

Janis, Irving L. *Victims of Groupthink*. Boston: Houghton Mifflin Co., 1972.

Joesten, Joachim. *Nasser: The Rise to Power*. London: Odhams Press, 1960.

Johnson, P. *The Suez War*. London: MacGibbon and Kee, 1957.

Kent, Marian. *Oil and Empire: British Policy and Mesopotamian Oil, 1900–1920*. New York: Harper, 1976.

Kerr, Malcolm. *Regional Arab Politics and Conflict with Israel*. Santa Monica, Calif.: RAND Corporation, 1969.

––––––. *The Arab Cold War: Gamal Abd Al-Nasir and His Rivals, 1958–1967*. 3rd ed. London: Oxford University Press, 1971.

Khadduri, Majid. *Independent Iraq: A Study in Iraqi Politics From 1932 to 1958*. 2nd ed. London: Oxford University Press, 1960.

————. *Republican Iraq: A Study of Iraqi Politics Since the Revolution of 1958.* London: Oxford University Press, 1969.

Khoury, Fred J. *The Arab-Israeli Dilemma.* Syracuse, N.Y.: Syracuse University Press, 1968.

Kissinger, Henry. *White House Years.* Boston: Little, Brown and Co., 1979.

Klass, Michael W., et al. *International Minerals: Cartels and Embargoes.* New York: Praeger, 1980.

Klebanoff, Shoshana. *Middle East Oil and U.S. Foreign Policy: With Special Reference to the U.S. Energy Crisis.* New York: Praeger, 1974.

Klieman, Aaron. *Foundations of British Policy in the Arab World: The Cairo Conference of 1921.* Baltimore: Johns Hopkins University Press, 1970.

Klinghoffer, Arthur Jay. *The Soviet Union and International Oil Politics.* New York: Columbia University Press, 1977.

Knorr, Klaus, and Frank N. Trager, eds. *Economic Issues and National Security.* Lawrence, Kansas: Allen Press, Inc., 1977.

Kohl, Wilfrid L. *After the Second Oil Crisis.* Lexington, Mass.: Lexington Books, 1982.

Kohler, Foy D., Goure Leon, and Harvey Mose. *The Soviet Union and the October 1973 Middle East War: The Implications for Detente.* Coral Gables, Fla.: University of Miami, 1974.

Kosut, Hal, ed. *Israel and the Arabs: The June 1967 War.* New York: Facts on File, 1967.

Kraemer, Joel L., ed. *Jerusalem: Problems and Prospects.* New York: Praeger, 1980.

Krapels, E. N. *Oil and Security: Problems and Prospects of Importing Countries.* Adelphi Papers, 136. London: International Institute for Strategic Studies, 1977.

Kubbah, Abdul Amir. *The Libyan Kingdom: Its Oil Industry and Economic System.* Beirut: Arab Center for Oil and Economic Studies, 1963; Rihani Press, 1964.

————. *OPEC: Past and Present.* Vienna: Petro-Economic Research Center, 1974.

Lackner, Helen. *A House Built on Sand: The Political Economy of Saudi Arabia.* London: Ithaca Press, 1979.

Lacouture, Jean. *Nasser: A Biography.* Translated by Daniel Hofstadter. New York: Knopf, 1973.

Landen, Robert G. *Oman Since 1856: Disruptive Modernization in a Traditional Arab Society.* Princeton, N.J.: Princeton University Press, 1967.

Landis, Lincoln. *Politics and Oil: Moscow in the Middle East.* New York and London: Dunellen, 1973.

Landis, Robin C., and Michael W. Klass. *OPEC: Policy Implications for the United States.* New York: Praeger, 1980.

Laqueur, Walter. *The Struggle for the Middle East.* London: Routledge and Kegan Paul, 1969.

————. *Confrontation: The Middle East and World Politics.* New York: Quadrangle, 1974.

Lebkicker, Roy. *Aramco and World Oil.* New York: Moore, 1952.

Leeman, Wayne A. *The Price of Middle East Oil: An Essay in Political Economy.* Ithaca, N.Y.: Cornell University Press, 1962.

Lenczowski, George. *Oil and State in the Middle East.* Ithaca, N.Y.: Cornell University Press, 1960.

_____. *U.S. Interests in the Middle East.* Washington, D.C.: American Enterprise Institute for Public Policy Research, 1968.

LeVine, Victor T., and Timothy W. Luke. *The Arab-African Connection: Political and Economic Realities.* Boulder, Colo.: Westview Press, 1979.

Little, Tom. *Modern Egypt.* New York: Praeger, 1967.

Long, David E. *Saudi Arabia.* Washington, D.C.: Center for Strategic and International Studies, Georgetown University, 1976.

Longrigg, Stephen Hemsley. *Oil in the Middle East: Its Discovery and Development.* 3rd ed. London and New York: Oxford University Press for the Royal Institute for International Affairs, 1968.

Love, Kenneth. *Suez: The Twice-Fought War.* New York: McGraw-Hill, 1960.

Luethy, Herbert, and David Rodnick. *French Motivation in the Suez Crisis.* Princeton, N.J.: Institute for International Social Research, 1956.

Lutfi, Ashraf T. *Arab Oil: A Plan for the Future.* Beirut: Middle East Research and Publishing Center, 1960.

_____. *OPEC Oil: A Plan for the Future.* Beirut: Middle East Research and Publishing Center, 1960.

Lyon, Peter. *Eisenhower: Portrait of the Hero.* Boston: Little, Brown and Co., 1974.

MacAvoy, Paul W. *Energy Policy: An Economic Analysis.* New York: W. W. Norton and Company, 1983.

Mackintosh, J. M. *Strategy and Tactics of Soviet Foreign Policy.* London: Oxford University Press, 1963.

Macmillan, Harold. *Riding the Storm: 1956–1959.* London: Macmillan, 1971.

Madelin, Henri. *Oil and Politics.* Translated by Margaret Totman. Lexington, Mass.: Lexington Books, D. C. Heath, 1973.

Mancke, Richard B. *The Failure of U.S. Energy Policy.* New York: Columbia University Press, 1974.

_____. *Squeaking By: U.S. Energy Policy Since the Embargo.* New York: Columbia University Press, 1976.

Mangold, Peter. *Superpower Intervention in the Middle East.* New York: St. Martin's Press, 1978.

Mangone, Gerald J. *Energy Policies of the World.* New York: Elsevier, 1976.

Mansfield, Peter. *The British in Egypt.* New York: Holt, Rinehart and Winston, 1971.

Maull, Hanns. *Oil and Influence: The Oil Weapon Examined.* Adelphi Papers, No. 118. London: International Institute for Strategic Studies, Summer 1975.

Mendershausen, Horst. *Coping With the Oil Crisis: French and German Experiences.* Baltimore: Johns Hopkins University Press, 1976.

Merlin, Samuel. *The Search for Peace in the Middle East: The Story of President Bourguiba's Campaign for a Negotiated Settlement Between Israel and the Arab States.* South Brunswick, N.J.: Yoseloff, 1968.

The Middle East and North Africa: Survey and Directory of Lands of Middle East and North Africa, 1973–1974. London: Europa Publications, 1973.

Mikdashi, Zuhayr. *A Financial Analysis of Middle Eastern Oil Concessions: 1901–1965.* New York: Praeger, 1966.

———. *The Community of Oil Exporting Countries: A Study in Governmental Cooperation.* Ithaca, N.Y.: Cornell University Press, 1972.

Mikesell, Raymond F., et al. *Foreign Investment in the Petroleum and Mineral Industries: Case Studies of Investor–Host Country Relations.* Baltimore: Johns Hopkins University Press for Resources for the Future, 1971.

Miller, Aaron David. *Search for Security: Saudi Arabian Oil and American Foreign Policy, 1939–1949.* Chapel Hill: University of North Carolina Press, 1980.

Moncrieff, Anthony, ed. *Suez Ten Years Later.* London: British Broadcasting Corporation, 1967.

Mosley, Leonard. *Power Play: Oil in the Middle East.* New York: Random House, 1973; Baltimore: Penguin Books, 1974.

Mughraby, Muhamad A. *Permanent Sovereignty Over Oil Resources: A Study of Middle East Oil Concessions and Legal Change.* Beirut: Middle East Research and Publishing Center, 1966.

Murphy, Robert. *Diplomat Among Warriors.* London: Doubleday, 1964.

Nakhleh, Emile. *The United States and Saudi Arabia, A Policy Analysis.* Washington, D.C.: American Enterprise Institute, 1975.

Nash, Gerald. *United States Oil Policy, 1890–1964.* Pittsburgh, Pa.: University of Pittsburgh Press, 1968.

Nasser, Gamal, Abd El-. *The Philosophy of the Revolution.* Cairo: Dar Al-Maaref, 1954.

———. *Egypt's Liberation: The Philosophy of the Revolution.* Washington, D.C.: Public Affairs Press, 1955.

Nathan, James A., and James K. Oliver. *United States Foreign Policy and World Order.* Boston: Little, Brown and Co., 1976.

Neff, Donald. *Warriors at Suez: Eisenhower Takes America Into the Middle East.* New York: Simon and Schuster, 1981.

Noreng, Oystein. *Oil Politics in the 1980s: Patterns of International Cooperation.* New York: McGraw-Hill, 1978.

Nutting, Anthony. *No End of a Lesson: The Story of Suez.* New York: Clarkson N. Potter, 1967.

———. *Nasser.* London: Constable, 1972.

O'Ballance, Edgar. *The War in Yemen.* Hamden, Conn.: Archon, 1971.

O'Connell, D. P. *The Law of State Succession.* Cambridge: The University Press, 1956.

Odell, Peter R. *Oil and World Power: Background to the Oil Crisis.* New York: Taplinger, 1971.

Odell, Peter R., and Luis Vallenilla. *The Pressures of Oil: A Strategy for Economic Revival.* New York: Harper and Row, 1978.

OPEC, Selected Documents—1968. Vienna: Organization of Petroleum Exporting Countries, June 1969.

Organization of Arab Petroleum Exporting Countries. *A Brief Report of the Activities and Achievements of the Organization, 1968–1973.* Kuwait: OAPEC, 1974.

Organization of European Economic Co-Operation. *Europe's Growing Needs of Energy: How Can They Be Met?* (Harley Report). Paris: OEEC, 1956.

———. *Europe's Need for Oil: Implications and Lessons on the Suez Crisis.* Paris: OEEC, 1958.

———. *Towards a New Energy Pattern in Europe* (Robinson Report). Paris: OEEC, 1960.

Paterson, Thomas G., J. Garry Clifford, and Kenneth J. Hagan. *American Foreign Policy: A History.* Lexington, Mass.: D. C. Heath and Co., 1977.

Paust, Jordan, et al. *The Arab Oil Weapon.* Dobbs Ferry, N.Y.: Oceana Publications, 1977.

Penrose, Edith. *The Large International Firm in Developing Countries.* London: Allen and Unwin, 1968.

———. *The Growth of Firms, Middle East Oil and Other Essays.* London: Cass, 1971.

Penrose, Edith, and E. F. Penrose. *Iraq: International Relations and National Development.* Boulder, Colo.: Westview Press, 1978.

Petroleum Commission of Libya. *Petroleum Development in Libya, 1954 Through Mid-1961.* Tripoli: Government Printing Office, 1961.

Pfaff, R. H. *Jerusalem: Keystone of an Arab-Israeli Settlement.* New York: American Enterprise Institute for Public Policy Research, 1969.

Philby, H.St.J.B. *Arabian Oil Ventures.* Washington, D.C.: Middle East Institute, 1974.

President Gamal Abdel Nasser's Speeches and Press-Interviews. Cairo: Information Department, 1961.

Protopopov, A. S. *The Soviet Union and the Suez Crisis of 1956.* Moscow: "Nanka," 1969.

Pugh, Dave, and Mitch Zimmerman. *The "Energy Crisis" and the Real Crisis Behind It.* San Francisco: United Front Press, June 1974.

Quandt, William B. *Decade of Decisions: American Policy Toward the Arab-Israeli Conflict, 1967–1976.* Berkeley and Los Angeles: University of California Press, 1977.

———. *Saudi Arabia in the 1980s: Foreign Policy, Security, and Oil.* Washington, D.C.: Brookings Institution, 1981.

Ra'anan, Uri. *The USSR Arms the Third World: Case Studies in Soviet Foreign Policy.* Cambridge, Mass.: MIT Press and the Research Institute on Communist Affairs, Columbia University, 1969.

Rahmy, Ali Abdel Rahman. *The Egyptian Policy in the Arab World: Intervention in Yemen 1962–1967 Case Study.* Lanham, Md.: University Press of America, 1983.

Ramazani, P. K. *The Persian Gulf and the Strait of Hormuz.* Rockville, Md.: Sijthoff and Noordhoff, 1979.

Ray, George F. *Western Europe and the Energy Crisis.* London: Trade Policy Research Center, 1975.

Reich, Bernard. *Quest for Peace: United States-Israel Relations and the Arab-Israeli Conflict.* New Brunswick, N.J.: Transaction Books, 1977.

Revolutionary Iraq 1968–1973. Baghdad: Al-Thawrah Publications, 1974.

Rihani, Ameen. *Maker of Modern Arabia.* New York: Houghton and Mifflin Company, 1928.

Robertson, Charles L. *The Emergency Oil Lift to Europe in the Suez Crisis.*
Indianapolis: Bobbs-Merrill, 1965.

Robertson, John Henry. *The Most Important Country: The True Story of the Suez
Crisis and the Events Leading Up to It.* London: Cassell, 1957.

Robertson, Terence. *Crisis: The Inside Story of the Suez Conspiracy.* New York:
Atheneum, 1965.

Roosevelt, Kermit. *Countercoup: The Struggle for Control of Iran.* New York:
McGraw-Hill, 1979.

Rouhani, Fuad. *A History of OPEC.* New York: Praeger, 1971.

Rubin, Barry M. *The Great Powers in the Middle East, 1941–1947.* London: Cass,
1980.

Rubin, Jeffrey Z., ed. *Dynamics of Third Party Intervention: Kissinger in the Middle
East.* New York: Praeger, 1981.

Sadat, Anwar el-. *Revolt on the Nile.* London: Wingate, 1957.

_____. *In Search of Identity: An Autobiography.* New York: Harper and Row,
1977.

Safran, N. *From War to War: The Arab Israeli Confrontation 1948–1967.* New York.
Western Publishing Company, 1969.

St. John, Robert. *The Boss: The Story of Gamal Abdel Nasser.* New York: McGraw-
Hill, 1960.

Salman, Hasan. *Toward Nationalization of Iraqi Petroleum.* Beirut: Dar al-Talia,
1967. [In Arabic]

Samo, Elias, ed. *The June 1967 Arab-Israeli War: Miscalculation or Conspiracy?*
Wilmette, Ill.: Medina University Press International, 1971.

Sampson, Anthony. *The Seven Sisters: The Great Oil Companies and the World
They Made.* New York: Viking Press, 1975.

Sarkis, Nicholas. *Le Petrole à l'Heure Arabe.* Paris: Editions Stock, 1975.

Sayegh, Kemal S. *Oil and Arab Regional Development.* New York: Praeger, 1968.

Schmidt, Dana Adams. *Journey Among Brave Men.* Boston: Little, Brown and
Co., 1964.

_____. *The Yemen: Unknown War.* New York: Holt, Rinehart and Winston, 1968.

_____. *Armageddon in the Middle East.* New York: John Day Co., 1974.

Schurr, Sam H., and Paul T. Homan. *Middle-Eastern Oil and the Western World:
Prospects and Problems.* New York: American Elsevier, 1971.

Shamsedin, Ezzedin. *The Arab Oil Embargo and the United States Economy.*
London: Middle East Economic Digest Monographs, 1974.

_____. *Arab Oil and the United States: An Admixture of Politics and Economics.*
Columbia: University of South Carolina, 1974.

Sharabi, Hisham. *Government and Politics of the Middle East in the Twentieth
Century.* New York: D. Van Nostrand Co., 1962.

Shavarsh, Toriguian. *Legal Aspects of Oil Concessions in the Middle East.* Beirut:
Hamaskaine Press, 1972.

Sheehan, Michael Karl. *Iran: The Impact of United States Interests and Policies,
1941–1954.* Brooklyn, N.Y.: Theo. Gaus' Sons, 1968.

Sherbiny, Naim A., and Mark A. Tessler, eds. *Arab Oil: Impact on the Arab
Countries and Global Implications.* New York: Praeger, 1976.

Shichor, Yitzhak. *The Middle East in China's Foreign Policy, 1949-1977.* Cambridge: Cambridge University Press, 1979.

Shihata, Ibrahim F. I. *The Case for the Arab Oil Embargo.* Beirut: The Institute for Palestine Studies, 1975.

Shwadran, Benjamin. *The Middle East, Oil, and the Great Powers.* 3rd rev. ed. New York and Toronto: Halsted, 1973.

_____. *Middle East Oil: Issues and Problems.* Cambridge, Mass.: Schenkman, 1977.

Siksek, Simon G. *The Legal Framework of Oil Concessions in the Arab World.* Beirut: Middle East Research and Publishing Center, 1960.

Solomon, Lawrence. *Energy Shock, After the Oil Runs Out.* New York: Doubleday and Company, Inc., 1980.

Sowagagh, Abdulaziz. *Oil and Arab Politics.* Riyadh: Gulf Center for Documentation and Information, 1981. [In Arabic]

Spanier, John. *American Foreign Policy Since World War II.* 7th ed. New York: Holt, Rinehart and Winston, 1977.

Stephens, Robert. *Nasser: A Political Biography.* London: Allen Lane, 1971.

Stewart, Desmond. *Young Egypt.* London: Wingate, 1958.

Stock, Ernest. *Israel on the Road of Sinai, 1949-1956.* Ithaca, N.Y.: Cornell University Press, 1967.

Stocking, George Ward. *Middle East Oil: A Study in Political and Economic Controversy.* Nashville, Tenn.: Vanderbilt University Press, 1970.

Stoff, Michael B. *Oil, War, and American Security: The Search for a National Policy on Foreign Oil, 1941-1947.* New Haven, Conn., and London: Yale University Press, 1980.

Stone, Russell A., ed. *OPEC and the Middle East.* New York: Praeger, 1977.

Stookey, Robert W. *America and the Arab States: An Uneasy Encounter.* New York: John Wiley and Sons, 1975.

_____. *Yemen: The Politics of the Yemen Arab Republic.* Boulder, Colo.: Westview Press, 1978.

Study on the Fifth Arab Petroleum Congress, 1965. Beirut: Lebanese and Arab Documentations Office, 1965.

Sylvester, Anthony. *Arabs and Africans: Cooperation for Development.* London: Bodley Head, 1981.

Szyliowicz, Joseph S., ed. *The Energy Crisis and U.S. Foreign Policy.* New York: Praeger, 1975.

Tanzer, Michel. *The Political Economy of International Oil and the Underdeveloped Countries.* Boston: Beacon Press, 1969.

_____. *The Energy Crisis: World Struggle for Power and Wealth.* New York: Monthly Review Press, 1974.

Tetreault, Mary Ann. *The Organization of Arab Petroleum Exporting Countries: History, Policies, and Prospects.* Westport, Conn.: Greenwood Press, 1981.

Thomas, Hugh. *Suez.* New York: Harper and Row, 1967.

Tugendhat, Christopher. *Oil: The Biggest Business.* London: Eyre and Spottiswoode, 1968.

Turner, Louis. *Oil Companies in the International System.* London: Institute of International Affairs, 1978.

Udovitch, A. L. *The Middle East: Oil, Conflict and Hope.* Lexington, Mass.: Lexington Books, 1976.

Urquhart, Brian. *Hammarskjold: The Years of Decision.* New York: Alfred A. Knopf, 1972.

U.S. Congress. House. Committee on Foreign Affairs. *Data and Analysis Concerning the Possibility of a U.S. Food Embargo as a Response to the Present Arab Oil Boycott.* 93rd Cong., 1st sess. 21 November 1973.

U.S. Congress. House. *The United States Oil Shortage and the Arab-Israel Conflict.* 93rd Cong., 1st sess. Study mission report, 20 December 1973.

U.S. Department of the Interior. Office of Oil and Gas. *The Middle East Petroleum Emergency of 1967.* 2 vols. Washington, D.C.: Government Printing Office, 1969.

U.S. Federal Energy Administration. *The Relationship of Oil Companies and Foreign Governments.* Washington: FEA, 1975.

———. *U.S. Oil Companies and the Arab Oil Embargo: The International Allocations of Constricted Supplies.* Prepared for the Subcommittee on Multinational Corporations of the Committee on Foreign Relations, U.S. Senate. Washington, D.C.: Government Printing Office, 1975.

U.S. Federal Trade Commission. *The International Petroleum Cartel.* Staff Report. Washington, D.C.: Government Printing Office, 1952.

U.S. Library of Congress. Congressional Research Service. *Oil Fields as Military Objectives.* Washington, D.C.: Government Printing Office, 1975.

Vatikiotis, P. J. *Nasser and His Generation.* New York: St. Martin's Press, 1978.

Vernon, Raymond, ed. *The Oil Crisis.* New York: Norton, 1976.

Waddams, Frank C. *The Libyan Oil Industry.* Baltimore and London: Johns Hopkins University Press, 1980.

Walton, Richard J. *The Power of Oil: Economic, Social and Political.* New York: Seabury, 1977.

Wendzel, Robert L. *International Politics, Policymakers and Policymaking.* New York: John Wiley and Sons, 1981.

Wenner, Manfred. *Modern Yemen: 1918–1966.* Baltimore: Johns Hopkins University Press, 1967.

Wheelock, Keith. *Nasser's New Egypt.* New York: Praeger, 1960.

Whitson, William W., ed. *Foreign Policy and U.S. National Security.* New York: Praeger, 1976.

Williams, Ann. *Britain and France in the Middle East and North Africa.* New York: St. Martin's Press, 1968.

Wilson, E. M. *Jerusalem: Key to Peace.* Washington, D.C.: Middle East Institute, 1970.

Wint, Guy, and Peter Calvocoressi. *Middle East Crisis.* Harmondsworth, England: Penguin, 1957.

Wise, David, and Thomas B. Ross. *The Invisible Government.* New York: Random House, 1964.

World Energy Demands and the Middle East. Washington, D.C.: The Middle East Institute, 1972.

Wu, Yuan-Li. *Japan's Search for Oil: A Case Study on Economic Nationalism and International Security.* Stanford, Calif.: Hoover Institution, 1977.

Wynn, Wilton. *Nasser of Egypt: The Search for Dignity.* London: Arlington, 1959.
Yeganah, Mohamed, and Charles Issawi. *The Economics of Middle East Oil.* New York: Praeger, 1962.
Yodfat, A., and M. Abir. *In the Direction of the Gulf: The Soviet Union and the Persian Gulf.* London: Cass, 1977.
Zonis, Marvin. *The Political Elite of Iran.* Princeton, N.J.: Princeton University Press, 1971.

Articles in Books and Journals

Abdel Nasser, Gamal. "Ours Is the Side of Peace and Freedom," in *World Perspectives on International Politics,* pp. 187–192. Edited by Walter C. Clemens, Jr. Boston: Little, Brown and Co., 1965.
Abu-Rudeneh, O. "The Oil Weapon: From Slogan to Reality." *Shu'un Filastiniyya* [Palestine affairs] 43 (March 1975):33–58. [In Arabic]
Adelman, M. A. "Is the Oil Shortage Real? Oil Companies as OPEC Taxcollectors." *Foreign Policy* 8 (Winter 1972–73):69–107.
————. "Politics, Economics, and World Oil." *The American Economic Review* 64 (May 1974), pp. 58–68.
Adelman, M. A., and Soren Friis. "Changing Monopolies and European Oil Supplies." *Energy Policy* (December 1974), pp. 275–292.
Ahrari, Mohammed. "OAPEC and 'Authoritative' Allocation of Oil: An Analysis of the Arab Oil Embargo." *Studies in Comparative International Development* 14, no. 1 (Spring 1979):9–21.
Akins, James E. "The Oil Crisis: This Time the Wolf Is Here." *Foreign Affairs* 51, no. 3 (April 1973):462–490.
Akinsanya, A. "The Afro-Arab Alliance: Dream or Reality?" *African Affairs* 75 (October 1976).
Alnasrawi, Abbas. "The Collective Bargaining Power of Oil Producing Countries." *Journal of World Trade Law* 7 (March-April 1973):188–207.
Amuzegar, Jahangir "Nationalism Versus Economic Growth." *Foreign Affairs* 44, no. 4 (July 1966):651–661.
Anderson, Lisa. "Libya and American Foreign Policy." *Middle East Journal* 36, no. 4 (Autumn 1982):516–534.
Attiqa, A. "The Future for Oil: A View from OAPEC." *Arab Perspectives* 2 (Summer 1981):31–40.
Ball, W. M. "Problems of Australian Foreign Policy, July-December 1956: The Australian Reaction to the Suez Crisis." *Australian Journal of Politics and History* 2 (1957):129–150.
Becker, Abraham S. "Oil and the Persian Gulf in Soviet Policy in the 1970's," in *The U.S.S.R. and the Middle East,* pp. 173–214. Edited by M. Confino and S. Shamir. New York: John Wiley and Sons, 1973.
Berry, John A. "Oil and Soviet Policy in the Middle East." *Middle East Journal* 26, no. 2 (Spring 1972):149–160.
Bilder, Richard. "Comments on the Legality of the Arab Oil Boycott." *Texas International Law Journal* 12 (1977):41–46.

Bill, James A. "The Military and Modernization in the Middle East." *Comparative Politics* 2 (October 1969):41–62.

Blechman, Barry M., and Andrew M. Kuzmack. "Oil and National Security." *Naval War College Review* (May-June 1974):8–25.

Boorman, James A. "Economic Coercion in International Law: The Arab Oil Weapon and the Ensuing Legal Issues." *Journal of International Law and Economics* 9 (1974):205–222.

Brecher, M. "Jerusalem: Israel's Political Decisions, 1947–1977." *Middle East Journal* 32, no. 1 (Winter 1978):13–34.

Brewer, John V. E. "Petropolitics." *School of Advanced International Studies Review* 18, no. 2 (1974):24–31. Letter by Jeffrey R. Cooper and Reply by John Brewer in *SAIS Review* 18, no. 3 (1974):59–63.

Brosche, Harmut. "The Arab Oil Embargo and United States Pressure Against Chile: Economic and Political Coercion and the Charter of the United Nations." *Case Western Reserve Journal of International Law* 7, no. 3 (1974):3–35.

Brown, W. "The Oil Weapon." *Middle East Journal* 36, no. 3 (1982):301–318.

Burchard, Hans-Joachim. "OPEC Oil Policy Since 1973," in *Oil Shock Five Years Later*, ed. Manfred Tietzel (Bonn: Friedrich-Ebert-Stiftung, 1979), pp. 99–103.

Burrell, R. M. "The Oil Weapon: Who Gains Most?" *Soviet Analyst* 2, no. 23 (1973):1–3.

Caldwell, Malcolm. "Russian Oil Policy and the Middle East," in *Israel and the Palestinians*, pp. 177–185. Edited by Uri Davis, Andrew Mack, and Nira Yuval-Davis. London: Ithaca Press, 1975.

Campbell, Lawrence. "Middle Eastern Oil: The Multinational Firm Challenged." *School of Advanced International Studies Review* 15, no. 4 (Fall 1971):31–34.

Chandler, Geoffrey. "The Myth of Oil Power—International Groups and National Sovereignty." *International Affairs* 46, 4 (October 1970):710–718.

————. "The Changing State of the Oil Industry." *Petroleum Review* (June 1974):375–381.

Church, Frank. "The Impotence of Oil Companies." *Foreign Policy* 27 (Summer 1977):27–51.

Crecelius, Daniel. "Sa'udi-Egyptian Relations." *International Studies* (New Delhi) 14 (October-December 1975):563–586.

Daoudi, M. S., and M. S. Dajani. "Contending Approaches to Social Change and Political Development—A Comparative Analysis," *Indian Political Science Review* 17, no. 2 (July 1983):117–130.

————. "Sanctions: The Falklands Episode," *World Today* 39, no. 4 (April 1983):150–160.

————. "Exploring at the Fringes: The Bibliography as Database," *Teaching Political Science* 11, no. 3 (Spring 1984):106–109.

————. "The 1967 Oil Embargo Revisited." *Journal of Palestine Studies* 13, 2 (Winter 1984):65–90.

Davis, Jerome D. "The Arab Use of Oil." *Cooperation and Conflict* 2 (1976):57–67.

Dawisha, A. I. "Intervention in the Yemen: An Analysis of Egyptian Perceptions and Policies." *Middle East Journal* (Winter 1975).

Dougherty, J. "The Aswan Decision in Perspective." *Political Science Quarterly* 74, no. 1 (March 1959):21–45.

Drambyants, G. "The Oil Embargo." *New Times* (Moscow) (22 March 1967):20–22.

Duguid, Stephen. "A Biographical Approach to the Study of Social Change in the Middle East: Abdullah Tariki as a New Man." *International Journal of Middle East Studies* 1, no. 3 (July 1970):195–220.

Eagleton, C. "The United Nations and the Suez Crisis," in *Tensions in the Middle East*, pp. 273–296. Edited by P. W. Thayer. Baltimore: Johns Hopkins University Press, 1958.

Eayrs, J. G. "Canadian Policy and Opinion During the Suez Crisis." *International Journal* (Toronto) 12 (1957):97–108.

Feith, D. "The Oil Weapon De-mystified." *Policy Review*, no. 15 (1981):19–39.

Frankel, P. H. "Oil Supplies During the Suez Crisis—On Meeting a Political Emergency." *Journal of Industrial Economics* (February 1958).

Friedland, Edward, Paul Seabury, and Aaron Wildavsky. "Oil and the Decline of Western Power." *Political Science Quarterly* 90, no. 3 (Fall 1975):437–450.

Gamal, M. B. "Israel and the Suez Canal, A New Approach." *Egyptian Review of International Law* (1961):103–130.

Georgescu-Rogen, Nicholas. "Energy and Economic Myths." *Southern Economic Journal* 41, no. 3 (January 1975):347–381.

Ghobashy, O. Z. "Israel and the Suez Canal." *Egyptian Economic and Political Review* 4 (1960):9–13.

Gilman, E. "Israel and the Iranian Oil Embargo: The Search for Alternative Sources of Energy." *Round Table* 276 (October 1979):291–307.

Gitelson, A. "Why Do Small States Break Diplomatic Relations With Outside Powers? Lessons From the African Experience." *International Studies Quarterly* 18 (December 1974):451–484.

Goldstein, H. N. "The World Oil Crisis: A Portfolio Interpretation Reexamined." *Economic Inquiry* (January 1977):125–131.

Griffith, William E. "The Fourth Middle East War, the Energy Crisis and U.S. Policy." *Orbis* 17, no. 4 (Winter 1974):1161–1188.

Grosser, A. "Suez, Hungary and European Integration." *International Organization* 11 (1957):470–480.

Gumpel, Werner. "USSR—Energy Policy and Middle East Crisis." *Aussen Politik* (1st quarter 1974):31–41.

Halliday, Fred. "Saudi Arabia: Bonanza and Repression." *New Left Review* 80 (July-August 1973):3–28.

Hameed, K. A. "The Oil Revolution and African Development." *African Affairs* 75, no. 300 (July 1976):349–358.

Hani, Kamal. "The Disengagement Between Oil and the Interest of the Arab People." *Al-Tariq* (Beirut), no. 4 (April 1974):16–17. [In Arabic]

Hartshorn, J. E. "A Diplomatic Price for Oil?" *Pacific Community* 5, no. 3 (April 1974):363–379.

———. "From Tripoli to Teheran and Back: The Size and Meaning of the Oil Game." *The World Today* 27, no. 7 (July 1973):291–301.

Hoyt, Monty. "Middle East Oil: Hobson's Choice for the West." *Middle East International*, No. 7 (October 1971):41–45.

Itayim, Fuad. "Arab Oil—The Political Dimension." *Journal of Palestine Studies* 3, no. 2 (Winter 1974):84–97.

————. "Strengths and Weaknesses of the Oil Weapon," in *The Middle East and the International System II: Security and the Energy Crisis*, pp. 1–7. Adelphi Papers, No. 115. London: The International Institute for Strategic Studies, 1975.

Jacoby, Neil H. "Oil and the Future: Economic Consequences of the Oil Revolution." *Journal of Energy and Economic Development* (Autumn 1975).

Jarada, G. "The Organization of Arab Oil Producing Countries, OAPEC." *Shu'un Arabiya* 3 (May 1981):201–226. [In Arabic]

Johnson, W. A., and R. E. Messick. "Vertical Divestiture of U.S. Oil Firms: The Impact on the World Oil Market." *Law and Politics of International Business* 8 (1976):963–989.

Kalymon, B. A. "Economic Incentives in OPEC Oil Pricing Policy." *Journal of Development Economics* 2, no. 4 (1975).

Karpov, S. "The Closure of the Suez Canal: Economic Consequences." *International Affairs* (Moscow) (April 1974):83–85.

Kedourie, Elie. "Continuity and Change in Modern Iraqi History." *Asian Affairs* 61, no. 2 (June 1974):140–146.

Kelidar, Abbas. "Iraq: The Search for Stability." *Conflict Studies* 59 (July 1975).

Kelly, J. B. "Of Valuable Oil and Worthless Policies." *Encounter* 52, no. 6 (June 1979):74–80. Reprinted in *At Issue: Politics in the World Arena*, 3rd ed., pp. 265–277. Edited by Steven L. Spiegel. New York: St. Martin's Press, 1981.

Kemezis, P. "The Permanent Crisis: Changes in the World Oil System." *Orbis* 23, no. 4 (1980):761–784.

Kerr. Malcolm H. "The Arabs and Israelis: Perceptual Dimensions to Their Dilemma," in *The Middle East: Quest for an American Policy*, pp. 3–31. Edited by Willard A. Beling. Albany: State University of New York Press, 1973.

Khadduri, W. "Factors in Arab-American Oil Relations." *Qadaya Arabiyah* [Arab causes] 7, no. 4 (April 1980):53–62. [In Arabic]

Kimche, J. "After Sadat—With the Oil Weapon Gone." *Midstream* 27, no. 10 (December 1981):3–6.

Klinghoffer, Arthur Jay. "The Soviet Union and the Arab Embargo of 1973–74." *International Relations* 3 (May 1976).

Krasner, Stephen D. "The Great Oil Sheikdown." *Foreign Policy* 13 (Winter 1973/74):123–138.

————. "Oil Is the Exception." *Foreign Policy* 14 (Spring 1974):68–83.

————. "A Statist Interpretation of American Oil Policy Toward the Middle East." *Political Science Quarterly* 94, no. 1 (Spring 1979):77–96.

Kuczynski, Pedro-Pablo. "The Effects of the Rise in Oil Prices on the Third World." *Euromoney* (May 1974):37–41.

Laoussine, Mordine Ait. "The Political Dimension of Oil." *OPEC Review* 3 (Autumn 1979):39–45.

Levy, Walter. "Oil Power." *Foreign Affairs* 49, no. 4 (July 1971):652–668.

Lewinson, G. "Suez and Its Consequences: The Israeli View." *World Today* 13, no. 4 (April 1957):152–161.

Lewis, Bernard. "The Consequences of Defeat." *Foreign Affairs* 46, no. 2 (January 1968):321–335.

Linder, W. "Oil and the Future of Iran." *Swiss Review of World Affairs* 24, no. 5 (August 1974):22–24.

Magnus, Ralph. "Middle East Oil and the OPEC Nations." *Current History* 70 (January 1976):22–26.

Malone, J. J. "Germany and the Suez Crisis." *Middle East Journal* 20 (1966):20–30.

Maull, Hans. "The Control of Oil." *International Journal* 36, no. 2 (1981):273–293.

Mazrui, A. A. "Black Africa and the Arabs." *Foreign Affairs* 53, no. 4 (July 1975):725–742.

Mead, Walter J. "An Economic Analysis of Crude Oil Price Behavior in the 1970s." *The Journal of Energy and Development* 4 (Spring 1979):212–228.

Mikdashi, Zuhayr. "Cooperation Among Oil Exporting Countries With a Special Reference to Arab Countries: A Political Economy Analysis." *International Organization* 28 (Winter 1974):1–30.

Mingst, Karen. "Regional Sectorial Economic Integration: The Case of OAPEC." *Journal of Common Market Studies* 16, no. 2 (December 1977):95–113.

Mohan, J. "India, Pakistan, Suez and the Commonwealth." *International Journal* (Toronto) 15, no. 3 (Summer 1960):185–199.

———. "South Africa and the Suez Crisis." *International Journal* 16, no. 4 (Autumn 1961):327–357.

Morano, Louis. "Multinationals and Nation-States: The Case of Aramco." *Orbis* 23, no. 2 (Summer 1979):447–468.

Muhammad, A. "The Position of Arab Oil in the Map of International Conflict." *Qadaya Arabiyah* 6, no. 8 (December 1979):203–218. [In Arabic]

Ninmer, B. "Dulles, Suez and Diplomatic Diplomacy." *Western Political Quarterly* (1959):784–798.

Odell, Peter. "Toward a Geographically Reshaped World Oil Industry." *World Today* 37, no. 12 (December 1981):447–453.

Park, T. W., F. Abolfathi, and M. Ward. "Resource Nationalism in the Foreign Policy Behavior of Oil Exporting Countries (1947-1974)." *International Interactions* 2 (November 1976):247–262.

Paust, Jordan J., and Albert P. Blaustein. "The Arab Oil Weapon—A Threat to International Peace." *American Journal of International Law* 68 (1974):410–439.

———. "The Arab Oil Weapon: A Reply and Reaffirmation of Illegality." *Columbia Journal of Transnational Law* 15 (1976):57–73.

Penzin, D. "Oil and Independence." *International Affairs* (Moscow) 10 (October 1972):34–40.

———. "New Moves by Oil Imperialism." *International Affairs* (Moscow) 5 (May 1973):47–53.

Polk, William R. "The Middle East: Analyzing Social Change." *Bulletin of Atomic Scientists* (January 1967).

Pollack, Gerald A. "The Economic Consequences of the Energy Crisis." *Foreign Affairs* 52 (April 1974):402–471.

Qazzaz, A. al-. "Arab Oil." *Arab Perspectives* 2 (October 1981):6–13.

Rachkov, B. "The Future of Arab Oil." *International Affairs* (Moscow) 8 (1970):32–37.

Rothschild Intercontinental Bank. "Coping With the Oil Deficit." *Euromoney* (May 1974):115–118.

Rugh, William A. "Arab Media and Politics During the October War." *Middle East Journal* 29 (Summer 1975):310–328.

Rustow, Dankwart A. "Petroleum Politics 1951-1974: A Five-Act Drama Reconstructed." *Dissent* 21 (Spring 1974):144–153.

S., H., and G. "The First Arab Petroleum Congress." *World Today* 15, no. 6 (June 1959):246–253.

Salant, S. W. "Exhaustible Resources and Industrial Structure: A Cournot-Nash Approach to the World Oil Market." *Journal of Political Economy* 84 (October 1976):1079–1093.

Sankari, Farouk A. "The Character and Impact of Arab Oil Embargoes," in Naiem Sherbiny and Mark Tessler, eds., *Arab Oil* (New York: Praeger, 1976):265–278.

Savory, D. L. "Sequel to the Suez Crisis." *Contemporary Review* (1961):80–83, 254–257, 416–418.

Sayegh, Fayez A. "The Camp David Agreements and the Palestine Problem." *Journal of Palestine Studies* 8, no. 2 (Winter 1979):3–40.

Sayigh, Yusif. "Arab Oil in the Strategy of Arab-Israeli Confrontation." *Shu'un Filastiniya* [Palestine affairs] 16 (December 1972).

———. "Arab Oil and the Palestine Question: A Dialectical Relationship." *Shu'un Filastiniya*, no. 41/42 (January-February 1975).

———. "Arab Oil Policies: Self-Interest Versus International Responsibility." *Journal of Palestine Studies* 4, no. 3 (Spring 1975):59–73.

Schneider, Carl J. "The Arab-Israeli Conflict: The Impact of the Six-Day War," in *Problems in International Relations*, 3rd ed., pp. 228–247. Edited by Andrew Gyorgy, H. Gibbs, and R. Jordan. Englewood Cliffs, N.J.: Prentice-Hall, 1970.

———. "The Suez Crisis of 1956 and Its Aftermath," in *Problems in International Relations*, 3rd ed., pp. 304–318. Edited by Andrew Gyorgy, H. Gibbs, and R. Jordan. Englewood Cliffs, N.J.: Prentice-Hall, 1970.

Shihata, Ibrahim. "Destination Embargo of Arab Oil: Its Legality Under International Law." *American Journal of International Law* 68 (October 1974):591–627.

———. "Arab Oil Policies and the New International Economic Order." *Virginia Journal of International Law* 16 (Winter 1976):261–288.

Shwadran, Benjamin. "Middle East Oil 1961—II, Iraq-IPC Negotiations." *Middle Eastern Affairs* (November 1962):258–267.

Silbey, Franklin R. "Will Arab Oil Change the U.S. Middle East Stance?" *Middle East Information Series*, 23 (May 1973):40–52.

Singer, S. Fred. "Limits to Arab Oil Power." *Foreign Policy* (Spring 1978):53–67.

Smart, Ian. "Uniqueness and Generality." *Daedalus* 104, no. 4 (Fall 1975):259–282.

———. "Communicating With the Oil Exporters: The Old Dialogue and the New." *Trialogue* 22 (Winter 1980).

Smith, Stephen N. "Re 'The Arab Oil Weapon': A Skeptic's View." *American Journal of International Law* 69 (1975):136.

Smolansky, O. M. "Moscow and the Suez Crisis 1956: A Reappraisal." *Political Science Quarterly* 80 (1965):581–605.

Snyder, Julian M. "The Biggest Problem of the Arabs Getting Into the Club." *Vital Speeches of the Day* 41, no. 11 (15 March 1975):326–331.

Stevens, Harley C. "Some Reflections on the First Arab Petroleum Congress." *Middle East Journal* (Washington) (Summer 1959).

Stork, Joe. "Middle East Oil and the Energy Crisis." *Middle East Research and Information Project* (Washington) (September 1973).

Szyliowicz, Joseph S. "The Embargo and U.S. Foreign Policy," in *The Energy Crisis and U.S. Foreign Policy*, pp. 183–232. Edited by Joseph S. Szyliowicz and Bard E. O'Neil. New York: Praeger, 1975.

Tarzian, P. "The Early Oil Concessions." *Qadaya Arabiya* 8, no. 5 (May 1981):5–28. [In Arabic]

Torrey, Gordon H. "The Ba'th Ideology and Practice." *Middle East Journal* 23 (Autumn 1969):445–470.

Trabulsi, Fawwaz. "The Palestine Problem: Zionism and Imperialism in the Middle East." *New Left Review* 57 (September-October 1969).

Tueni, Ghassan. "After October." *Journal of Palestine Studies* 3, no. 4 (Summer 1974):114–130.

Tuma, Elias H. "Strategic Resources and Viable Interdependence: The Case of Middle Eastern Oil." *Middle East Journal* 33, no. 3 (Summer 1979):269–287.

Venkataramani, M. S. "Oil and U.S. Foreign Policy During the Suez Crisis 1956-57." *International Studies* (New Delhi) 2, no. 2 (October 1960):105–152.

Venu, S. "Oil Prices and the Indian Economy." *Euromoney* (May 1974):105–107.

Vital, David. "Israel and the Arab Countries," in *Conflict in World Politics*, pp. 221–239. Edited by Steven L. Spiegel and Kenneth N. Waltz. Cambridge: Winthrop Publishers, 1971.

Watt, D. C. "The Arab Summit Conference and After." *World Today* 23, no. 10 (October 1967):443–450.

Waverman, Leonard. "Oil and the Distribution of International Power." *International Journal* (Autumn 1974):619–635.

Weinberg, Alvin M. "Reflections on the Energy Wars." *American Scientist* (March/April 1978):153–158.

Wenner, Lettie M. "Arab-Kurdish Rivalries in Iraq." *Middle East Journal* 17 (Winter-Spring 1963).

Werner, Roy A. "Oil and U.S. Security Policies." *Orbis* 21, no. 3 (Fall 1977):651–670.

Wilton, T. "Arabs and Oil." *Asian Affairs* 11, no. 2 (June 1980):127–133.

Wright, Quincy. "Intervention, 1956." *American Journal of International Law* 51, no. 2 (April 1957):257–276.

Wright, W., M. Schupe, N. Fraser, and K. Hipel. "A Conflict Analysis of the Suez Canal Invasion of 1956." *Conflict Management and Peace Science* 5, no. 1 (1980):1–27.

Wrong, Dennis. "Oil, the Marines, and Prof. Tucker." *Dissent* (Spring 1975):111–113.

Yamani, Ahmad Z. "Towards a New Producer-Consumer Relationship." *World Today* 30, no. 11 (November 1974):479–486.

Yershov, Y. "The 'Energy Crisis' and Oil Diplomacy Manoeuvres." *International Affairs* (Moscow) 11 (November 1973):54–62.

Yost, Charles W. "The Arab-Israeli War: How It Began." *Foreign Affairs* 46 (January 1968):304–320.

Index